The Company in Law and Practice: Did Size Matter?
(Middle Ages–Nineteenth Century)

Legal History Library

VOLUME 23

Studies in the History of Private Law

VOLUME 12

The titles published in this series are listed at *brill.com/shpl*

The Company in Law and Practice: Did Size Matter? (Middle Ages–Nineteenth Century)

Edited by

D. De ruysscher
A. Cordes
S. Dauchy
H. Pihlajamäki

BRILL

LEIDEN | BOSTON

Cover illustration: Interior of a London Coffee-house. Anonymous. 1650–1750, courtesy of the British Museum.

Library of Congress Cataloging-in-Publication Data

Names: Ruysscher, Dave de, editor.
Title: The company in law and practice : did size matter? (Middle Ages – nineteenth century) / Edited by D. De Ruysscher, A. Cordes, S. Dauchy, H. Pihlajamaki.
Description: Leiden : Brill, 2017. | Series: Legal history library ; volume 23 | Includes bibliographical references and index.
Identifiers: LCCN 2017028902 (print) | LCCN 2017031401 (ebook) | ISBN 9789004351868 (e-book) | ISBN 9789004348493 (hardback : alk. paper)
Subjects: LCSH: Commercial law–Europe–History. | Business enterprises–Law and legislation–Europe–History.
Classification: LCC KJC6415 (ebook) | LCC KJC6415 .C66 2017 (print) | DDC 346.40709/03–dc23
LC record available at https://lccn.loc.gov/2017028902

Typeface for the Latin, Greek, and Cyrillic scripts: "Brill". See and download: brill.com/brill-typeface.

ISSN 1874-1793
ISBN 978-90-04-34849-3 (hardback)
ISBN 978-90-04-35186-8 (e-book)

Contents

Acknowledgments

This book is based on the papers that were presented at the workshop "The Small, Medium-Sized and Large Company in Law and Economic Practice (Middle Ages-Nineteenth Century)", which was held in Brussels in May 2015. This workshop was organized within the framework of the project "The Making of Commercial Law. Common Practices and National Legal Rules from the Early Modern to the Modern Period" under the supervision of Heikki Pihlajamäki (University of Helsinki). This was the second in a series of five workshops focusing on different subjects: they include the historiography and sources of commercial law (Helsinki, September 2014); commercial law in the colonies (Fiskars, Finland, January 2016); and migrating merchants, words and laws (Frankfurt, September 2016). A final conference in Helsinki (September 2017) regarding the theme of historiography of commercial law will gather the results together and present new topics for research. The mentioned project, conferences, as well as this book, are funded by the Academy of Finland and the Finnish Cultural Foundation.

We'd like to thank the authors, the language editor Sara Roberts, and Jennifer Obdam and Wendel Scholma at Brill, for helping in the preparation of this volume. With regards to the organization of the workshop and the preparation of this volume, the help of Kaat Cappelle, Maarten Colette, Marco In 't Veld, Stephanie Plasschaert, Jussi Sallila, Gorik Van Assche, and Marianne Vasara-Altonen was most appreciated.

Dave De ruysscher, Albrecht Cordes, Serge Dauchy and Heikki Pihlajamäki
Brussels, 1 February 2017

List of Figures and Tables

Figures

Tables

Introduction

Dave De ruysscher, Albrecht Cordes, Serge Dauchy and Heikki Pihlajamäki

Over the past two decades the history of commercial law has witnessed a revival. Nowadays, research on this topic is vibrant. Studies on old commercial law tie in with debates on the interactions between the economy, institutions and private actors that are all pervasive in many academic disciplines, including legal studies, economic history, business studies and comparative political analysis.

The angles from which historical commercial law can be considered are many. Historical analysis of mercantile actions (e.g. in the contents of contracts) can be combined with scrutiny of norms that are found in legislation, the judgments of courts, legal doctrine and the customs of merchants. The agency that traders and entrepreneurs had when devising the structures that were relevant for their activities was often considerable, which invites thorough consideration of the interactions between law and practice. Contextual methods are often applied in order to detect the ideas, incentives and attitudes underlying commercial arrangements and their use in the past. Even so, functional approaches are preferred when old legal materials are examined for their contribution to present-day legal solutions. Moreover, since merchants and entrepreneurs engaged in trade on an international scale, and were inspired by what their peers in other regions and countries did, looking beyond borders in comparative research is most natural.

This volume brings together nine chapters that address the topic of the scale and size of companies, in the Middle Ages, the Early Modern Period, and in the nineteenth century, from these many perspectives.

In this regard, this book seeks to reinvigorate a scholarly tradition. The subfield of legal-historical analysis of company law indeed has a long history. In the third quarter of the nineteenth century, academics, and legal authors in particular, started to study commercial law from a historical point of view. In their writings, the theme of company law was fundamental. In the 1860s, 1870s and 1880s, many European countries embarked on a thorough revision of their legislation concerning companies (France in 1867, Belgium in 1873, Germany in 1861, 1870 and 1884, Italy in 1882). Legal reforms served as a strong incentive to look back and trace the historical roots and nature of contemporary legal arrangements. On the European continent, this development came after a thorough re-elaboration of scholarly views regarding the legal status of the

 | DOI: 10.1163/9789004351868_002

firm (legal personhood)[1] and corporate governance, in particular, concerning the liability of directors and the powers of shareholders.[2] The reforms of the 1860s, 1870s and 1880s aimed at modernizing the then out-dated contents of the codes. Until the middle of the 1800s, academic and legislative ideas on firms had still largely been marked by older legal literature on *societas* (general partnership). Moreover, codifications of the later eighteenth and early nineteenth century that had envisaged organizational structures for business ventures (the *Allgemeines Landrecht für die Preussischen Staaten*, the *Code de commerce*) had not been very supportive, mostly because they had linked investment protection to strict control.

As a result, in the later nineteenth century, histories of company law mainly highlighted the development of the rules that were enacted in new national laws. Limited liability was a theme that attracted much attention. Authors such as Levin Goldschmidt,[3] Willy Silberschmidt,[4] Gustav Lastig[5] and many others, including the important French jurist Raymond Saleilles,[6] devoted historical monographs and articles to the theme. Moreover, the new legislation detailed many aspects of corporations (*sociétés anonymes, Aktiengesellschaften*), and as a result legal-historical studies on this topic saw the light of day. Occasionally, prominent legal scholars such as Edmond-Eugène Thaller delved into the history of shareholder companies.[7] Moreover, even the less appealing ordinary

1 Malte Diesselhorst, "Zur Theorie der juristischen Person bei Friedrich Carl von Savigny," and Jan Schröder, "Zur älteren Genossenschaftstheorie. Die Begründung des modernen Körperschaftsbegriffs durch Georg Beseler," *Quaderni Fiorentini per la storia del pensiero giuridico moderno* 11/12 (1982/83), 319–337 and 399–459 respectively; Edouard Richard, ""Mon nom est personne". La construction de la personnalité morale ou les vertus de la patience," *Entreprises & Histoire* 57 (2009), 14–44.

2 Hervé Joly, "La direction des sociétés anonymes depuis la fin du XIXe siècle: le droit entretient la confusion des pratiques," *Entreprises & Société* 57 (2009), 111–125. See also the chapter by Annamaria Monti in this volume.

3 Levin Goldschmidt, *De societate en commandite specimen I* (PhD thesis, University of Halle, 1851).

4 Wilhelm Silberschmidt, *Die Commenda in ihrer frühesten Entwicklung bis zum XIII. Jahrhundert. Ein Beitrag zur Geschichte der Commandit- und der stillen Gesellschaft* (Würzburg: Stuber, 1884).

5 Gustav Lastig, *Die Accomendatio. Die Grundform der heutigen Kommanditgesellschaften in ihrer Gestaltung vom XIII. bis XIX: Jahrhundert* (Halle a. d. S.: Buchhandel des Waisenhauses, 1907).

6 Raymond Saleilles, "Études sur l'histoire des sociétés en commandite," *Annales de droit commercial* (1895), 10–26, 49–79, and (1897), 29–49.

7 Edmond-Eugène Thaller, "Les sociétés par actions dans l'ancienne France," *Annales de droit commercial* (1901), 183–201.

partnership (*société en nom collectif*, *Offene Handelsgesellschaft*) was analyzed, most notably in Max Weber's dissertation.[8] Many of the studies that were written by these scholars are still useful, but they must be read from within their contemporary legal settings in order to be appreciated fully.

A common approach by the aforementioned researchers was to consider the legal characteristics of business associations as pertaining to "ideal types" of companies. These constructed types of companies served as methodological vehicles, clustering certain legal features together. Even though they were built up from within contemporary legal definitions, they were projected onto the past. This meant that in the course of historical analysis idiosyncrasies, temporal shifts and contextual elements were often overlooked.[9] Moreover, linking the contemporary characteristics of companies to Southern-European medieval examples became a trend. It was generally held that these properties were, over a long period of time, received and perfected in North-Western European legal arrangements, a view that has contributed to the "out-of-Italy" approach which has marked the field of historical commercial law ever since.

During the twentieth century, the broad nineteenth-century panorama of legal-historical studies on companies became narrow. Legal historians usually paid attention only to corporations and their (alleged) precursors, such as the *Verenigde Oost-Indische Compagnie* (1602).[10] Business and economic historians continued to analyze business ventures of all types and forms, but the legal aspects receded into the background; corporations became a dominant subject for them as well.[11] Scholars such as Alfred Chandler proffered the idea that cor-

8 Max Weber, *Zur Geschichte der Handelsgesellschaften im Mittelalter. Nach südeuropäischen Quellen* (Stuttgart: Enke, 1889). For a scientific edition see Gerhard Dilcher and Susanne Lepsius (eds.), *Max Weber Gesamtausgabe. Band I/1: Zur Geschichte der Handelsgesellschaften im Mittelalter. Schriften 1889–1894* (Tübingen: Mohr, 2008). For an English translation, see Max Weber, *The History of Commercial Partnerships in the Middle Ages*, Lutz Kaelber (trans.) (Lanham: Rowman & Littlefield, 2003).

9 See on these problems, in general: Albrecht Cordes and Katharina Jahntz, "Aktiengesellschaften vor 1807?," in Walter Bayer and Mathias Habersack (eds.), *Aktienrecht im Wandel*, vol. 1 (Tübingen: Mohr, 2007), 1–22, here 4–5, and for companies in late medieval Hanseatic areas: Albrecht Cordes, "Die Anfänge des Gesellschaftshandels im Hanseraum bis zur Mitte des 14. Jahrhunderts," in Nils Jörn, Detlef Kattinger and Horst Wernicke (eds.), *Genossenschaftliche Strukturen in der Hanse* (Cologne: Böhlau, 1999), 65–78, here 67–68.

10 See Egidius J.J. van der Heijden, *De ontwikkeling van de naamloze vennootschap in Nederland voor de codificatie* (Amsterdam: van der Vecht, 1908); Simon van Brakel, *De Hollandsche handelscompagnieën der zeventiende eeuw: hun ontstaan, hunne inrichting* (The Hague: Nijhoff, 1908).

11 See, for example, Aloys Schulte, *Geschichte der grossen Ravensburger Handelsgesellschaft*

porations provided the optimal organizational structure for large enterprises in need of finance.[12]

Over the past three decades, however, a broader analysis of company law in history has emerged, both among legal historians,[13] and economic and business historians. Since then, economic and business history has increasingly stepped away from proclaiming the corporation as the best company form possible. The obvious distortion deriving from research focusing on a few exceptionally big companies has been corrected. Much attention is now being paid to small entities and organizational structures in legislation that allowed for choice by and support for entrepreneurs. Moreover, the characteristics of the corporation, which is still commonly portrayed as an autonomous entity with limitedly liable shareholders, have been nuanced from a historical perspective.[14] In addition, for the legal history of smaller companies, new studies have been published, and some of those were already published before the 1990s. Legal historians such as Albrecht Cordes and Carlos Petit have demonstrated anachronisms in the present-day understanding of the characteristics of companies, for the late medieval and Early Modern periods, and both in mercantile practice and in legislation.[15] A new strand of legal-historical scholarship delves into the

---

1380–1530, 3 vols. (Stuttgart: Deutsche Verlags-Anstalt, 1923). Late twentieth-century emphasis on corporations is clear in many publications by business and economic historians, for example: Ann M. Carlos and Stephen Nicholas, "Theory and History: Seventeenth-Century Joint-Stock Chartered Trading Companies," *The Journal of Economic History* 56 (1996), 916–924. Detailed economic-historical analysis of (small) partnerships can be found in: Ernst Pitz, "Kapitalausstättung und Unternehmensformen in Antwerpen 1488–1514," *Vierteljahrschrift für Sozial- und Wirtschaftsgeschichte* 53 (1966), 53–91; Michael Postan, "Partnership in Medieval English Commerce," in *Medieval Trade and Finance* (Cambridge: CUP, 1973), 65–91.

12 Alfred D. Chandler, *The Visible Hand. The Managerial Revolution in American Business* (Cambridge (Ma.): Belknap, 1977).

13 Reference can be made to the session on companies which was held by the *Société Jean Bodin* in 2003, and to the workshop "Companies and company law in late medieval and early modern Europe", held at Leuven in 2012. See Bram Van Hofstraeten and Wim Decock (eds.), *Companies and Company Law in Late Medieval and Early Modern Europe* (Leuven: Peeters, 2016).

14 See the bibliography in the chapter by Dave De ruysscher in this volume. To this can be added: Oscar C. Gelderblom, Abe de Jong and Joost P.B. Jonker, "The Formative Years of the Modern Corporation. The Dutch East India Company VOC, 1602–1623," *Journal of Economic History* 73 (2013), 1050–1076.

15 Albrecht Cordes, *Spätmittelalterlicher Gesellschaftshandel im Hanseraum* (Cologne: Böhlau, 1998); Carlos Petit, *La compañia mercantil bajo el régimen de las Ordenanzas del Consulado de Bilbao, 1737–1829* (Seville: Universidad de Sevilla, 1979).

contents of academic doctrine in the later Middle Ages and the Early Modern period concerning partnerships. Recent research has, for example, pointed to a divide between personal partnerships (*societas*) and corporations (*universitas*).[16] New approaches towards chartered and shareholder companies, such as the EIC and the VOC, are also prominent.[17]

The chapters in this book are centred on the theme of the size and scale of companies as a legal and economic variable. They focus on regions of continental Europe (Germany, Belgium, Italy and Spain) and they tackle different periods from the late Middle Ages up to the nineteenth century. The new outlooks in literature have invited a reappraisal of the structuring of modest business ventures, of company structures lacking entity features, or involving few entrepreneurs or traders. The editors have selected chapters that focus on the idea that historical analysis of the features of both large and smaller companies is the best method to track down the origin of such legal notions as limited liability and legal personhood.

This book aims to offer nuanced views concerning these themes. Many chapters in the book provide materials supporting the idea that in the seventeenth century, large and smaller companies were, in legal terms, not all that different when it came to the liability of investors or entity-like properties (see the chapters by Stefania Gialdroni and Carlos Petit). During the Early Modern period, the view that partners shared risks since they were involved in a common enterprise, and which went back to the *societas* of Roman law, still prevailed, and this was also visible within the larger companies such as the English East India Company. Moreover, some chapters emphasize specific motives, including economic ones, for setting up business associations that were not entities, and this not only for the Early Modern era but also for the nineteenth century. This is

16 Luisa Brunori, *"Societas quid sit". La société commerciale dans l'élaboration de la Seconde Scolastique. Personnes et capitaux entre le XVIe et le XVIIe siècle* (Paris: Mare & Martin, 2015); J.M. de Jongh, *Tussen* societas *en* universitas. *De beursvennootschap en haar aandeelhouders in historisch perspectief* (Deventer: Kluwer, 2014); Ralf Mehr, *Societas und Universitas. Römischrechtliche Institute im Unternehmensgesellschaftsrecht vor 1800* (Cologne: Böhlau, 2008).

17 Stefania Gialdroni, *East India Company: una storia giuridica (1600–1708)* (Bologna: Il Mulino, 2011). One can add de Jongh's dissertation (see previous footnote), Katharina Jahntz, *Privilegierte Handelscompagnien in Brandenburg und Preußen. Ein Beitrag zur Geschichte des Gesellschaftsrechts* (Berlin: Duncker & Humblot, 2006), and Martijn Punt, *Het vennootschapsrecht van Holland. Het vennootschapsrecht van Holland, Zeeland en West-Friesland in de rechtspraak van de Hoge Raad van Holland, Zeeland en West-Friesland* (Dordrecht: Wolters Kluwer, 2013).

one of the reasons why companies with weaker protection for investors, such as the ordinary partnership, could thrive in the face of "stronger" alternatives that were available, in particular the limited company and the corporation (see the chapters by Ulla Kypta, Carlos Petit and Dave De ruysscher). Complementary institutions and networks can equally explain why certain company structures were not always chosen (see the chapter by Bart Lambert).

Some chapters go into the contents of company statutes and their relation to the official law. They yield results that encompass economic factors as well. In his contribution concerning companies in seventeenth-century Liège, Bram Van Hofstraeten underlines how company statutes differed according to the branches of business. Mining associations were of a different form to trading ventures, for example. Such divergence in contractual practice seems to have been typical not only in seventeenth-century Liège, but also in other localities and during other periods. In his chapter on company statutes in nineteenth-century Antwerp, Dave De ruysscher demonstrates how a tradition of structuring firms in a flexible way was maintained, notwithstanding the new and often conflicting rules of the *Code de commerce* (1807). The lenient and mediating approaches of the supervising courts facilitated this continuity. Hence, partnerships remained diverse, and their organizational features were different according to the branch of industry or the purpose of the venture. The chapters by Van Hofstraeten and De ruysscher show how interactions between contractual practice and law (in the broad sense, including legislation, judicial and academic interpretation) were important. Yet, whereas Van Hofstraeten points out that provisions concerning the external liability of partners were largely absent in seventeenth-century Liège company statutes, the opposite was true for nineteenth-century Antwerp. An explanation lies in the fixedness and acceptance of legal norms. In seventeenth-century Liège, the joint and several liability of associates in mining partnerships was a widely held rule, and was therefore uncontested, and was implied in partnership contracts. In Antwerp during the 1800s, by contrast, contractual provisions on the external liability of partners were ubiquitous. They were used for all sorts of companies, even when they were at odds with the rules of the *Code de commerce*, and they were more important in partnerships for purposes of manufacturing than they were in trading associations.

Both Van Hofstraeten and De ruysscher stress the fact that limited liability in the periods they study was not a central issue for parties to a company contract. The same view is expressed by Carlos Petit, who underscores incremental change in this regard. Stefania Gialdroni also makes it evident that partners in the early seventeenth-century East India Company were not limitedly liable, because they could be held to provide new investments in a situation where the company faced a shortage of capital. Both Carlos Petit and Gialdroni stress that the limited liability of shareholders was fully acknowledged in English and Spanish law only over the course of the nineteenth century. Limited liability grew from modest beginnings. The transferability of shares developed in England near the end of the seventeenth century. In eighteenth-century Spain, sales of stock were possible for chartered public companies, but many companies with shareholders did not provide for the transferability of equity stakes. Yet, in seventeenth-century Liège, shares in mining partnerships could be easily passed on from one partner to the next, but one might add that due to the limited number of transactions, no secondary market arose. This happened elsewhere, in the Dutch Republic of the early seventeenth century, and some time later in England, when stakes in the chartered public companies of the VOC and EIC developed into shares to bearer.

Carlos Petit demonstrates that the nineteenth-century corporation, with its clustered features of legal personhood and the limited liability of investors, cannot be transposed to before 1848. In the contributions of Anja Amend-Traut and Carlos Petit, it is highlighted that the chartered companies of the Old Regime were state enterprises, which differed from contractual partnerships. The idea of reciprocal support, which had its basis in the family enterprise, marked these partnerships. Shareholders in public companies were more remote than family members, but a complete separation of capital and personal ties was not yet present in the seventeenth and eighteenth centuries.

The aforementioned chartered public companies are often considered to be the precursors of the present-day corporation. This evokes the question of how changes in the type, scope and size of business triggered adaptations in company statutes and law. The size of companies and its impact are difficult to define, as Ulla Kypta mentions in her text. Still, many chapters demonstrate how differences in organization reflected scale. Bart Lambert for example contends that in late medieval Bruges, the size of firms mattered in respect of their access to information, and that merchant guilds were crucial in supporting smaller firms. Anja Amend-Traut defines the growing scale of businesses and the need for heavy financing as incentives to leave the late medieval *accommendatio* for larger and chartered companies. By contrast, in his chapter, De ruysscher presents the argument that codifications could impose different types of companies, which were considered to be fit for smaller or larger entrepreneurial activities, but also that in contractual and judicial practice generic legal concepts could be used for ventures of all size and purpose.

Some chapters in this volume analyze longer periods of time. Ulla Kypta advocates a reassessment of the development of associations in the late medieval German territories, from a temporal rather than a geographical perspective. Whereas undisclosed associations were used more in the fourteenth century, this way of structuring business ventures became juxtaposed with publicly known associations in the fifteenth century. Anja Amend-Traut depicts the evolution from personal partnerships in the later Middle Ages to chartered public companies in the seventeenth and eighteenth centuries.

In Van Hofstraeten's chapter, the point of geographical divergence is prominent: the contents of company statutes in seventeenth-century Liège differed in many respects from those contracts that were drafted in early modern Antwerp and Maastricht. In periods when the applicable law was fragmented, because of the co-existence of legal orders (local, regional, national), local contractual practice was closely connected to the law of the locality, which could be composed of many layers as well. But it seems that even with a uniform and codified law, differences in interpretation could remain. Scholarly and judicial interpretations of sections of codes could differ, among legal actors, and from region to region, as the contributions of Annamaria Monti and Dave De ruysscher show.

Some chapters explore the doctrinal understanding of companies. Luisa Brunori states that the authors of the *Secunda Scholastica* were forerunners in separating capital from the venture, thus marking the beginnings of modern capitalized companies. The debates among nineteenth-century French and Italian scholars over the nature of partnerships, ownership and legal personhood are analyzed in the contributions of Dave De ruysscher and Annamaria Monti.

Research questions arising from the contributions to this volume will incite new analyses. It can be questioned, for example, whether it was jurists (notaries, advocates and legal scholars) or merchants who devised the features that became so crucial in the development of Western capitalism: legal personhood and limited liability. The chapters by Luisa Brunori and Dave De ruysscher suggest creative influence from legal scholars and judges; in turn, Anja Amend-Traut, as well as Ulla Kypta and Bram Van Hofstraeten, exhibit the organizational agency of merchants. From their chapters, it might be inferred that doctrine and the official legal framework were either irrelevant in business practice, or that they developed into embracing the solutions first introduced in mercantile environments. But, however, one gains the impression that merchants/entrepreneurs and jurists were mostly co-operating in devising legal structures that were fit for the needs of trade (see foremost the chapters of Annamaria Monti and Dave De ruysscher). There is little evidence supporting the view that in the late Middle Ages, merchants' conceptions of a restricted liability of investors long preceded facilitating positions in court decisions, municipal bylaws, statutes and legal doctrine. The time lag that existed between the factual limitation of investors' liability and its juridical conceptualization, which often was only perfected in the nineteenth century, does not provide arguments as to a gap between official law and mercantile practice. Several chapters demonstrate how investors could be shielded, even without opting for an organizational scheme that was based on "limited liability". Moreover, questions on the interactions between law and practice, with regard to companies, must take into account that the organizational features of firms were the result of many incentives. Carlos Petit in his contribution highlights the importance of the sovereign's position with regard to the characteristics of chartered companies. Dave De ruysscher stresses that not all company statutes were drafted for the purpose of locking in capital. As a result, neither the law nor the contractual schemes of co-operation in trade and industry should be explained in terms of rational choice and profitability only.

Another question relates to the temporal changes: for example, why did late medieval merchants collaborate in international ventures that often remained informal (see the contribution of Ulla Kypta), whereas in the eighteenth and nineteenth centuries, written company statutes were more widespread, even for modest enterprises? This development has no parallel in the official law, which over this long period between the Middle Ages and the present day became more detailed, and which—so one would suspect—must have reduced the necessity to stipulate the contracts of a company to a large extent. From different chapters in this volume, it becomes apparent that commercial practice itself became increasingly juridified. As mentioned, as early as the later Middle Ages, trade was subject to rules, and the features of companies were circumscribed in municipal bylaws and legal doctrine early on. The professionalization of merchants since the later Middle Ages has often been highlighted, but it has not often been pointed out that this also entailed that the structuring of business ventures became increasingly sophisticated. At the same time, law became more commercial. Once merchants and jurists (notaries, advocates, legal scholars) began interacting, legal explanation and the facilitation of merchants' initiatives by jurists were integrated into mercantile practice. The increase in detail was then a snowball-effect of these interactions. This for example is clear in the development of the formulas in charters of English incorporated companies (see the chapter by Stefania Gialdroni). But, again, the cooperation between traders and jurists could be different from one region to the next: whereas in early nineteenth-century Antwerp the mercantile and legal practice with regard to partnerships were very much intertwined, in seventeenth-century Liège an important practice of selling equity in mining companies remained outside the scope of the official law, even though it was condoned.

CHAPTER 1

What is a Small Firm? Some Indications from the Business Organization of Late Medieval German Merchants

Ulla Kypta

1 Introduction

During the last decades, business studies has undergone a paradigmatic shift. In the second half of the twentieth century, an ideal company was believed to be large, long-living, hierarchical, and endowed with a large bureaucracy handling double entry bookkeeping. In the twenty-first century, companies regarded as progressive are small, flexible, decentralized and reputation-based.[1] Despite this change from "big is beautiful" to "small is beautiful", it is not completely clear which companies are regarded as "big" and which ones are regarded as "small". Different organizations employ different measures to decide whether a firm is big, small or medium. The European Commission, for example, defines a small company as a company with less than 50 employees and a turnover and balance sheet total of no more than €10 million.[2] This definition, however, sounds more clear-cut than it is. For example, who exactly counts as one of the 50 employees? Who works for a company and thus belongs to it; who works merely with a company and should thus not be regarded as an employee?[3]

If we turn from business studies to business history, the question gets more complicated, especially for premodern history. Neither the political institutions

---

1 Hartmut Berghoff and Jörg Sydow, "Unternehmerische Netzwerke—Theoretische Konzepte und historische Erfahrungen," in Hartmut Berghoff and Jörg Sydow (eds.), *Unternehmerische Netzwerke. Eine historische Organisationsform mit Zukunft?* (Stuttgart: Kohlhammer, 2007), 9–43; Hartmut Hirsch-Kreinsen, "Dezentralisierung: Unternehmen zwischen Stabilität und Desintegration," *Zeitschrift für Soziologie* 24 (1995), 422–435; John Child, "Trust. The Fundamental Bond in Global Colloboration," *Organizational Dynamics* 29 (2001), 274–288.

2 http://ec.europa.eu/growth/smes/business-friendly-environment/sme-definition/ (consulted on 17 January 2017).

3 Stephen N.S. Cheung, "The Contractual Nature of the Firm," *Journal of Law and Economics* 26 (1983), 386–405, here 402–403.

 | DOI: 10.1163/9789004351868_003

of premodern Europe nor many of today's researchers bother to give an exact definition of "small" as compared to "large" firms. Studies employing these labels do not always make it clear whether they regard a firm as large on the basis of a large number of partners and/or employees (and which number is a "large" number), or by considering high capital stock (and what is meant with "high"), a large trade volume (and again, what "large" means), or the scope of its trading activities, etc. This is probably a wise choice, since it is even more complicated for premodern companies than it is for modern companies to decide who their members were, let alone make more than mere guesses about their turnover and balance sheets. For instance, Donald Harreld in his study on German trade in late medieval Antwerp distinguishes between large, mid-level and small merchants without saying how a merchant is qualified as "large". Large firms according to Harreld held "the most prominent (…) presence in Antwerp and were responsible for the lion's share of the trade between Antwerp and the various German cities".[4] Mid-level merchants had "substantial means, but not quite to the extent of the great firms".[5] Anyone who could dispose of neither great nor substantial means is regarded to be a small-scale merchant.

The question of whether a company was large or small, however, is of certain interest for historians of premodern times, because some of their assumptions about the development of the premodern European economy rest on a differentiation between small and large firms. The latter ones are sometimes characterized as the modern, progressive vehicles for doing business.[6]

In this article, I focus on one specific example, namely, merchants from the Holy Roman Empire during the Late Middle Ages (fourteenth to sixteenth century). The size of their enterprises is usually regarded as the crucial variable of difference between merchants from higher and merchants from lower Germany. The southern German merchants are supposed to have learnt how to run a large firm from their Italian trading partners, thereby leading the path of the German economy into the future.[7] "Low German" and "High German" in this paper refer to merchants speaking Middle Low and Middle High German,

4 Donald J. Harreld, *High Germans in the Low Countries: German Merchants and Commerce in Golden Age Antwerp* (Leiden: Brill, 2004), 71.

5 Harreld, *High Germans*, 75.

6 Francesca Trivellato, *The Familiarity of Strangers. The Sephardic Diaspora, Livorno, and Cross-Cultural Trade in the Early Modern Period* (New Haven: Yale University Press, 2009), criticizes this judgement, at 272.

7 See, for example, on information management, Markus A. Denzel, "Professionalisierung und sozialer Aufstieg bei oberdeutschen Kaufleuten und Faktoren im 16. Jahrhundert," in Günther

respectively. Thus, the label of "German" encompasses merchants not only from territories of present-day Germany but also from Basel and Riga, for example. I use the attributes "Hanseatic" and "northern German" as synonyms here, which is not entirely correct since not every merchant from northern Germany enjoyed the Hanseatic trading privileges. Both groups however overlapped significantly.

Research of the past decades suggests that in Northern Germany, Hanseatic merchants organized their trade via networks of independent merchants, setting up small associations with partners on an equal footing with a limited number of fellow merchants. In Southern Germany, on the other hand, large hierarchical corporations, most notably the Fugger Company, are said to have dominated the landscape.[8] The description of trading enterprises in late medieval Germany mirrors the abovementioned shift in business history. During the 1970s, when large corporations were seen as the vanguard of business organizations, Wolfgang von Stromer wrote his famous praise of the southern German trading houses as the largest business enterprises of the Holy Roman Empire.[9] Consequently, he regarded the organization of Hanseatic trade as "backward".[10] Hanseatic historians responded to Stromer with studies arguing that the Hanseatic merchants could not be characterized as, for example, hostile to credit techniques or as pushing out merchants from other cities.[11]

Schulz (ed.), *Sozialer Aufstieg. Funktionseliten im Spätmittelalter und in der frühen Neuzeit* (Munich: Oldenbourg, 2002), 413–442, see 432.

8 See, for example, Stephan Selzer and Ulf Christian Ewert, "Netzwerke im europäischen Handel des Mittelalters. Konzepte—Anwendungen—Fragestellungen," in Gerhard Fouquet and Hans-Jörg Gilomen (eds.), *Netzwerke im europäischen Handel des Mittelalters* (Ostfildern: Thorbecke, 2010), 21–47, see 10.

9 Wolfgang von Stromer, *Oberdeutsche Hochfinanz 1350–1450. Teil 1* (Wiesbaden: Steiner, 1970).

10 Wolfgang von Stromer, "Konkurrenten der Hanse: Die Oberdeutschen," in *Hanse in Europa. Brücke zwischen den Märkten* (Cologne: Kölnisches Stadtmuseum, 1973), 331–340; Wolfgang von Stromer, "Der innovatorische Rückstand der Hansischen Wirtschaft," in Knut Schulz (ed.), *Beiträge zur Wirtschafts- und Sozialgeschichte des Mittelalters. Festschrift für Herbert Helbig zum 65. Geburtstag* (Cologne: Böhlau, 1976), 204–217.

11 Stuart Jenks, "War die Hanse kreditfeindlich?," *Vierteljahrschrift für Sozial- und Wirtschaftsgeschichte* 69 (1982), 305–338; Stuart Jenks, "Zum hansischen Gästerecht," *Hansische Geschichtsblätter* 114 (1996), 3–60. Other famous reactions to Stromer are, for example, Rolf Sprandel, "Die Konkurrenzfähigkeit der Hanse im Spätmittelalter," *Hansische Geschichtsblätter* 102 (1984), 21–38; Stephan Selzer and Ulf Christian Ewert, "Verhandeln und Verkaufen, Vernetzen und Vertrauen. Über die Netzwerkstruktur des Hansischen Handels," *Hansische Geschichtsblätter* 119 (2001), 135–161.

Hanseatic trade functioned differently, but nonetheless efficiently. At the beginning of the twenty-first century, different aspects of this answer were combined with the view that every function of a large trading house provided for by southern German merchants, for example the exchange of information, was present within the Hanseatic world as well. Instead of hierarchical companies, northern German trade was regarded as being structured with networks of independent merchants including some important organizations such as the Kontors and the Hanseatic Diet.[12] In short, Hanseatic firms and associations very much resembled the ideal which business studies proclaimed at the beginning of the twenty-first century.[13]

Thus, German trade in the Late Middle Ages seems to offer a suitable case study if one wants to study the problem of the size of a company in premodern times. The question of whether a company or association is large or small quite quickly leads to the problem of defining what a company or association is. Before delving into the Middle Ages, the following part explores the general discussion on the question "what is a firm?". One answer to this question consists of focusing not on the firm as a unit, but on the relations between merchants instead. Part three deals with some problems concerning the description of these relations for premodern times, and offers a possible solution. Part four shows how this new definition could result in a new interpretation of the development of premodern trade. In part five, the question of how and when the cooperation between merchants turned into an entity that could act on its own is discussed. Part six argues that even if we can regard companies as entities in their own right, that does not mean that they were exclusive: merchants could work for and with different companies at the same time. Part seven concludes by returning to the initial question: what is a firm? And which firms are small and large?

---

12 Stuart Jenks, "Die Hanse als kybernetische Organisation," in Oliver Auge (ed.), *Hansegeschichte als Regionalgeschichte* (Frankfurt am Main: Lang, 2014), 59–84; Stuart Jenks, "Small Is Beautiful. Why Small Hanseatic Firms Survived in the Late Middle Ages," in Justyna Wubs-Mrozewicz and Stuart Jenks (eds.), *The Hanse in Medieval and Early Modern Europe* (Leiden: Brill, 2013), 191–214.

13 For a discussion of these ideal types, see Ulf Christian Ewert and Stephan Stelzer, "Wirtschaftliche Stärke durch Vernetzung. Zu den Erfolgsfaktoren des hansischen Handels," in Mark Häberlein and Christof Jeggle (eds.), *Praktiken des Handels. Geschäfte und soziale Beziehungen europäischer Kaufleute in Mittelalter und früher Neuzeit* (Konstanz: UVK, 2010), 39–69.

2 What is a Firm?

Before deciding whether a firm is large or not, the first step consists of determining what a firm is. The question of the "nature of the firm" was first raised by Ronald Coase,[14] but, as Lawson remarks, Coase did not inquire much into the nature of the firm but rather into the reason as to why there are firms.[15] Would it not be more efficient to allocate resources via the price-mechanism of a market instead of via the decisions of a firm's manager? Coase gave the answer that high transaction costs could make market transactions less efficient. He thus distinguished between market transactions, and transactions carried out inside the firm, which results in the need to decide whether a transaction is regarded as a market or as an internal transaction. But what about, for example, leased labourers? Can they be seen as part of the firm, or is it more accurate to state that the firm hired their labour force via a market transaction from another firm? A similar question arises if we look at a firm's turnover. Do we have to include, for example, business transactions with branch offices or sister companies? Coase himself remarked that it is difficult to draw the line between market and firm.[16] He sets out reasons as to why firms exist, but he does not define what a firm is.

In the German legal system, a "firm" (in German "Firma") refers to the legal name of a business. In German economic history however, the term is often used as a synonym for company.[17] The terms firm and company both connote an association that could somehow act on its own, for example, sending representatives to important trading centres. Lutz brings both strands together when he argues that late medieval merchants bound together in a company or firm did business under the same name.[18] But Lutz also stresses the point that speaking of a firm in the Middle Ages is anachronistic. The term "firm" in the sense of a business organization stems from the eighteenth century.[19] Contemporary names such as *gesellschaft*, *compagnia* or *company* could refer

14 Ronald Harry Coase, "The Nature of the Firm," *Economica* 4 (1937), 386–405.

15 Tony Lawson, "The Nature of the Firm and Peculiarities of the Corporation," *Cambridge Journal of Economics* 39 (2015), 1–32.

16 Coase, "Nature," 392.

17 See for example Joachim Riebartsch, *Augsburger Handelsgesellschaften des 15. und 16. Jahrhunderts. Eine vergleichende Darstellung ihres Eigenkapitals und ihrer Verfassung* (Bergisch-Gladbach: Eul, 1987).

18 Elmar Lutz, *Die rechtliche Struktur süddeutscher Handelsgesellschaften in der Zeit der Fugger. 1: Darstellung* (Tübingen: Mohr, 1976), 449.

19 Lutz, *Darstellung*, 445.

to all kinds of groups of people. For example, Lübeck's most famous fraternity was called "Zirkel-Gesellschaft", in low German *selschop der circuler*,[20] just as trading enterprises were called *selschop*. Depending on the region, the sources contain different names for trading enterprises, for example *commenda, collegantia, societas, geselschaft, selscop, compagnia, widerlegung*, and *vulle mascopei*.[21] If one only focuses on entities that could act on their own and comprised of merchants who all did business under the same trade name, one misses an important part of medieval business organization. As will be demonstrated below, merchants very often cooperated with one another without using the same trade name or even without pooling their capital.

Research in business studies has come up with a solution that seems well suited for premodern studies as well. Instead of trying to analyze the firm as an entity, contracts are taken as benchmarks, or, to be more precise, the number of contracts connecting a number of people (thus turning them into a group) is analyzed.[22] A firm, then, can be defined as a nexus of contracts,[23] or as a "particularly dense intersection of contracts"[24] with necessarily fuzzy boundaries. This definition removes the need for a dichotomic distinction between the inside and the outside of a firm. To start the analysis with the relationship between two persons seems to be appropriate for medieval business studies as well, since a trading enterprise was started by at least two merchants agreeing to cooperate in a certain business transaction. For example, on 8 February 1491, Wilhelm Weißhaupt and Hans Schreiber from Bibrach and Valentin Dietmar from Ulm agreed to invest 1,000 guilders each in order to form a company (*gesellschafft*), thus pooling resources for trade between Southern Germany and Italy for four years.[25] In 1558, Kraft Stalburg from Frankfurt and

---

20 *Urkundenbuch der Stadt Lübeck*, vol. 7 (Lübeck: Asschenfeldt, 1885), 302 (no. 322, *Statuten der Zirkelgesellschaft*).

21 Albrecht Cordes, *Spätmittelalterlicher Gesellschaftshandel im Hanseraum* (Cologne: Böhlau, 1998), 315–326; Michael Rothmann, "Unternehmensformen und Formen von Unternehmungen zwischen Spätmittelalter und Früher Neuzeit," *Jahrbuch für Wirtschaftsgeschichte* 53 (2012), 25–37, see 27.

22 Armen A. Alchian and Harold Demsetz, "Production, Information Costs, and Economic Organization," *American Economic Review* 62 (1972), 777–795.

23 Michael C. Jensen and William H. Meckling, "Theory of the Firm. Managerial Behavior, Agency Costs and Ownership Structure," *Journal of Financial Economics* 3 (1976), 305–360.

24 Richard N. Langlois and Paul L. Roberston, *Firms, Market and Economic Change. A Dynamic Theory of Business Institutions* (London: Routledge, 1995), 10. For this "nexus-of-contracts view of the firm", see Cheung, "Contractual Nature".

25 Elmar Lutz, *Die rechtliche Struktur süddeutscher Handelsgesellschaften in der Zeit der Fugger. II: Urkunden* (Tübingen: Mohr, 1976), 9–20.

Jacob von Botzheim from Hagenau agreed to work together for ten years, Kraft Stalburg trading between Frankfurt and Italy and Jacob von Botzheim trading between Frankfurt and Straßburg. Each party contributed 14,000 guilders.[26]

In short, the search for medieval firms in the sense of entities does not take us very far because it always borders on anachronism. Instead, I want to start by analyzing the smallest possible unit of cooperation between merchants for organizing trade, that is, associations between two merchants whereby one represents the other. If a merchant wanted to carry out business at places where he was not physically present, he had to rely on a representative. I use the word "association" here in the sense of a cooperation between at least two merchants to carry out trade, without implying any special economic or juridical definition. "Association" can then encompass agency-based cooperation or an equity-oriented enterprise; both agents and investors are "associated" with trading merchants. This broad definition is important because in the mercantile practice of the German territories of the later Middle Ages, a clear distinction between equity and agency was not present (as will be demonstrated below).

With the association between two merchants, a basic economic question arose. Did this cooperation save more costs than it incurred?[27] Did correspondence, supervision, accounting etc. cost less than the opportunity costs of the merchant doing everything by himself? Likewise, legal questions arose. Who was responsible for the acts carried out by one of the partners? Who was entitled to which share of gains and losses? In short, the association between two merchants is a very basic starting point, but it is the point to which all the interesting questions can be linked. I use the term company only if merchants formed an entity that could act on its own. The following sections analyze the different associations merchants formed to carry out their business, which leads to a historically sensitive definition of a firm.

3 Four Types of Associations

The description and systematization of associations poses some challenges. Neither in current research nor in the sources does the labelling of different forms of association follow a consistent pattern. Studies describing ideal

26 Georg Ludwig Kriegk, *Deutsches Bürgerthum im Mittelalter. Nach urkundlichen Forschungen* (Frankfurt am Main: Rütten & Löning, 1871), 451–452.

27 See Coase, "Nature".

types normally label the employees of large companies as factors (*Faktoren*) or trading servants (*Handelsdiener*), in contrast to the partners (*Partner*) linked together in a network.[28] It proves difficult, however, to define exactly who could qualify as factor or partner. If a researcher provides a clear-cut definition, the criteria he lists are normally nothing more than abstractions from the specific case the researcher is analyzing. For example, Reinhard Hildebrand in his study on the Fugger company sets forth seven detailed criteria that should help to decide whether a servant could qualify as a factor.[29] But these seven criteria can only be applied to the Fugger factors, and probably only to an ideal type of those, too. For instance, criterion seven holds that a factor was required to get the approval of his superiors if he wanted to do side business. Some Fugger factors, however, engaged in business other than that of their company. For example, Andreas Hyrus, who worked as a Fugger factor in Spain, became rich in dealing in letters of exchange on his own behalf, which was strictly forbidden according to his contract with the Fugger company.[30] At vibrant trading posts like Antwerp it is hard to find any representative of a trading house working for one trading house only,[31] and it is open to speculation as to whether their respective headquarters had approved all of their activities. Thus, it is difficult to judge whether there were any factors according to Hildebrandt's definition of the term, particularly outside the Fugger company. Studies that do not construct ideal types but analyze cases seldom explain their assumptions as regards labels. For example, Hans-Jürgen Vogtherr uses the term factor for independent partners, and even as a synonym for brokers.[32] Hans Pohl, on the other hand, categorizes the merchants who

---

28 See for example Ewert and Selzer, "Stärke"; Jenks, "Small Is Beautiful".

29 Reinhard Hildebrandt, *Die "Georg Fuggerischen Erben". Kaufmännische Tätigkeit und sozialer Status 1555–1600* (Berlin: Duncker & Humblot, 1966), 47: *"Er war a) Leiter einer vom Hauptsitz der Firma räumlich getrennten Niederlassung, b) Inhaber einer weitreichenden Vollmacht, die bei Tod, Krankheit oder Ortsabwesenheit meistens übertragbar war ("Instrumentum procuratorii substituendi"), c) unmittelbar dem "Regierer" gegenüber verantwortlich, d) direkter Vorgesetzter aller anderen Bediensteten an der von ihm geleiteten Faktorei, e) angewiesen, über die berufliche Arbeit und private Lebensführung seiner Untergebenen zu wachen und gegebenenfalls darüber zu berichten, f) Repräsentant der Gesellschaft im Geschäftsbereich der von ihm geleiteten Niederlassung, g) verpflichtet, jede eventuelle Nebenbeschäftigung sich von der Firmenleitung genehmigen zu lassen".*

30 Denzel, "Professionalisierung," 424.

31 Harreld, *High Germans*, 73.

32 See, for instance, Hans-Jürgen Vogtherr, "Hamburger Faktoren von Lübecker Kaufleuten des 15. und 16. Jahrhunderts," *Zeitschrift des Vereins für Lübeckische Geschichte und Altertumskunde* 73 (1993), 39–138, see 41.

traded in Antwerp on behalf of Cologne merchants interchangeably as factors, commissioners and innkeepers ("*Wirte*").[33] For the Ravensburger trading company, Jürgen Schneider distinguishes between different forms of representation ("*Gelieger*", "*Gesellen*", "*Agenten*", "*Vertreter*") without making it clear in which respect these labels differed.[34]

Turning to late-medieval documents offers no solution. Labels vary from region to region, and it is difficult to assign certain categories to certain terms. For example, most servants (*diener*, *knechte*) can be distinguished from partners because they did not invest money in the enterprise. However, some servants are explicitly urged to invest any profits they had made.[35] For example, Johann Rauchfass was explicitly called the servant of a Frankfurt company, which was founded by the associates Kraft Stalburg, Daniel Bromm, Claus Stalburg and Hans Bromm. Even though he was called a servant (*Diener*), he owed a share in the company's capital, thereby partaking in wins and losses.[36] It can thus become difficult to tell the difference between a servant and an associate.[37]

The term "*Faktor*" in German texts obviously stands in close connection to the Italian term *fattore*, but *fattore* could refer to almost any kind of employee.[38] A *lieger* is generally said to be the lower German equivalent of factor,[39] but since factor is an ill-defined term, this equation does not lead us very far. In English sources, the names factor and servant are used more or less interchangeably: either of them could or could not be answerable to a superior, and both could or could not have a share in gains and losses.[40]

---

33 Hans Pohl, "Köln und Antwerpen um 1500," in Hugo Stehkämper (ed.), *Köln, das Reich und Europa. Abhandlungen über weiträumige Verflechtungen der Stadt Köln in Politik, Recht und Wirtschaft im Mittelalter* (Cologne: Neubner, 1971), 469–553.

34 Jürgen Schneider, "Die Bedeutung von Kontoren, Faktoreien, Stützpunkten (von Kompagnien), Märkten, Messen und Börsen im Mittelalter und Früher Neuzeit," in Hans Pohl (ed.), *Die Bedeutung der Kommunikation für Wirtschaft und Gesellschaft* (Wiesbaden: Steiner, 1989), 37–63, see 44.

35 Rudolf Ortner, *Der Handlungsgehilfe, im Besonderen der Faktor des süddeutschen Kaufmanns im 15. und 16. Jahrhundert* (Munich: Höfling, 1932), 28–29.

36 Kriegk, *Deutsches Bürgerthum*, 439.

37 Ortner, *Handlungsgehilfe*, 31.

38 Ortner, *Handlungsgehilfe*, 10.

39 Hermann Kellenbenz, "Faktor," in *Lexikon des Mittelalters*, vol. 4 (Munich: Artemis, 1989), cols. 234–235.

40 Michael M. Postan, "Partnerships in English Medieval Commerce," in Michael M. Postan (ed.), *Medieval Trade and Finance* (Cambridge: CUP, 1973), 65–91, see 74.

Neither the names we read in the sources nor the names given to a merchant's representative by present-day researchers can thus help us to figure out the different forms in which representation could be organized. Instead of searching for words, however, we can distinguish different types of association by looking for the basic differences that characterized all partnerships. The differences can be systematized on the basis of two criteria. First, did a merchant who made a deal with a fellow merchant know that this merchant was the representative of another merchant? In other words, was it an undisclosed or a disclosed partnership? I assume that a merchant did know that his counterpart worked with another merchant if this is explicitly stated in the sources. For instance, an Antwerp notary recorded that Jakob Perilleux came to Alexius Grimel, presented him a letter of exchange and demanded immediate payment. The notary explicitly stated that Jakob Perilleux acted on behalf of Thomas de Chardes from Tournay ("*honestus vir Jacobus Prilleux tamquam procurator factor institor et seu negotiorum gestor spectabilis viri Thome de Chordes mercatoris Tornacensis principalis*"). Alexius Grimel, on the other hand, is identified as working for Bartholomeus Welser and his associates from Augsburg ("(…) *Alexio Grimel factori institori et seu negotiorum gestori Bartholomei Welzer et sociorum mercatorum de Augusta*").[41] The notary knew and deemed it important enough to mention that both parties acted on behalf of someone else. The association between Jakob Peirilleux and Thomas de Chardes as well as the one between Alexius Grimel and Bartholomeus Welser can thus be regarded as disclosed.

Secondly, did every participant or only a number of them invest capital into the association? According to Postan, the question of whether the stock of a company consisted of joined capital or not was a crucial one for late medieval merchants. It did not matter whether one or all partners engaged in activities of trade. Only a joint stock company was regarded as a mutual partnership.[42] Every elaborate discussion on the sharing of gains and losses, or concerning questions of liability, differentiated between partnerships involving partners that had joined their capital on the one hand and one-sided partnerships on the other.[43] But this did not only concern partnerships or partners, since also agents and even servants could invest in associations.

41 Jakob Strieder (ed.), *Aus Antwerpener Notariatsarchiven. Quellen zur Deutschen Wirtschaftsgeschichte des 16. Jahrhunderts* (Wiesbaden: Steiner, 1962; reprint of Stuttgart: Deutsche Verlags-anstalt, 1930), 52–54 (no. 47).

42 Postan, "Partnerships," 88–90.

43 Lutz, *Darstellung*, 279.

The two criteria can be combined into four types of associations. The first type of association was undisclosed, and only one participant contributed capital. This can be labelled "commission trade". The principal sent goods to a commission agent who sold them in his own name, but on behalf of the principal. Commission trade is regarded as more efficient than one merchant traveling around with merchandise all by himself if the commissioner had a better knowledge of prices and the quality of goods. This was possible when he had lived for some time in the city in which the principal wanted to do business. Commission trade could become even more profitable if the commissioner could buy or sell on better terms than the principal, for example if he had citizen rights at the place of business. For instance, Bruges merchants did not have to pay pound toll.[44] In Bruges, merchants from northern as well as southern Germany employed as commissioners either brokers and hostellers or merchants that had come from their own hometown but had transferred their offices to Bruges.[45] Merchants from Cologne sent wine to innkeepers in Antwerp who sold the wine on their principals' behalf.[46]

The second type of association was also undisclosed, but both participants contributed capital. The Hanseatic *societas* falls into this category. It was called *wedderlegginge* because both associates, who were partners, put their capital together (the capital of one partner was "laid" (*leggen*) "against" (*wedder*) that of the other).[47] One of the partners took the whole amount of money, bought goods, sold them and then rendered account for gains and losses. But not only Hanseatic merchants, such as for example Hans Selhorst from Tallin and Laurens Molsen from Gdansk, joined in this type of association.[48] Merchants from Nuremberg established such societies with merchants from Antwerp.[49] Ulrich

---

44 Cordes, *Gesellschaftshandel*, 247.

45 Oscar Gelderblom, *Cities of Commerce. The Institutional Foundations of International Trade in the Low Countries, 1250–1650* (Princeton: Princeton University Press, 2013), 46–50, and 79. For the Hanseatic merchants in Bruges, see Anke Greve, *Hansische Kaufleute, Hosteliers und Herbergen im Brügge des 14. und 15. Jahrhunderts* (Frankfurt am Main: Lang, 2011).

46 Pohl, "Köln," 490, and 502; Bernd Ulrich Hucker, "Der Köln-Soester Fernhändler Johann von Lunen (1415–1443) und die hansischen Gesellschaften Falbrecht & Co. und v.d. Hosen & Co.," in Gerhard Köhn (ed.), *Soest. Stadt—Territorium—Reich. Festschrift zum 100 jährigen Bestehen des Vereins für Geschichte und Heimatpflege Soest* (Soest: Mocker & Jahn, 1981), 383–421, see 398.

47 Cordes, *Gesellschaftshandel*, 121.

48 Carsten Jahnke, *Geld, Geschäfte, Informationen. Der Aufbau hansischer Handelsgesellschaften und ihre Verdienstmöglichkeiten* (Lübeck: Schmidt-Römhild, 2007), 9–10.

49 Harreld, *High Germans*, 82.

Meltinger from Basel was part of a network of southern German merchants that were linked together by such undisclosed partnerships.[50]

Associations of the third type were visible to the outside world, and these were always partnerships. Someone buying merchandise from a merchant belonging to such a partnership knew that the merchant he was buying from was member of a company. The partners put their capital together, and then distributed it among themselves. With their share of money, the partners went to different places, bought and sold goods, sent each other letters of exchange to balance differences in money supply, and rendered account at normally fixed intervals.[51] One of the most famous of this type of association was the *Ravensburger Handelsgesellschaft*, which was based in the fustian region of Upper Germany and which was involved in trade at, for instance, Antwerp, Lyon and Genoa.[52] Other examples from southern Germany are the Tucher Company, with partners among other in Nuremberg and Lyon,[53] or the Halbysen society, which was based in Basel and which engaged in business not only in Germany but also in Italy, Spain, France, England and the Netherlands.[54] In the Hanseatic area, the Falbrecht-Morser-Rosenfeld Company did not only trade between Flanders and Prussia, but was also involved in monetary transactions between these areas, and it had shares in copper mines in Sweden and Hungary.[55] Some companies covered both North and South. For example, the Carstens-von-Brocke society had trading outposts at Lübeck, Antwerp, Amsterdam, Gdansk and Nuremberg.[56] The Venetian society, infamous for its lack of success, tried to establish trading connections between Lübeck, Bruges and

50 Matthias Steinbrink, "Netzwerkhandel am Oberrhein—Kaufmännische Buchhaltung und Organisationsformen am Beispiel Ulrich Meltingers," in Gerhard Fouquet and Hans-Jörg Gilomen (eds.), *Netzwerke im europäischen Handel des Mittelalters* (Ostfildern: Thorbecke, 2010), 317–331, see 326–327.

51 For such trading societies in general see Lutz, *Darstellung*; for Augsburg in particular see Riebartsch, *Handelsgesellschaften*.

52 Aloys Schulte, *Geschichte der Großen Ravensburger Handelsgesellschaft 1380–1530*, 3 vols. (Stuttgart: Deutsche Verlags-anstalt, 1923).

53 Walter Bauernfeind, "Marktinformationen und Personalentwicklung einer Nürnberger Handelsgesellschaft im 16. Jahrhundert. Das Briefarchiv von Anthoni und Linhart Tucher in der Zeit von 1508 bis 1566," in Angelika Westermann and Stefanie von Welser (eds.), *Beschaffungs- und Absatzmärkte oberdeutscher Firmen im Zeitalter der Welser und Fugger* (Husum: Matthiesen, 2011), 23–60, see 28.

54 Franz Ehrensperger, *Basels Stellung im internationalen Handelsverkehr des Spätmittelalters* (Zürich: Aku, 1962), 58; Steinbrink, "Netzwerkhandel," 328.

55 Hucker, "Johann von Lunen," 391.

56 Rolf Hammel-Kiesow and Matthias Puhle, *Die Hanse* (Darmstadt: Primus, 2009), 100.

Venice.[57] Based in the Hansa town of Cologne, the Stralen Company traded between Barcelona, Bruges, London, Antwerp, the Frankfurt fairs and Italy.[58]

In an association of the fourth type, a merchant working for a company was known to belong to the company, but he did not contribute capital. He thus did not have a share in gains or losses. His rights and obligations were often recorded in an employment contract. The factors, or "*Handelsdiener*" (tradings servants) as they are described in the ideal picture of a southern German company, belong to this category.[59] Hierarchical companies such as the Fugger employed such factors to trade at their outposts. The partners of a type three association often appointed type four employees to work for them. The *Ravensburger Handelsgesellschaft*, for instance, consisted of partners contributing capital, and they recruited employees who did not invest money into the *Handelsgesellschaft*.[60] The outposts of the Grimmel Company, based in Konstanz and Memmingen, were also staffed partly by type three-partners and partly by type four-employees.[61] Merchants who were joined together in an undisclosed partnership also did not always carry out trade by themselves; they sometimes instructed servants to do so.[62]

Even though at first glance it seems pretty straightforward to distinguish "associations" into these four types, a second glance reveals some challenges. The last example illustrates that the four types should not be regarded as strictly separated. Associates of all the types of trading societies could engage type four employees. The associates of a partnership could not only be individual persons, but also other partnerships. For example, Johannes Ghesmer and

57 Rolf Hammel, "Veckinchusen, Hildebrand," in *Biographisches Lexikon für Schleswig-Holstein und Lübeck*, vol. 9 (Neumünster: Wachholtz, 1991), 358–364, see 360–361; a description of its failure is given by Mathias Franc Kluge, "Zwischen Metropole, Fürst und König. Die Venedische Handelsgesellschaft der Kaufleute Veckinchusen und ihr Niedergang," *Hansische Geschichtsblätter* 131 (2013), 33–76.

58 Gunther Hirschfelder, *Die Kölner Handelsbeziehungen im Spätmittelalter* (Cologne: Kölnisches Stadtmuseum, 1994), 549.

59 For an overview, see Reinhard Hildebrandt, "Diener und Herren. Zur Anatomie großer Unternehmen im Zeitalter der Fugger," in Johannes Burkhardt (ed.), *Augsburger Handelshäuser im Wandel des historischen Urteils* (Berlin: Akademie Verlag, 1996), 149–174.

60 Schneider, "Bedeutung," 44.

61 Frank Göttmann, "Die Bedeutung des textilen Verlagswesens und die Konstanz-Memminger Handelsgesellschaft Grimmel Mitte des 16. Jahrhunderts," in Angelika Westermann and Stefanie von Welser (eds.), *Beschaffungs- und Absatzmärkte oberdeutscher Firmen im Zeitalter der Welser und Fugger* (Husum: Matthiesen, 2011), 143–158, see 151.

62 Steinbrink, "Netzwerkhandel," 325 describes this case for the merchant Ulrich Meltinger from Basel.

Thidemann Guzstrowe founded a Hanseatic *societas*. This *societas* in turn set up a *wedderlegginge* in which Johannes was the second partner.[63] The question of who invested capital could also be more complicated. In some associations with two participants who each contributed capital, one of the participants lent the other one the necessary investment capital. This happened in Hanseatic companies[64] as well as in southern German ones, where it was called *"Fürlegung"*.[65]

4 Changes in Business Organization in Northern and Southern Germany

Even though the four types—like all attempts of systematization—oversimplify some of the complexities of associations, they provide us with a means of disentangling and classifying the different associations of which a merchant could be part. Since they combine only two very basic characteristics, they allow for a simple but effective first approach to separating different associations. They are effective in as much as they enable us to see empirical findings in a new light. As mentioned above, the research of the past decades rests on the assumption that the organization of trade differed according to geography. Merchants from the North worked with associates in networks—in type one and type two associations—whereas merchants from Southern Germany normally belonged to a trading house, which was a combination of type three and type four associations. After some forty year of discussions as to whether the Hanseatic merchants must be regarded as backward because they did not establish trading houses, a consensus seems to have been reached among researchers studying northern German trade and the ones investigating southern German merchants. All agree that both northern and southern German trade functioned quite differently, but obviously also efficiently, since northern and southern merchants did not outcompete each other.[66] If we look at the evidence in the light of the four types, however, there does not seem to be need for the mentioned consensus, since the development of merchants' organizations in the South probably did not differ so much from the changes that happened in the North.

---

63 Cordes, *Gesellschaftshandel*, 135.

64 Ib., 172.

65 Schneider, "Bedeutung," 43.

66 Ewert and Selzer, "Stärke," 60; Stuart Jenks, "Transaktionskostentheorie und die mittelalterliche Hanse," *Hansische Geschichtsblätter* 123 (2005), 31–42, see 31–32.

When we group the empirical evidence cited above according to the four types, a chronological dimension instead of a geographical dichotomy becomes evident. In the fourteenth century, merchants joined mostly undisclosed associations (type 1 and 2). In the fifteenth century, in northern as well as in southern Germany, type three partnerships emerged alongside the undisclosed associations. Some of these sharpened their internal hierarchy at the end of the fifteenth and at the beginning of the sixteenth century, thus placing greater emphasis on type four employees. This study will now briefly elaborate on this new narrative. In the fourteenth century, the commercial revolution during which merchants became sedentary came to a close.[67] For a sedentary merchant, the question arose as to how he could organize his business at places where he was no longer physically present. As a first solution he cooperated with a merchant residing at or travelling to another city. He gave the other merchant merchandise to sell (type one), or both of them pooled capital (type two). The merchant who did the actual trading did so in his own name, but on behalf of his principal (type one), or on behalf of the association he had founded together with his colleague (type two). These types of associations operated all over Europe including in northern and southern Germany.[68] Nikolaus Eisvogel can serve as a more or less random example for an Upper German merchant who was not part of a company, but carried out trade with partners, probably family members, to Flanders, Lombardy and Hungary.[69] Numerous examples for Hanseatic undisclosed associations are recorded in the *Lübecker Niederstadtbuch*.[70] Johann Wittenborch from Lübeck acted as principal, sending his goods with several fellow merchants to trade on his behalf.[71] Vicko van Geldersen formed different undisclosed partnerships, including one with his uncle Albert Luneborch.[72]

67 Robert Lopez, *The Commercial Revolution of the Middle Ages 950–1350* (Cambridge: CUP, 1976).

68 On the European level, the Italian "super-companies" of the Bardi, Peruzzi, Acciaiuoli etc. are often mentioned as examples of the fact that in Italy large corporations existed as early as the late thirteenth century. However, they all went bankrupt during the first decades of the fourteenth century. Thus, they cannot be considered as marking the first step to a Europe-wide phenomenon of large companies, but rather as short-term solutions to short-term problems only, as Hunt and Murray argue: Edwin S. Hunt and James M. Murray, *A History of Business in Medieval Europe, 1200–1500* (Cambridge: CUP, 1999), 122.

69 Stromer, *Oberdeutsche Hochfinanz*, 32.

70 Albrecht Cordes, Klaus Friedland and Rolf Sprandel (eds.), *Societates. Das Verzeichnis der Handelsgesellschaften im Lübecker Niederstadtbuch 1311–1361* (Cologne: Böhlau, 2003).

71 Cordes, *Gesellschaftshandel*, 219–220.

72 Ib., 231–235.

During the fifteenth century, merchants decided not only to cooperate with each other, but also to band together to found companies that were not undisclosed. In the South, examples include the famous *Ravensburger Handelsgesellschaft*, the Imhoff or the Welser trading company in Nuremberg, the company of the Manlich in Augsburg, or the Vöhlin in Memmingen. In northern Germany, examples include the Falbrecht-Morser-Rosenfeld Company, which was based in Toruń and Gdansk, and the Loitz Company in Stettin. The rulings of the city council of Lübeck indicate that at the close of the fifteenth century, Lübeck merchants began to form partnerships with shared external liability, called *vulle mascopei*, as Albrecht Cordes has demonstrated.[73] At least two large corporations, the *Stralengesellschaft* and the *Kalthofgesellschaft*, were based in Cologne.[74] The case of Cologne is a very good example of how the paradigm of networks in the north and trading houses in the south have shaped researchers' findings. Gunther Hirschfelder put forward a development from smaller undisclosed associations to larger companies that took place in Cologne during the fifteenth century. However, as he defines the former as Hanseatic and the latter as upper German, he concludes that business in Cologne must have changed its focus from northern to southern Germany.[75] If we supersede this equation (Hanseatic equals small, undisclosed associations; upper German equals large companies), Hirschfelder's results confirm the hypothesis that during the fifteenth century, business structures changed. Alongside the trading houses, numerous merchants still carried out trade without belonging to a company, for instance the Zeringer brothers, who successfully carried out their trade via diverse associations between Nuremberg, Genoa and Antwerp.[76] Hildebrand Veckinchusen based himself in Bruges and carried out commission trade, for example for his brother Sievert, who did business in Lübeck, and for his father-in-law Engelbrecht Witte from Riga.[77]

In the late fifteenth and sixteenth century, some of the companies underwent organizational change. Instead of a large circle of type three partners, only a very limited number of partners were allowed to invest capital and discuss the strategy of the company. This development corresponds with a growing number of type four employees carrying out business at the outposts of the

---

73 Ib., 266.

74 Franz Irsigler, "Kölner Wirtschaft im Spätmittelalter," in Hermann Kellenbenz (ed.), *Zwei Jahrtausende Kölner Wirtschaft*, vol. 1 (Cologne: Greven, 1975), 217–319, see 284 and 294.

75 Hirschfelder, *Handelsbeziehungen*, 549.

76 Marco Veronesi, *Oberdeutsche Kaufleute in Genua, 1350–1490. Institutionen, Strategien, Kollektive* (Stuttgart: Kohlhammer, 2014), 294.

77 Cordes, *Gesellschaftshandel*, 244.

company, instead of type three partners representing their company at the important trading hubs. The most famous example of this new kind of company is the Fugger Company, which developed a "quasi-monarchical structure" with one sole disposer ("*Regierer*") at the top.[78] To a lesser degree, the Welser Company based at Augsburg or the Paumgartner from Nuremberg underwent the same changes. The same is true for the Loitz Company from Stettin in the Hanseatic area. However, there were still plenty of type three companies and undisclosed associations doing business. The Hochstetter or the Imhof Company did not strengthen their hierarchical structures to the same extent as did the Fugger Company.[79] Other merchants still relied mostly on undisclosed associations. For example, Herden Dude's vibrant trading network stretched from Southern Germany over Cologne to the Netherlands.[80] Ulrich Meltinger traded on commission for his brother Martin from their hometown Basel, to France and Flanders, whereas his brother Martin served as Ulrich's commissioner in trade with France.[81] Based in Tallinn, Hans Selhorst set up undisclosed associations with merchants from Lübeck as vehicles for trade to England and the Netherlands.[82] Donald Harreld's study of High Germans in Antwerp shows that even though the bulk of trade was carried out by large trading houses, the majority of southern German merchants traded only small amounts of merchandise and mostly only to their home towns.[83]

In sum, by employing two very basic criteria—was the association disclosed or undisclosed? did one or both participants contribute capital?—the empirical evidence can be grouped into four types. These four types enable us to consider the development of trading organizations in a different light. We do not see networks in the north and trading houses in the south, but a development that happened in both regions. Disclosed partnerships emerged alongside undisclosed associations during the fifteenth century. At the end of the fifteenth and the beginning of the sixteenth century, some of the undisclosed

78 Reinhard Hildebrandt, "Unternehmensstrukturen im Wandel. Personal- und Kapitalgesellschaften vom 15.–17. Jahrhundert," in Hans Jürgen Gerhard (ed.), *Struktur und Dimension. Festschrift für Karl-Heinrich Kaufhold zum 65. Geburtstag. 1: Mittelalter und Frühe Neuzeit* (Stuttgart: Steiner, 1997), 93–110, see 99.

79 Riebartsch, *Handelsgesellschaften*, 226–228.

80 Hirschfelder, *Handelsbeziehungen*, 550.

81 Steinbrink, "Netzwerkhandel," 324.

82 Carsten Jahnke, *Netzwerke in Handel und Kommunikation an der Wende vom 15. zum 16. Jahrhundert am Beispiel zweier Revaler Kaufleute* (*Habilitations*-thesis University of Kiel, 2004), chapter 3.4.

83 Harreld, *High Germans*, 75–80.

partnerships began to employ greater numbers of servants who did not invest capital into the partnership and thus did not have a share in gains and losses.[84]

5 Companies

The systematization of associations into four types does not by itself answer the question "what is a company?", but it can help to get a clearer picture of what we are looking for. In some cases, one of the partners of a partnership was not a person, but a group of persons. Such a group of persons could even be called a *compagnia*, a company. To be precise, the deeds of Antwerp notaries show that the associate of a merchant could be considered in three different ways. A merchant could be authorized to act (1) on behalf of another person, (2) on behalf of a person and his associates, or (3) on behalf of a company. For example, (1) Johannes Ralander, a German merchant in Antwerp, commissioned Peter Amsteghen to carry out trade of all sorts and to collect his debts in lower and upper Germany.[85] (2) Martin Lombairt from Basel, in his own name and on behalf of his associate Jakob Hanradt, authorized Peter Nouts to collect debts in the Westphalian towns of Minden, Münster and Osnabrück.[86] (3) Jakob Rembold acted on behalf of the company of Bartholomeus Welser when paying off debts.[87] Thus, notaries at Antwerp obviously had a notion of a company as an entity that could authorize someone to act on its behalf. A possible definition could therefore hold a company as an entity that did not equal a single merchant but which could nonetheless act as a merchant in entering partnerships.

But what changed if one of the associates was not a single merchant, but a company? Did it make a difference for merchants if they were employed by one person, several persons or by a company? Looking at the tasks they had to fulfil, it is not possible to see any difference. Regardless of the person, persons or company for whom they worked, they bought and sold, arranged deliveries, organized legal support, and accepted or refused letters of exchange. Most agents even employed servants of their own for doing the actual buying, selling or collecting of debts.

84 This hypothesis is based on empirical data collected by the researchers I mentioned above. My current research project is going to test the hypothesis with source materials from Antwerp.

85 *Aus Antwerpener Notariatsarchiven*, 57 (no. 51).

86 Ib., 59 (no. 57).

87 Ib., 62–63 (no. 65).

It is not clear whether the merchants and notaries of late medieval Antwerp regarded the three cases as different. For example, Hans Pruner carried out business in Lisbon and Andalusia for his brother Joachim Pruner, a merchant who was from Berlin but was based in Antwerp.[88] In 1525, Joachim Pruner went into a type three partnership with Kilian Rietwieser from Leipzig.[89] They then employed Hans to carry out trade in Lisbon. In the corresponding contract, Hans is sometimes mentioned as working for Pruner and Rietwieser, sometimes as acting on behalf of the company of Pruner and Rietwieser.[90] The notary obviously did not see any difference between describing Hans as agent of two persons or as an agent of a company.

In conclusion, it seems that merchants of the fifteenth and sixteenth century did not see a big difference between "a merchant (who was part of a company) who employs a servant" and "a company which employs a servant". A servant who worked for a company was not an idea that the Italians had invented and which had been copied by everyone else afterwards,[91] but something that emerged slowly out of the well-known practice that someone acted on behalf of another merchant.

The contracts in which merchants agreed to join their capital for certain enterprises provide some hints as to when a group of merchants turned into someone acting as one single entity under the name of a company. Servants changed from being servants of one of the partners to being servants of the company as a whole when they were paid out of the joined capital of the associates. If their salary and, more importantly, their board and lodging, was not paid by a single merchant, but they were paid out of the joined capital of the company, they were called servants of the company.[92] A company began to act as a unity, not as a buyer or seller, since buying and selling were still done by individual merchants on behalf of the company. A company acted as a unity in employing servants, because the company as an entity paid them. The

88 Ib., 18–21 (no. 13). Johannes is called the *comiss* of Joachim Pruner.

89 Lutz, *Urkunden*, 49–59.

90 *Aus Antwerpener Notariatsarchiven*, 43–46 (no. 36). He is alternatively said to be employed by "*Joachim Pruner (…) tam suo proprio et privato nomine quam nomine sue societatis cantantis et intitulate Joachim Pruner et Kilianus Rietwieser*", or by "*Joachim Pruner pro se et dicto Kyliano Rietwieser eius socio*".

91 See Amend-Traut, "Handelsgesellschaften".

92 See for example the contract between Anton Haug Senior, Hand Langenauer and Ulrich Link in 1531: "The servants who are called "our servants" ("*unnsere dienner*") shall be paid out of the joined capital ("*sollen mit seys klaidung unnd belonung auß gemeynem handel bezahlt warden*")": Lutz, *Urkunden*, 81.

company also formed an entity in owning horses, presumably because horses were quite expensive. For example, the associates Wilhelm Weißhaupt, Hans Schreiber and Valentin Dietmar from Ulm each had their own servants, but their company bought, fed and owned the horses.[93] In short, the company as a unit acting on its own did not originate from the associates' question "do we regard our company as a "person" in its own right?" but rather from the question: "Who has to pay the bill for the horses or the servants?".

6 Companies as Associations of Capital

That an association could evolve into an entity that could act on its own behalf should not lead to the conclusion that every merchant that was associated with it belonged to this one company alone. A merchant could be part of different types of associations, either successively or at the same time. It was very common for a merchant to play different roles over the course of his lifetime. A typical career path led from being a trading servant (type four) to being admitted as an independent partner in a disclosed or undisclosed partnership (type three or two). For example, Bertold started as a servant of Johann Wittenborch in Lübeck and later became one of his most important partners.[94] Some of the Fugger employees, notably Mathias Oertel, Wolff Haller and Bernhard Stecher in Antwerp, went from being type four employees to investing their own money in the Fugger company and in other enterprises.[95]

But a merchant could also fulfil different roles at the same time. Examples can be found in the South as well as in the North of the late medieval Holy Roman Empire. Ulrich Meltinger from Basel entered different undisclosed partnerships with his brother and with other merchants from Basel; and he took part in a type three partnership, the "*Große Gesellschaft*", which consisted of multiple partners contributing large amounts of money.[96]

The Hanseatic merchant Hildebrandt Veckinchusen was both principal and agent in commission trade (type one), for his brother Sivert who was based in Lübeck and for his father-in-law Engelbrecht Witte in Riga. He engaged in numerous undisclosed partnerships, for example with his brother Sivert,

93 "(…) *den habern zu den Pfarten, wem oder wie vil wir der hetten, den sollen wir den rossen von unnser gemain unnd gesellschafft die bestimmpen anzall jaur selbs kauffen und bezallen*": Lutz, *Urkunden*, 14.

94 Cordes, *Gesellschaftshandel*, 217.

95 Ortner, *Handlungsgehilfe*, 52.

96 Steinbrink, "Netzwerkhandel," 324–330.

with Hinrich Tyte and Hans van der Woesten in Tallinn, and with his brother and two merchants from Gdansk, Gottschalk von dem Bokel and Lodewich Buggendal. Besides, he was one of the partners of the Venetian society, a disclosed partnership that traded furs to and spices from Venice over land, with little success.[97] Johann von Lunen from Cologne served as type four employee for the *vogt* of Vyborg, traded on commission for merchants from Tallinn, founded a number of undisclosed partnerships with other merchants from Cologne, and was a member of the type three Falbrecht Company.[98] He also joined capital with Gerhard van der Hosen and Johann van Roide to form a disclosed company that traded cloth between Cologne and Breslau. Another merchant from Cologne, Godard Stertzgin, employed several type four servants to do business for him in the Netherlands and Southern Germany, as well as forming a type two or type three partnership with Gottschalk van Gilse and the Frankfurt merchant Johann van Melem for trade to Southern Italy.[99]

Merchants worked for different disclosed companies at the same time. Harreld shows that in the case of Antwerp, factors served different trading houses.[100] Numerous merchants from Leipzig situated in Antwerp received orders from different companies of Leipzig, Nuremberg and Augsburg. Lazarus Tucher worked for different companies in Upper Germany—the Fugger, the Höchstätter, the Manlich and the Welser—as well as founding the Antwerp branch of the company belonging to his own family.[101] At the mine of Falkenstein in Northern Tyrol, the Fugger Company employees Jakob Sauerzopf and Jörg Hörmann did business for the Prechter Company as well. In the Upper Rhine region, type four servants worked for the Prechter as well as for the Fugger company.[102]

Merchants obviously did not favour one type of cooperation over another. Present-day researchers sometimes consider undisclosed partnerships to be

97 Rolf Hammel-Kiesow, "Hildebrand Veckinchusen—ein Kaufmann an der Zeitenwende," in Gisela Graichen and Rolf Hammel-Kiesow (eds.), *Die deutsche Hanse. Eine heimliche Supermacht* (Reinbek bei Hamburg: Rowohlt, 2011), 219–246, see 231–235; Cordes, *Gesellschaftshandel*, 244.

98 Hucker, "Johann von Lunen," 395–400.

99 Hirschfelder, *Handelsbeziehungen*, 550.

100 Harreld, *High Germans*, 73.

101 Bauernfeind, "Marktinformationen," 26.

102 Angelika Westermann and Ekkehard Westermann, "Der Papier-, Kupfer- und Silberhandel der Straßburger Prechter in der ersten Hälfte des 16. Jahrhunderts," in Angelika Westermann and Stefanie von Welser (eds.), *Beschaffungs- und Absatzmärkte oberdeutscher Firmen im Zeitalter der Welser und Fugger* (Husum: Matthiesen, 2011), 253–271, see 257–259.

an old-fashioned type of business organization, whereas large disclosed companies are seen as signposts of modern times.[103] Late medieval merchants, in contrast, apparently did not regard disclosed associations as the absolute best way to do business. Even merchants who knew such companies from first-hand experience chose to organize other business activities in another form, for example as commission trade. This finding accords with Frederic Lane's observation that merchants always choose more than one institution to deal with challenges, since every institution serves a different purpose.[104] Lane analyzes how merchants dealt with the threat of violence, but his conclusions seem to apply for the case of business organization as well.

The categorization of the four types enables us to see that merchants could be part of different trading organizations at the same time. Hence, we cannot define a firm on the basis of the merchants who belonged to it. A firm is not the sum of a merchant's or some merchants' activities. Rather, a firm can be seen as a number of different kinds of alliances, while neither the number nor the type of the alliances must remain the same over time. As I discussed in the previous section, a firm became an entity not as a sum of people, but as a sum of capital. A company acted as an entity when something or someone was paid out of its shared capital.

7 Conclusion: What is a Small Firm?

This short investigation of late medieval trading organizations provides us with some indications as to how we can—and how we cannot—grasp what a firm is. A short overview of the names given to trading organizations by contemporaries and in current research reveals that different names did not necessarily correspond to different types of organizations. The term *compagnia* does not carry any implications about the specific nature of the company in question. Since it proved difficult to find a clear-cut definition of different types of business organizations, I followed the suggestion that was made by researchers of modern firms, namely, to focus not on trading organizations, but rather on the basic unit of cooperation between merchants, which is the agreement between parties. Empirical studies analyzing late medieval trade offer a number of case studies for such agreements. Comparing these agreements, it turns out that

---

103 Trivellato, *The Familiarity of Strangers*.

104 Frederic Lane, "Economic Consequences of Organized Violence," *Journal of Economic History* 18 (1958), 401–417, see 409–410.

they can be grouped into four categories, combining two criteria. First, was it an undisclosed or a disclosed association? Secondly, did each partner or only a number of them invest capital into the association?

The systematization—as with every systematization—does not level out some complications, but it turns out to be an efficient tool for analyzing how merchants from the Holy Roman Empire organized their business activities, since it helps to see the picture of late medieval trade more clearly. First, it proves difficult to find the dividing line between northern and southern Germany, which, according to scholarly tradition, marked the landscape of trading organizations. In the northern part undisclosed partnerships would have abounded, and in the southern part large companies would have compounded into type three and type four partnerships. Instead, a chronological process becomes evident. Disclosed companies emerged alongside undisclosed associations during the fifteenth century, with some of them employing a larger number of type four servants at the end of the century. Secondly, partners agreeing to cooperate could be individual merchants, but they could also be a group of merchants that had been formed with an earlier agreement and which was given one of the possible labels for a company (*compagnia, selscop, societas* etc.). In this instance, thus, we can view companies acting as entities. The entity comes into being by disposing of the shared capital. When something or someone is paid out of the joined capital which the partners had pooled, this is done not by one merchant or by a group of merchants, but by the company itself. Third, a merchant could be part of different forms of associations at the same time.

In conclusion, a firm can be characterized as cluster of alliances, which can in turn be of different types, and changing over time. Some associations could come to an end, others could be added, and partnerships could change in structure. For example, a type four associate could be hired or fired, or he could at some point start to invest capital in the business and thus turn into a type three partner. This cluster of alliances acted as an entity when it disposed of the joint capital of the associates, that is, when it paid something (a horse, lodging) or someone (a servant), or when it joined capital with another partner to form a new partnership. Since it was a cluster of alliances, the firm was a cluster of capital; furthermore, it acted as an entity by disposing of the joint capital. The appropriate benchmark for the largeness or smallness of a firm thus seems to be the amount of its capital. A large firm was one with a large capital stock. But how large was a large capital stock? This question was discussed at the Imperial Diet in Nuremberg in 1522/23. During the previous years, prices had risen, especially for spices, and the large trading companies were blamed for it. A committee of the Imperial Diet proposed a number of regulations that were intended to break the market power of the Fugger, Welser and a few others. The committee recommended that it should be forbidden for trading houses to have a capital stock of more than 50,000 guilders.[105] It would have been interesting to see how this regulation was enforced, but the proceedings never went that far. The question was discussed over the next couple of years, with the number of 50,000 guilders popping up a few times during the discussions, but the regulations were never enacted since the trading houses under suspicion were important sources of credit for the Emperor.[106]

The excursion into the Late Middle Ages thus offers a new perspective on the quest to find the nature of the firm. A firm consisted of a number of different associations, but the merchants that were joined in these associations were highly likely to be linked to other merchants in other associations at the same time. A firm can therefore not be defined on the basis of the merchants belonging to it. Instead, it was the joining of capital that constituted a firm or company, in the sense of an entity. Contemporaries regarded a firm with more than 50,000 guilders of stock as a large company. Such companies emerged during the end of the fifteenth and at the beginning of the sixteenth century, probably in southern as well as in northern Germany. They were not considered to be the one best solution to all challenges merchants faced when trading across Europe, since most merchants, even the ones working for prominent trading houses, at the same time carried out part of their trading activities in other types of business associations, for example as commission trade. Small firms with a small capital stock obviously served a need that almost all late medieval merchants across Europe felt.

---

105 Bernd Mertens, *Im Kampf gegen die Monopole. Reichstagsverhandlungen und Monopolprozesse im frühen 16. Jahrhundert* (Tübingen: Mohr, 1996), 46.

106 Mertens, *Im Kampf gegen die Monopole*, 100 and 153.

CHAPTER 2

Making Size Matter Less: Italian Firms and Merchant Guilds in Late Medieval Bruges

Bart Lambert

1 Introduction

In the past few decades, the role played by merchant guilds in the pre-modern European economy has been at the centre of historical debate. In the wake of Douglass North and the New Institutional Economics, many scholars have argued that corporate associations of merchants only existed for such a long period of time because they were efficient institutions that benefited general economic growth. Some, most notably Avner Greif, have claimed that merchant guilds promoted commercial security by making rulers commit to the protection of traders' property, by providing mechanisms for contract enforcement or by sorting out principal-agent relationships.[1] Others have stated that merchant organizations were essential for the distribution of market information[2] or that they had a stabilizing effect on prices. In a 2010 article, Regina Grafe and Oscar Gelderblom concluded that, depending on a set of variables, merchant guilds were used in combination with other institutions to solve a multitude of commercial problems.[3] A completely opposite view on the role of these associations was advanced by Sheila Ogilvie. In her *Institutions and European Trade*, Ogilvie characterized merchant guilds as institutions that prevented, rather than facilitated, economic development. Only interested in seeking rents in favour of their own members, they established monopolies

---

1 Avner Greif, Paul Milgrom and Barry Weingast, "Coordination, Commitment, and Enforcement: The Case of the Merchant Guild," *Journal of Political Economy* 102:4 (1994), 912–950; Avner Greif, *Institutions and the Path to the Modern Economy: Lessons from Medieval Trade* (Cambridge: CUP, 2006), 58–90, and 318–349.

2 Don Harreld, *High Germans in the Low Countries: German Merchants and Commerce in Golden Age Antwerp* (Leiden: Brill, 2004), 41, 45, and 58.

3 Regina Grafe and Oscar Gelderblom, "The Rise and Fall of the Merchant Guilds: Re-thinking the Comparative Study of Commercial Institutions in Premodern Europe," *Journal of Interdisciplinary History* 40:4 (2010), 477–511.

 | DOI: 10.1163/9789004351868_004

while barring others from accessing the market, reducing overall well-being and growth.[4]

A variable that is not taken into account in any of these assessments is company size. Most merchant guilds in pre-modern Europe were made up of individuals who, first and foremost, were involved in a variety of commercial partnerships. Even in one and the same guild, these partnerships could differ considerably in size and in functionality. It would be premature to assume that merchant guilds would have served the same interests for members with such different affiliations. This chapter will investigate whether company size impacted the way in which Italian merchants in late medieval Bruges made use of merchant guild structures.

During the fourteenth and fifteenth centuries, Bruges, a city of about 40,000 inhabitants in the county of Flanders, served as a meeting point for traders from all over Europe.[5] Many of them were organized in foreign merchant guilds or so-called nations, according to their places of origin. Prominent amongst those guilds were the nations of merchants from the Italian cities of Venice, Genoa, Lucca and Florence.[6] For shorter periods of time, associations were also set up by traders from Siena and Sicily. The members of these nations engaged in businesses that ranged from one-man enterprises to colossal monster firms. During the fourteenth century, Bruges was a crucial node in the commercial networks of the so-called Florentine super companies such as the Bardi and the Peruzzi, who employed hundreds of members of staff and had branches all over the Western world.[7] Following their collapse, Lucchese firms took over and evolved into smaller and more decentralized entities.[8] The biggest merchant house in fifteenth-century Europe, the Florentine Medici bank, managed

---

4 Sheilagh Ogilvie, *Institutions and European Trade: Merchant Guilds, 1000–1800* (Cambridge: CUP, 2011).

5 See James M. Murray, *Bruges: Cradle of Capitalism, 1280–1390* (Cambridge: CUP, 2005).

6 For the Venetians, see Peter Stabel, "Venice and the Low Countries. Commercial Contacts and Intellectual Inspirations," in Bernard Aikema and Beverly L. Brown (eds.), *Renaissance Venice and the North: Crosscurrents in the Time of Bellini, Dürer and Titian* (New York: St Martins Press, 1999), 31–43. For the Genoese Giovanna Petti Balbi, *Mercanti e nationes nelle Fiandre. I genovesi in età bassomedievale* (Pisa: GISEM, 1996). For the Lucchese Raymond De Roover, "La communauté des marchands Lucquois à Bruges de 1377 à 1404," *Annales de la Société d'Emulation de Bruges* 86 (1949), 23–89.

7 Edwin S. Hunt, *The Medieval Super-Companies. A Study of the Peruzzi Company of Florence* (Cambridge: CUP, 1994), 145–146.

8 John F. Padgett and Paul D. McLean, "Organizational Invention and Elite Transformation. The Birth of Partnership Systems in Renaissance Florence," *American Journal of Sociology* 111:5 (2006), 1463–1568, here 1479.

interests all over Europe, including Bruges, through a holding-like structure of connected companies.[9] Unlike the Tuscans, the Genoese relied on combinations of short-term individual partnerships[10] and the Venetians remained more sedentary while commission agents did the work abroad.[11] Even within these groups of traders from the same cities, company sizes and structures could differ endlessly. Did the way in which these merchants used their merchant guilds vary accordingly?

2 Monopolies and Rent Seeking

According to Sheila Ogilvie, merchant guilds in pre-modern Europe should be considered to be monopolists, created with the intention of claiming and enforcing exclusive legal rights over particular lines of trade for their members.[12] While this might have been true for many guilds of local traders, Ogilvie's model is more difficult to apply to the Italian nations in late medieval Bruges. Upon their establishment, the associations of Italian merchants were granted legal privileges, first by the count of Flanders, after 1385 by the duke of Burgundy: the Venetians obtained their first charter in 1358, the Lucchese in 1369, the Genoese in 1395 and the Florentines in 1427.[13] All of these grants were later renewed, extended or restricted, depending on the circumstances. The privileges entitled the nations to specific series of fiscal exemptions that could significantly lower transaction costs. Yet none of them gave any of the Italian merchant guilds in Bruges the exclusive right to trade in certain goods or areas. The fact that princely privileges were preferable but not essential to engage

9 For the Medici bank, see Raymond De Roover, *The Rise and Decline of the Medici Bank, 1397–1494* (Cambridge (Ma.): Harvard University Press, 1963), 338–346.

10 Roberto S. Lopez, "Le marchand génois: un profil collectif," *Annales: Economies, Sociétés, Civilisations* 13/3 (1958), 505–515.

11 Stabel, "Venice and the Low Countries," 32.

12 Ogilvie, *Institutions and European Trade*, 94–159.

13 For the Lucchese, Eugenio Lazzareschi, "Gli statuti dei Lucchesi a Bruges e ad Anversa," in *Ad Alessandro Luzio. Gli Archivi di Stato italiani. Miscellanea di studi storici*, vol. 2 (Florence: Le Monnier, 1933), 75–88, here 85. For the Genoese, Andrée Van Nieuwenhuysen and John Bartier (eds.), *Ordonnances de Philippe le Hardi et de Marguerite de Male du 17 janvier 1394 au 25 février 1405* (Brussels: Commission royale des anciennes lois et ordonnances, 1974), 791–794. For the Florentines, Armand Grunzweig, "Le fonds du Consulat de la Mer aux Archives de l'Etat à Florence," *Bulletin de l'Institut Historique Belge de Rome* 10 (1930), 5–121, here 105–106.

in commercial exchange is corroborated by the activities in the city of merchants without guilds. Some groups of traders originating from places that did not have a merchant guild of their own did join one of the existing nations: the Bolognese associated with the Lucchese, the Piacentines with the Genoese and those coming from smaller towns in Tuscany with the Florentines.[14] Others, however, traded in the city for substantial periods without the support of a guild: the Florentines only received their first privileges in the Low Countries in 1427, but were active in Bruges for decades before. Outside the Italian communities, merchants from France visited the city throughout the whole late medieval period without ever founding a nation.[15]

Neither did the Italian merchant guilds in late medieval Bruges obtain *de facto* monopolies in the way that the German Hansa, which controlled nearly all trade with Northern Europe, did.[16] The divisions between the Italian cities and their specialization in similar ranges of high value goods always allowed for sufficient competition. During the last quarter of the fourteenth and the first quarter of the fifteenth centuries, the Lucchese dominated the market in silks but luxury fabrics could still be purchased from the Venetians or Genoese as well.[17] Before the middle of the fifteenth century, alum, a raw material that was indispensable in the Flemish textile industries, was mainly provided by Genoese traders but could also be procured from the Venetians.[18] The Italian nations could and did exclude merchants who did not adhere to their internal regulations and prohibited other members of the guild in Bruges and sister associations in other places to continue working with them. What the evildoers were denied in these cases, however, was not so much access to a legal or factual monopoly, but the support and collaboration of colleague merchants. Being ostracized could be particularly damaging to smaller businesses, who could not

14 For the Piacentines, see Giovanna Petti Balbi, "I piacentini tra Genova e i Paesi Bassi," in *Precursori di Cristoforo Colombo. Mercanti e banchieri piacentini nel mondo durante il medioevo. Atti del convegno internazionale di studio* (Piacenza: Analisi, 1994), 69–88.

15 Émile Coornaert, *Les Français et le commerce international à Anvers, fin du XVe–XVIe siècle* (Paris: Rivière, 1961), 113.

16 Philippe Dollinger, *The German Hansa* (London: Routledge, 1970), 370–371.

17 Bart Lambert, ""Se fist riche par draps de soye". The Intertwinement of Italian Financial Interests and Luxury Trade at the Burgundian Court (1384–1481)," in Bart Lambert and Katherine A. Wilson (eds.), *Europe's Rich Fabric. The Consumption, Commercialisation and Production of Luxury Textiles in Italy, the Low Countries and Neighbouring Territories (Fourteenth-Sixteenth Centuries)* (Farnham: Ashgate, 2016), 91–106.

18 Léone Liagre, "Le commerce de l'alun en Flandre au moyen âge," *Le Moyen Age* 61 (1955), 177–206.

fall back on elaborate firm structures with branches elsewhere, but had to rely on fellow citizens for their supplies and sales in other parts of Europe.[19]

When it came to rent seeking, Italian merchants in Bruges had more effective options at their disposal than the merchant guild had. As rulers did everywhere in medieval Europe, the princes of the Low Countries were in permanent need of liquidities to finance the administration of their dominions and the organization of military and dynastic projects. Certainly during the late fourteenth and the fifteenth centuries, the territorial ambitions of the Burgundian dukes created an enormous demand for ready cash.[20] Whoever was able to meet this demand could expect to be rewarded with fiscal and other privileges that far exceeded those obtained by the merchant guilds. Yet, because of the size of the princes' financial needs, government lending was primarily reserved for the largest firms with high turnovers and vast amounts of idle funds. The big Tuscan firms in particular, which were set up with a considerable inlay of capital, were contracted to function for several years and had access to a branch-based international payment system, proved themselves reliable creditors.

The Rapondi firm was a Lucchese company that had branches in Bruges, Paris, Avignon, Venice and Pisa and, in various compositions, continued to operate from the 1360s until at least the 1420s. From the middle of the 1370s onwards, they provided the first two Burgundian dukes, Philip the Bold and John the Fearless, with hundreds of thousands of pounds, either by supplying credit directly or by advancing the tax payments of the Flemish cities. The rewards were legion: apart from priority repayments of their loans, the Rapondi became the first choice suppliers of silks to the pomp-loving Burgundian court. Several members of the family were made ducal councillors and got a say in the princes' commercial and financial policy. They were invested with numerous honorary positions and were given lucrative fiscal revenues.[21]

From the 1460s until the early 1480s, Dukes Philip the Good and Charles the Bold borrowed extensively from Tommaso Portinari, manager of the local branch of the Medici Bank. Organized as a holding company, the Medici controlled offices in Bruges, London, Geneva, Lyons, Avignon, Pisa, Milan, Venice and at the papal court, and were involved in the silk and cloth business. Porti-

---

19 For examples, see Eugenio Lazzareschi (ed.), *Libro della Communità dei Merchanti Lucchesi in Bruges* (Milan: Malfasi, 1947), 43, 159–160.

20 Jelle Haemers and Bart Lambert, "Pouvoir et argent. La fiscalité d'État et la consommation du crédit des ducs de Bourgogne (1484–1506)," *Revue du Nord* 91:379 (2009), 35–59.

21 Lambert, "Se fist riche par draps de soye," 92–97; Bart Lambert, *The City, the Duke and their Banker. The Rapondi Family and the Formation of the Burgundian State (1384–1430)* (Turnhout: Brepols, 2006), 41–149.

nari, too, was appointed Ducal Councillor and was guaranteed a steady stream of ducal orders for the Medici silk shop. He was given the revenues of the wool toll in Gravelines and, in 1468, secured something which none of the merchant guilds had ever achieved. After deposits of alum had been discovered in the Papal States in Italy and the pope had engaged the Medici for its commercialization, Charles the Bold granted Portinari a legal monopoly on the sale of the raw material. At the frustration of all other suppliers, only alum of the papal-Medici cartel could be distributed in the duke's territories until 1473, when customers in the Low Countries were no longer prepared to pay the artificially high prices.[22] It was not through the membership of merchant guilds that companies were able to obtain the most significant commercial privileges, let alone monopolies that excluded others from the market, from rulers in late medieval Bruges; it was by making the best use of their individual financial reserves. Accordingly, firms with more capital at their disposal had far more opportunities for rent seeking.

Ogilvie argued that merchant guilds allowed smaller firms and merchants who did not have the capacities to meet the financial demands of rulers on their own to pool resources and contribute to loans in return for privileges anyway.[23] It is true that the Italian nations shared in the forced loans raised by the city of Bruges in 1379, 1411 and 1438, when the urban treasury was in desperate need of money.[24] The Genoese merchant guild also provided funds to the Burgundian duke in the hope of obtaining more extensive privileges in 1414 and agreed to pay a tax on all incoming Genoese ships when it sought the confirmation of its rights in 1434.[25] Yet the revenues from these isolated contributions were negligible compared to the constant credit provided by firms on an individual basis. Italian merchants teamed up to make collective loans to rulers outside the nation structures, working together with traders from other cities, more

22 De Roover, *The Rise and Decline of the Medici Bank*, 157–163; Marc Boone, "Apologie d'un banquier médiéval: Tomasso Portinari et l'Etat bourguignon," *Le Moyen Age* 105 (1999), 38–47; Richard J. Walsh, *Charles the Bold and Italy (1467–1477). Politics and Personnel* (Liverpool: Liverpool University Press, 2005), 129–133.

23 Ogilvie, *Institutions and European Trade*, 176.

24 Louis Gilliodts-Van Severen (ed.), *Inventaire des Archives de la Ville de Bruges. Section Première, Inventaire des Chartes*, vol. 2 (Bruges: Gaillard, 1873), 350; vol. 4 (Bruges: Gaillard, 1876), 90; vol. 5 (Bruges: Gaillard, 1876), 186–187.

25 Jonas Braekevelt, "Entre profit et dommage. Présence et privilèges de la nation génoise à Bruges sous les ducs de Bourgogne (1384–1477)," *Publications du Centre Européen d'Études Bourguignonnes* 49 (2009), 117–129.

frequently than they did within.[26] The merchant guilds did not have the means of their own to do more either: the members' contributions, amounting to about 0.5 per cent of their turnover, only allowed them to cover the costs of ceremonial activities and were not supposed to be used for other purposes. As vehicles for rent seeking, the foreign nations in late medieval Bruges were, thus, not particularly useful.

3 Legal Security and Contract Enforcement

Avner Greif, Paul Milgrom and Barry Weingast, as well as many others, claimed that the main contribution of merchant guilds lay in their capacity to force rulers to provide merchants with legal security.[27] The evidence suggests that this also applied to the Italian nations in late medieval Bruges. The privileges granted to the Genoese in 1395, for example, specified that in case of a Burgundo-Genoese conflict, merchants would not be held individually responsible and would be given sufficient time to leave the duke's territories with their belongings.[28] Many of the Italian guilds also negotiated with the duke or the city whenever the property of one of their members was at risk. The bargaining power to make the ruler commit to these clauses was limited, however. The divisions between the Italian nations and their partial interchangeability prevented them from resorting to embargoes, the weapon of choice of merchant guilds according to Greif, Milgrom and Weingast, in the same way as the German Hansa did. Among the Italians, only the Venetians tried to obtain a more favourable treatment by withdrawing their business from Bruges, in 1319.[29] In fact, the membership of a foreign merchant guild even made merchants particularly vulnerable in case of reprisals. In 1442, the Bruges aldermen seized the Genoese nation house, owned by all Genoese merchants in the city, after the authorities in Genoa had shown their dissatisfaction about the outcome of a court case between one of their subjects, Luca Spinola, and the Florentine Antonio di Francesco.[30]

---

26 See, for example, Lambert, "Se fist riche par draps de soye," 94–95.

27 Greif, Milgrom and Weingast, "Coordination, Commitment, and Enforcement". See also Oscar Gelderblom, *Cities of Commerce. The Institutional Foundations of International Trade in the Low Countries, 1250–1650* (Princeton: Princeton University Press, 2013), 170–180.

28 Van Nieuwenhuysen and Bartier, *Ordonnances de Philippe le Hardi et de Marguerite de Male*, no. 724.

29 Jan Van Houtte, *De Geschiedenis van Brugge* (Tielt: Lannoo, 1982), 171.

30 Genoa, State Archives, *Archivio Segreto, Litterarum*, 1788 (1441–1448), fol. 180^r, and fol. 181^v.

Also when it came to the protection of foreign merchants' property, the relationship between the larger individual firms and the ruler often proved more effective, sometimes even at the expense of the merchant guild. In 1395, houses belonging to the Rapondi family in their hometown of Lucca were confiscated by their political rivals. Drawing on their personal credit with the Burgundian dukes, the merchants agreed with Philip the Bold to transfer the property into his name. The prince subsequently addressed the authorities in Lucca, warning them that if the houses were not released within three months, he would confiscate the goods of all members of the Lucchese merchant guild in Bruges. Soon afterwards, the Rapondi got their property back.[31] The nations themselves were fully aware of the influence of some of their members and often made use of it. In 1394, the Lucchese merchant guild asked the Rapondi to intervene with the duke and the city in order to safeguard the inheritance of one of their merchants.[32] In these cases, the nation thus provided a framework in which members with more modest means could tap into the political and social capital of their more successful fellow citizens.

3.1 *Consular Jurisdiction*

The Italian merchant guilds in Bruges also provided commercial security in their roles as contract enforcing institutions. The privileges obtained from the prince granted most nations the right to judge all commercial disputes between their members themselves, according to the law of their home cities.[33] In the Italian guilds, sentences were ruled in the nation house by the consul, or the head of the community, often in agreement with a number of councillors and sometimes after consultation with all members. We are exceptionally well informed about the consular jurisdiction in the Lucchese nation in Bruges thanks to the preservation of its register, known as the *Libro della Comunità dei Mercanti Lucchesi in Bruges*.[34] The document covers the period 1377 to 1404 and gives a detailed account of the day-to-day business within the guild, including its court sessions. On 3 June 1378, for example, Jacopo del Bello sued Dino Sanocci before the consul in a dispute about an amount of money that was left from a disbanded partnership. Dino Panelli, another member of the nation, was appointed as arbitrator and asked to investigate the case. The next day, Panelli decided that half of the money should go to del Bello, half to Sanocci. His

---

31 Lambert, *The City, the Duke and their Banker*, 104.

32 Lazzareschi, *Libro della Communità*, 210.

33 Gelderblom, *Cities of Commerce*, 110–114.

34 Lazzareschi, *Libro della Communità*. See also De Roover, "La communauté des marchands Lucquois," 23–89.

decision was confirmed by the consul and recorded in the consulate register.[35] At the start of each year, members had to appoint a *pagatore* or guarantor who had to make sure that sentences were executed if parties were unable to do so. In 1378, Pietro Brunelli had to pay the debts of Guido dal Portico, for whom he acted as a *pagatore*.[36] If members could not appear before the consul in person, they were allowed to send a *procuratore* or proxy.[37] In the 27 years covered by the Lucchese register, 42 cases were judged by the consul. The number is remarkably low, though it should be stressed that the *Libro* was updated much less regularly after 1394 and that many disputes were probably settled amicably outside court.

Each year, the nation also recorded the composition of the companies in which its members were involved, or at least gave the names of their partners and factors, together with their trade marks. The register thus allows us to investigate the relationship between company size and the use of jurisdiction in the Lucchese merchant guild in Bruges at the end of the fourteenth century. The businesses ranged from merchants working without partners or factors to firms with multiple branches and over fifteen salaried members of staff. Of the 42 merchants who were involved in a court case between 1377 and 1404, either as a plaintiff or a defendant, 27, or nearly 65 per cent, worked for a firm that had fewer than three employees. The larger companies only appeared before the consul very occasionally. The Rapondi were involved twice in the 27 years of the register, once as a defendant, once when their books were consulted in a case between two other parties.[38] The Guinigi, the only Lucchese company that was bigger than the Rapondi, with branches in Lucca, Bruges, London and Rome, were mentioned three times, once after firing an employee and twice when their factor was made to pay for debts.[39] For these larger firms, the functionality of consular jurisdiction was limited. Unlike the smaller businesses, they mainly traded with non-Lucchese, who could not be prosecuted before the merchant guild. The accounts of the Rapondi with the Bruges money changer Collard de Marke in 1369–1370 make it clear that, even before the expansive growth of the company, fellow citizens only made up a minority of the people they dealt with.[40]

35 Lazzareschi, *Libro della Communità*, 29.

36 Ib., 24.

37 See the case in 1381 in which Pietro Brunelli acted as a proxy for Francesco Panichi. Lazzareschi, *Libro della Communità*, 87.

38 Lazzareschi, *Libro della Communità*, 8, and 66–67.

39 Ib., 111–115, 124–125, and 164–165.

40 Raymond De Roover, *Money, Banking and Credit in Medieval Bruges. Italian Merchant-*

Still, consular jurisdiction allowed the smaller Lucchese companies to sue larger firms when necessary and to expect a relatively impartial judgement. Unlike the Catalan nation, where the heads of the six biggest merchant houses automatically served as judges,[41] the consuls in the Lucchese guild were elected by all the community's members. Of the 21 consuls that served between 1377 and 1404, twelve were part of a business with two or fewer members of staff. The nation thus provided an environment in which the larger firms were prepared to give up a considerable part of their authority and in which company size might have mattered less. Appeals against the sentences of the consul could be lodged before the urban court of the Bruges aldermen, even though not all merchant guilds were equally keen to facilitate this. The Venetian Senate even threatened to fine its subjects who used the urban courts in Bruges and London to settle disputes with fellow Venetians in 1446.[42] Lucchese merchants who wanted to appeal needed to ask, and were usually given, their consul's permission. The *pagatori* of the cases in first instance were often maintained and the sentence of the *Loia di Bruges* was recorded in the consulate register.[43]

3.2 *Higher Jurisdiction*

Commercial disputes with merchants of different origins or with Bruges citizens, which, certainly for the larger companies, were much more frequent, had to be initiated before the courts of the city's aldermen. Cases in which less than £30 *parisis* was at stake were dealt with in the Chamber, and cases with more substantial claims were heard in the *Vierschaar*. Also before the urban courts, parties needed to appoint guarantors. Whereas merchants belonging to large scale companies had the option to call on partners or factors, this was much more difficult for Italians running small businesses. In these cases, membership of a merchant guild could prove very useful. When the Florentine Baptista de Gambaro was sued by Bruges citizen Thomas de Marquil in 1448, Agnolo Tani, consul of the Florentine nation, and seven of the guild's most prominent mer-

---

Bankers, Lombards and Money Changers. A Study in the Origins of Banking (Cambridge (Ma.): Harvard University Press, 1948), 376.

41 Louis Gilliodts-Van Severen (ed.), *Cartulaire de l'ancien Consulat d'Espagne à Bruges. Recueil de documents concernant le commerce maritime et intérieur, le droit des gens public et privé, et l'histoire économique de la Flandre* (Bruges: Plancke, 1901–1902), 98–99.

42 Louis Gilliodts-Van Severen (ed.), *Cartulaire de l'ancien estaple de Bruges. Recueil de documents concernant le commerce intérieur et maritime, les relations internationales et l'histoire de cette ville*, vol. 1 (Bruges: Plancke, 1904), 673.

43 See the case between Francesco Panichi and Fredo da Ghivizano in 1381. Lazzareschi, *Libro della Communità*, 86–95.

chants pledged their own assets to guarantee that the sentence would be duly executed.[44] Nation members could help each other out as proxies as well. The consul of the Venetian community, where trade was often conducted on commission and the number of resident traders was low, was particularly active as a representative of his colleagues in court.[45]

Eager to involve the foreign visitors as much as possible in the city's commercial policy and to make use of their expertise, the aldermen often delegated the authority to reach a verdict in cases brought before the *Vierschaar* to members of the merchant communities. A commission, consisting of two or three arbitrators both sides could agree on, was put together to work out a compromise. Most frequently the parties chose well-reputed and well-acquainted merchants from their own merchant guild. In other cases, the consul of the nation was asked to act as an arbitrator or to appoint one. In 1447, Jacopo Strozzi, Consul of the Florentines, suggested his fellow nation member Piero de Rabatta as part of the commission when Baptista de Gambaro, mentioned earlier, was made to appear.[46] To be part of a foreign merchant guild thus allowed merchants, including those without partners or staff, to mobilize the social, political and financial reputations of the whole community or of its most respected members to further their own case. If more general interests were at stake, the consul could also go to court in the name of all nation members. In 1460, the consul and the merchants of Genoa sued the consul and the merchants of Castile before the *Vierschaar* after Genoese goods had been arrested on Biscayan ships.[47] If merchants did not agree with a verdict reached before the urban courts, they could appeal before the central Burgundian courts of the Council of Flanders or the Great Council, or before the *Parlement de Paris*.[48]

---

44 Bruges, Municipal Archives (henceforth BMA), *Civiele Sententiën Vierschaar*, 1447–1453, fol. 46^{v}.

45 Stabel, "Venice and the Low Countries," 35. See also the case in which Alberto Contarini, consul of the Venetians, represented his late fellow citizen Marco Morosini in 1467. Gilliodts-Van Severen, *Cartulaire de l'ancienne estaple*, vol. 2 (Bruges: Plancke, 1905), 156–157.

46 BMA, *Civiele Sententiën Vierschaar*, 1447–1453, fol. 35^{r}.

47 BMA, *Civiele Sententiën Vierschaar*, 1453–1460, fol. 332^{v}.

48 Jan Dumolyn and Bart Lambert, "Cities of Commerce, Cities of Constraints. International Trade, Government Institutions and the Law of Commerce in Later Medieval Bruges and the Burgundian State," *Low Countries Journal of Social and Economic History* 11 (2014), 89–102, here 90–93.

4 Information Exchange

Several historians have underlined the role of merchant guilds as centres for the collection and exchange of market information.[49] Sheila Ogilvie has dismissed these claims by arguing that the guilds were nowhere as efficient as the individual firms when it came to the distribution of news.[50] It is, of course, true that the information networks of the larger Italian firms, with their branches and correspondents all over the Continent, their numerous *garzoni* or junior members of staff who spent most of their days writing and copying business letters, and their use of private couriers, reached standards that could not be met by anyone else in late medieval Europe. During the second half of the fifteenth century, the Medici agents, including those in Bruges, exchanged thousands of letters with the latest news on market conditions, shipments and exchange rates.[51] Managers such as the Rapondi brothers or Tommaso Portinari served as princely councillors and had access to the highest courtly circles, giving them inside information on political and military developments that could impact trade.[52]

Yet, once again, company size made a crucial difference. Most Italians in Bruges did not control companies such as the Medici firm. The Lucchese community did not only consist of the Rapondi and the Guinigi, but also of people like Ciecio da Colle who, in 1392, had no partners or factors[53] and for whom the collective services offered by the nation must have been welcome. The Lucchese and the Genoese merchant guild each operated their own *scarsella* or courier service.[54] The Venetian consul kept all correspondence in two chests that were sent to Venice each month.[55] For many, the nation house must have been the place where they picked up commercial news from colleagues and political rumours from more acquainted fellow members. It was also where

49 See, for example, Harreld, *High Germans*, 41.

50 Ogilvie, *Institutions and European Trade*, 378–381.

51 Armand Grunzweig (ed.), *Correspondance de la filiale de Bruges des Medici* (Brussels: Lamertin, 1931).

52 Eugenio Lazzareschi and Léon Mirot, "Lettere di mercanti lucchesi da Bruges e da Parigi, 1407–1421," *Bolletino Storico Lucchese* 1 (1929), 165–199.

53 Lazzareschi, *Libro della Communità*, 184.

54 See "*la nostra scarsella*" in Lazzareschi, *Libro della Communità*, 146, 148, 243, and 250. For the "*scarsella genovese*," see Lazzareschi, *Libro della Communità*, 31.

55 Louis Gilliodts-Van Severen (ed.), *Cartulaire de l'ancien estaple de Bruges. Recueil de documents concernant le commerce intérieur et maritime, les relations internationales et l'histoire de cette ville*, vol. 2 (Bruges: Plancke, 1905), 107.

the official directives arrived from merchants' hometowns, which kept their nations up to date with the latest developments in the diplomatic relations between Italy and the Low Countries.

5 Ceremony and Sociability

Ceremonial issues played an important part in the organization of the nations. They were the subject of many of its discussions and they were what nearly all members' contributions were spent on. Each of the Italian merchant guilds owned a chapel in one of the churches of the Bruges mendicant orders, where they regularly sang mass. That of the Lucchese, in the church of the Augustines, was dedicated to the *Volto Santo* or the Holy Cross, their hometown's patron saint. Religious services were attended by all nation members, both big and small, and those absent were fined. The merchant guild had its own livery, which had to be worn on feast days and had to be looked after carefully. In 1387, Simone Schiatta was heavily reprimanded and fined for losing his uniform in a game of dice.[56] Lengthy debates were held about whether or not it was a good idea to allow associate members to wear the livery as well.[57] Two *pacieri* were appointed each year, who had to coordinate all ceremonial matters.[58] When rulers made their Joyous Entry into the city, all foreign nations marched through the streets in solemn procession, fitted out in splendid dress and carrying flags or other ornaments.[59]

These activities were more than mere manifestations of empty pomp and circumstance. The nations' ceremonies cultivated a sense of community that could be economically beneficial. Shared religious devotion and the participation in collective activities reduced the chance of conflicts and created and reinforced bonds with people who could be your next partner, arbitrator or proxy. Taking part in the merchant guild's ceremonies also fostered symbolic

56 Lazzareschi, *Libro della Communità*, 139.

57 Ib., 68, 154, and 159.

58 All these issues were specified in the nation's statutes. See Lazzareschi, *Libro della Communità*, 271–279.

59 For an account of the festivities during Philip the Good's Joyous Entry in 1440, Nicolas Despars, *Cronijcke van den lande ende graefscepe van Vlaenderen*, Jean Antoine De Jonghe (ed.), vol. 3 (Bruges: De Jonghe, 1839), 431–432. For Charles the Bold's entry in 1468, Olivier de la Marche, *Mémoires d'Olivier de la Marche, maitre d'hôtel et capitaine des gardes de Charles le Téméraire*, Henri Beaune and Jules D'Arbaumont (eds.), vol. 3 (Paris: Renouard, 1885), 113–114.

capital. When the foreign nations welcomed Duke Charles the Bold in Bruges in 1468, Tommaso Portinari was allowed to ride on horseback in front of all other Florentine nation members.[60] His performance must have gained him respect in the circles whose clientele he tried to secure. Yet Portinari and many other managers of large Italian firms had alternative means of gaining honour and prestige: they rubbed shoulders with the courtly and urban high society, held honorary positions with the duke or offices in their hometowns. For smaller merchants, let alone factors or errand boys, the pathways to social recognition were scarcer. The nations' ceremonies, both internal and external, provided them with opportunities for ostentation which they would never have been able to generate themselves. Here, too, the collective goods of the merchant guilds benefited smaller companies differently to the way they benefited larger firms.

6 Conclusion: The Italian Merchant Guilds as Tools for Capital Redistribution

The Italian nations in late medieval Bruges were made up of merchants whose businesses ranged from one man enterprises to colossal multinational firms. The roles which the merchant guild structures played in their activities were also very diverse. The nations' privileges provided smaller companies with minimal fiscal rents and the basic protection of property rights in a foreign ruler's territories. Consular jurisdiction offered them a fairly impartial way of enforcing contracts with fellow citizens, which might still take up a large part of their business. Much more importantly, membership of a merchant guild and the sociability it promoted allowed them to compensate for their individual limitations and to draw on the social, economic, financial and symbolic capital of the whole community or its most prominent members. This could be highly profitable in urban courtrooms or when addressing local rulers, and give them access to information and social recognition that would never have been available otherwise.

The direct commercial interests of nation membership for larger Italian firms were more restricted. By providing financial services to rulers they could obtain more far reaching privileges and a more preferential settlement of property disputes than the merchant guild could offer. Engaged in business that involved more merchants from other cities than fellow nation members,

60 de la Marche, *Mémoires d'Olivier de la Marche*, 3, 113–114.

consular jurisdiction only gave them legal security for a small part of their work. The information networks of their own firms were definitely more efficient than the collective solutions of the nation were. Yet the merchant guild could also be beneficial to them. It provided them with an environment in which patron-client relationships could be fostered, that were useful both inside and outside the world of trade. Fellow nation members could be adopted into the business as factors or partners or could render services in merchants' hometowns. When, during the 1390s, the Rapondi family became involved in a factional conflict in Lucca, many of their partisans were people with whom they had worked together in the Lucchese nation in Bruges.[61] Through their link with the merchant guild, they could add to the symbolic capital which they tried to develop at court or within the urban and commercial elites. To be chosen as an arbitrator before the urban courts and to bring two arguing parties to a compromise could greatly boost merchants' reputations, both with other traders and with the Bruges aldermen. To be considered as the head of a foreign merchant community, either by serving as its consul or by acting as its main power broker, was not without prestige.

Supporting the views of Grafe and Gelderblom,[62] the Italian merchant guilds in late medieval Bruges did not serve one, but multiple purposes. Which of these was most important was partly dependent on the size and the nature of its members' businesses. It was exactly in this heterogeneity that the nations' main strength lay: they brought small, medium and large companies operated by merchants originating from the same cities together and, unlike any other commercial institution, redistributed their resources in a way that was beneficial to all.

---

61 Lambert, *The City, the Duke and Their Banker*, 56–57.

62 Grafe and Gelderblom, "The Rise and Fall of the Merchant Guilds".

CHAPTER 3

Late Scholasticism and Commercial Partnership: Persons and Capitals in the Sixteenth and Seventeenth Centuries

Luisa Brunori

1 Introduction

The Second Scholasticism is commonly studied for its fundamental contributions to the theory of natural rights and to the birth of international law,[1] but recent historiography is also discovering the importance of the doctrines of the Second Scholastics for the development of modern private law.[2]

The Late Scholastics, and in particular the younger members of that school, Molina, Lessius and Lugo, dedicated a large part of their studies to the solution of technical matters of private law; among them, those concerning the commercial law stand out for modernity and fineness. Their essays *De Iustitia et De Iure* are not only philosophical and theological works, but legal treatises in their own right, which observe with attention the reality of their era.[3] It is a "*jurisprudence spirituelle*", written by jurists who can be considered as half theologians

1 Dominique Bauer, "The Importance of Canon Law and Scholastic Tradition for the Emergence of an International Legal Order," in Randall Lesaffer (ed.), *Peace Treaties and International Law in History* (Cambridge: CUP, 2004), 198–221; Annabel S. Brett, *Liberty, Right and Nature. Individual Rights in Later Scholastic Thought* (Cambridge: CUP, 2003); Alessandro Ghisalberti, *Dalla prima alla seconda scolastica. Paradigmi e percorsi storiografici* (Bologna: Edizioni Studio domenicano, 2000); Jean-Barthélémy Haureau, *Histoire de la philosophie scolastique*, vol. 2/1 (New York: Franklin, 1966); Michel Villey, "Les fondateurs du droit naturel moderne au XVIIe siècle," *Archives de Philosophie du Droit* (1961), 73 *seq.*

2 Wim Decock, *Theologians and Contract law. The Moral Transformation of the Ius Commune (ca. 1500–1650)* (Leiden: Brill, 2013); Olivier Descamps, "Prolégomènes à l'affirmation du principe général de la responsabilité pour faute personnelle chez quelques auteurs de la Seconde Scolastique," in Damien Salles, Alexandre Deroche and Robert Carvais (eds.), *Études offertes à Jean-Louis Harouel. Liber amicorum* (Paris: Éditions Panthéon-Assas, 2015), 761–786; Paolo Grossi (ed.), *La Seconda Scolastica nella formazione del pensiero giuridico moderno* (Milan: Giuffrè, 1973).

3 Diego Alonso-Lasheras, *Luis de Molina's De Iustitia Et Iure. Justice as Virtue in an Economic Context* (Leiden: Brill, 2011).

 | DOI: 10.1163/9789004351868_005

or by theologians who were half jurist.[4] These theologians-jurists-economists succeeded in translating the new requirements of their time into new and suitable legal rules.

Molina, Lessius and Lugo built their private law systems from reflections on practice, and above all the practice of merchants departing from Spanish and Flemish harbours, who travelled the routes of the ocean, and who organized themselves into partnerships.[5] Commercial law became global for the first time. As a result, it had to be reinvented. It was necessary to categorize the numerous new contracts that were developed in the practice of the transatlantic trade (insurances, *cambia*, financial guarantees).[6] Among them, the contract of partnerships played a prominent role.[7]

2 The Investing Partner: An Infamous Usurer or a Precious Contributor?

One should not forget that in the extra-European trade, exchange was almost exclusively done through the legal tool of the commercial partnership, because

4 "This Second Scholastics, which was extremely erudite and based on the Church fathers and authors of the Middle Ages, recreated for some time a phenomenon that had already been seen before, reminding us of the mixture between theology and law of the period before Gratien": Pierre Legendre in "L'inscription du droit canon dans la théologie: remarques sur la Seconde Scolastique," in Stephan Kuttner and Kenneth Pennington (eds.), *Proceedings of the Fifth International Congress of Medieval Canon Law* (Vatican City: Bibliotheca Apostolica, 1980), 443–454, here 446.

5 André Azevedo Alves and José Manuel Moreira, *The Salamanca School* (London: Continuum, 2010); Angel García Sanz, "El contéxto económico del pensamiento escolastico," in Francisco Goméz Camacho et al. (eds.), *El pensamiento económico en la Escuela de Salamanca: una visión multidisciplinar* (Salamanca: Ediciones Universidad Salamanca, 1998).

6 Centre de recherches historiques, Louis Augustin Boiteux, *La fortune de mer. Le besoin de sécurité et les débuts de l'assurance maritime* (Paris: SEVPEN, 1968); Bartolomé Clavero Salvador, "Entre ocio de banco y negocio de cambio," in Vito Piergiovanni (ed.), *The Growth of the Bank as Institution and the Development of Money-Business Law* (Berlin: Duncker & Humblot, 1993), 191–224; Raymond de Roover, *L'évolution de la lettre d'échange, XIVe–XVIIIe siècle* (Paris: Collin, 1953); Dave De ruysscher, "L'acculturation juridique des pratiques commerciales à Anvers. L'exemple de la lettre de change (XVIe–XVIIe siècle)," in Bart Coppein, Fred Stevens and Laurent Waelkens (eds.), *L'acculturation juridique. Actes des Journées de la Société d'Histoire du Droit* (Brussels: Academy Palace, 2011), 151–160.

7 Luisa Brunori, *"Societas quid sit". La société commerciale dans l'élaboration de la Seconde Scolastique. Personnes et capitaux entre le XVIe et le XVIIe siècle* (Paris: Mare & Martin, 2015).

of its flexibility and the many advantages that it entailed.[8] In the first place, it offered to a large group of individuals the possibility of joining efforts in a situation where no single person had the necessary resources to undertake such a complex and onerous economic activity by himself. Secondly, it allowed the sharing of risk, an element of fundamental importance, considering that the crossing of the ocean brought with it a risk rate that was unknown in Mediterranean trade.[9] Nobody was willing to invest all his property into such hazardous ventures, but nonetheless many desired to take part in the exploitation of the wealth that had just been discovered, through entering into a partnership involving the sharing of profit, but also involving expenses and risk. Moreover, the contract of partnership had the advantage of facilitating a productive collaboration between merchants and non-merchants. The former had the necessary expertise; the latter could provide the resources to finance expensive expeditions to the Americas.

A new legal subject thus appeared: the merely monetary partner. Becoming a partner in a commercial partnership was an excellent method of investment for persons who had the means but who were not willing to commit themselves in person to the commercial activity.[10] The merely monetary partner therefore provided the money, while the merchant partner provided his labour.[11] The

8 Umberto Santarelli, *Mercanti e società tra mercanti* (Torino: Giappichelli, 1992).

9 Oscar Cruz Barney, *El riesgo en el comercio hispano-indiano. Préstamos y seguros marítimos durante los siglos XVI a XIX* (México D.F.: UNAM, 1998), 99–140.

10 The *socius stans* is defined as "*Vir honestus qui non habet negotiandi peritiam sed habet nummos, seu dotales seu adquisitos, qui collocat apud mercatorem ut pro rata pars sibi lucri pendatur*", by Domingo de Soto, *De Iustitia et de Iure* (Salamanca: Andreas à Portonariis, 1556), *quæstio* 6 "*De contractu societatis*", art. 1 ("An honest man who does not have any competence in merchant activities but who has money, received as dowry or acquired in another way, who invests with a merchant in order to receive a share in the profits").

11 Tomás de Mercado well describes the difference between *socius tractans* and *socius stans* in *Suma de tratos y contratos* (Seville: Fernando Diaz, 1571), *liber* (henceforth *lib.*) 2, *caput* (henceforth *cap.*) 9: "It is necessary to consider as investment not only the money but also the work and every activity that has a value. If it is gold, it is the value of that gold; therefore if someone invests care, sweat and zeal, it is as if he invests gold. In fact those people who go to the Indies do not invest money, or very little of it, however they earn a lot. It is necessary to consider the situation justly: it is essential to consider how much sacrifice it takes is to embark on such long and dangerous trips, to be estranged for a long time from his own lands, to reside in unpleasant places such as Nombre de Dios, Saint Domingo, Honduras, Vera Cruz. That is not the case for those that remain home with their wife and children" (my own translation).

first partner therefore participates in the profits without contributing with his own labour and without taking part in the concrete management of the business.[12] For this reason he is often designated as the *socius stans* (also called *procertans*).[13]

The role and position of the merely monetary partner challenged the medieval concepts of the productivity of money and labour.[14] Reconciling these differences became one of the most problematic issues in the reflections of the Late Scholastics on the partnership contract.[15] Most of the time, the partnership contract was treated within the general framework of usury, as is the case with Francisco De Vitoria,[16] because it was suspected to be a contract that concealed a usurious loan. Miguel de Palacio wrote in 1585: "The contract of business partnership is often compromised by usury".[17]

The medieval partnership was in fact a union of merchants, who at the same time were all financiers and workers in the enterprise.[18] It was fully congruent with medieval doctrine, above all Saint Thomas' teachings, and it was impregnated with the criterions of Aristotelian commutative justice.[19]

12 "*Societas contrahi aliquo, aut aliquibus, conferentibus capitale, et alio, vel aliis, apponentibus operam et industriam*": Luis de Molina, *De Iustitia et de Iure* (Cuenca, 1593–1600; edition consulted: Antwerp: Keerbergius, 1615), *tractatus* (henceforth *tract.*) 2, *disputatio* (henceforth *disp.*) 415, no. 1.

13 Fernand Braudel, *Civilisation matérielle, économie et capitalisme* (*XVe–XVIIIe siècles*) (Paris: Colin, 1979).

14 Amleto Spicciani, *Capitale e interesse fra mercatura e povertà nei teologi e canonisti dei secoli XIII–XV* (Rome: Jouvence, 1990).

15 José Barriento García, *Repertorio de moral económica* (*1536–1670*) (Pamplona: EUNSA, 2011).

16 Francisco de Vitoria, *In Secundam Secundæ—De Iustitia*, Vicente Beltrán de Heredía (ed.) (Madrid: Instituto Francisco de Vitoria, 1934), *quæstio* 78, art. 2, no. 26.

17 Miguel de Palacio, *Praxis theologia de contractibus et restitutionibus* (Salamanca: Ferdinandus, 1585), no. 360: "*Quoniam de usuris, disseritur, et contractus hic societatis sæpe vitiatur ex usura*". Also Juan Azor, *Institutionum moralium in quibus universæ quæstiones ad conscientiæ recte aut prave factorum pertinentes, breviter tractantur*, vol. 3 (Rome: Zanettum, 1600), 632–633. About the *ius commune* doctrine: Alberto Garcia Ulecia, "Las condiciones de licitud de la Compañia mercantil bajo el Derecho Común," in José Martínez Gijón, Luis Núñez Contreras, Manuel González Jiménez and Bartolomé Clavero Salvador (eds.), *Historia, Instituciones, Documentos*, vol. 7 (Seville: Universidad de Sevilla, 1980), 39–94.

18 Franz-Stefan Meissel, *Societas. Struktur und Typenvielfalt des römischen Gesellschaftsvertrages* (Frankfurt am Main: Lang, 2004); Santarelli, *Mercanti*.

19 Francisco Gómez Camacho, *Economía y filosofía moral, la formación del pensamiento económico europeo en la Escolástica Española* (Madrid: Sintesis, 1998).

Every exchange of goods within the community must result in an equal balance of value between what is given and what is received, and it must consist of an activity of the person within that community.[20] Above all, according to medieval doctrine, money, if not accompanied by any personal contribution from the individual who owned it, was by nature perfectly sterile. *Pecunia non parit pecuniam* was the adage.[21] Money was seen by legal scholars to be merely a medium to exchange, not a commodity in itself.[22] From that medieval postulation, the legitimacy of any profit was denied in the case of a purely monetary financing of any economic operation. In addition, also according to the medieval conceptions, if the capital provided by the merely monetary partner increased, the crime of usury was committed, because the simple passage of time did not alter the intrinsic sterility of money and could not produce a profit that was not usurious. The problem of usury was particularly relevant for the merely monetary partner in a commercial partnership, because he was remunerated exclusively for his monetary contribution:[23]

> With regard to this and other comparable contracts we must find out whether they can be made or if they are always illegitimate because of usury, which is when they are regarded as a loan rather than as a genuine business partnership.[24]

---

20 Italo Birocchi, *Alla ricerca dell'ordine. Fonti e cultura giuridica nell'età moderna* (Turin: Giappichelli, 2002); Decock, *Theologians and Contract Law*, especially 509 *seq.*

21 Bartolomé Clavero Salvador, *Usura: del uso económico de la religión en la historia* (Madrid: Tecnos, 1985); Auguste Dumas, "Intérêt et Usure," *Dictionnaire de Droit Canonique* (Paris: Letouzey & Ané, 1953), 1475–1518; Gabriel Le Bras, "La doctrine ecclésiastique de l'usure à l'époque classique," *Dictionnaire de Théologie Catholique*, vol. 15/2 (Paris: Letouzey & Ané, 1950), cols. 2316–2390.

22 James Davis, *Medieval Market Morality* (Cambridge: CUP, 2012).

23 St. Thomas Aquinas, *Summa Theologica. Secunda Secundæ* (Rome, 1265–1273; edition consulted: Padua: Typographia Seminaria, 1698), *quæstio* 78: "*Secundum se est illicitum pro usu pecuniæ mutuæ accipere pretium, quod dicitur usura*", "According to him it is illegitimate to accept a price for the use of borrowed money, which is called usury" (my own translation). See also Davis, *Medieval Market Morality*, 92.

24 Own translation of de Molina, *De Iustitia et de Iure, tract.* 2, *disp.* 417, no. 1: "*de ejusmodi ergo, et de aliis similibus contract*[*ibus*] *inquirimus, an licite celebrari possint, an vero semper illiciti sint, ac usurarij: eo quod id potius videatur mutuum cum pacto, ut aliquid insuper reddatur, quam vero societas*".

For instance the pontifical *bulla* of 1586, *Detestabilis avaritiæ*, condemned precisely the participation in a commercial partnership that was exclusively monetary.[25]

The doctors of the Late Scholasticism attempted to "rescue" this contract by overcoming the intertwined moral and legal objections. Late Scholasticism succeeded, in the first place by loosening the knot of the prohibition of usury with a new concept concerning the value of money, which in that new approach became a productive element in itself. In addition, the mentioned authors introduced a restrictive definition of usury according to which the capital injected into a partnership had full right of existence. Consequently, they crafted a modern theory of legitimate titles of profit: that is to say, all the cases in which the remuneration of a mere capital is justified.

I will not elaborate on the first, very important, aspect—the new value of the money—for which I refer to the many studies on the subject, foremost by economic historians.[26] As for the other two aspects, they concern the settling of conflicts between the traditional concept of usury, and the necessity to legitimate the profits of a merely monetary partner in a partnership.

The first argument is that the merely monetary partner cannot be suspected of usury, because usury exists only in cases of loans. Through a rigorous analysis

---

25 Paola Vismara, *Oltre l'usura. La Chiesa moderna e il prestito a interesse* (Milan: Rubbettino, 2004), 72 *seq.*; "*Religion is belief, representation and order. It is definitively a culture and as such it interests our history, mortgaged* ab initio *by a cultural debit*" (my own translation) says Carlos Petit in "*"Mercatvra"* y *"ivs mercatorvm"*," in Carlos Petit (ed.), *Del* ivs mercatorvm *al derecho mercantil. Actes du Seminario de Historia del Derecho Privado* (Madrid: Marcial Pons, 1997), 15–70, here 19.

26 André Azevedo Alves and José Manuel Moreira, *The Salamanca School* (London: Continuum, 2010); Louis Baeck, "Iberian monetarism and development theories of the sixteenth and seventeenth centuries," in Louis Baeck (ed.), *The Mediterranean Tradition in Economic Thought* (London: Routledge, 1994), 172–205, here 172 *seq.*; Donnis O. Flynn, Arturo Giráldez and Richard von Glahn (eds.), *Global Connections and Monetary History, 1470–1800* (Aldershot: Ashgate, 2003), especially 1–34; Francisco Belda, "Etica de la creación de créditos según la doctrina de Molina, Lesio y Lugo," *Pensamiento* 19 (1963), 53–92; Francisco Gómez Camacho (ed.), *El pensamiento económico en la Escuela de Salamanca. Una visión multidisciplinar* (Salamanca: Universidad Salamanca, 1998); Marjorie Grice-Hutchinson, *The School of Salamanca. Readings in Spanish Monetary Theory, 1544–1605* (Oxford: Clarendon Press, 1952); Ichiro Iizuka, *La Escuela de Salamanca en los primeros tiempos de la historia de la teoría monetaria* (Tokio: s.n., 1996); Fabio Monsalve, "Economics and Ethics: Juan de Lugo's Theory of the Just Price, or the Responsibility of Living in Society," *History of Political Economy* 42/3 (2010), 495–519, here 504 *seq.*; Murray N. Rothbard, *Economic Thought Before Adam Smith* (Auburn: Ludwig von Mises Institute, 2006).

of the two arrangements, the loan and the monetary partnership in a company, the doctors of Late Scholasticism underlined the autonomy of the contract of a merely monetary participation in a partnership in comparison to the contract of a loan. Their attention focused particularly on a fundamental distinctive aspect: in a loan, the ownership of the money passes on to the borrower, while the *socius stans* remains the owner of the provided money and he fully assumes the risk of losing it: "he who injects only capital into a partnership does not forfeit ownership as in a loan", wrote Luis de Molina.[27] Therefore, in order to justify the merely monetary participation in a partnership, the traditional doctrine on usury is not called into discussion: "Only money never earns. And if money earns it means that it is usury, and this profit is against nature and ill-omened" says Tomas de Mercado, talking precisely about the remuneration of capital in a partnership.[28]

The solution of the conflict with the prohibition of usury was sought through a formal distinction of the elements of the contract. But that formal argument made it possible to develop a second argument, which affected the very substance of the question: the legitimation of the profit made by the merely monetary partner. We have seen that, according to the medieval perspective, as was briefly set out above, the profit obtained by a merely monetary partner in a commercial partnership was suspected of being a usurious profit. Indeed this "capitalist partner" provided money and subsequently received a return on his capital without contributing with any personal labour, only waiting the passage of time.

At a time when religion and law were not completely separated, it was necessary to free the profit of the capitalist partner from the suspicion of usury. The release was operated by qualifying the *lucrum cessans* (the loss of profits) and the *periculum sortis* (the undertaking of the risk) as legitimate titles of

27 "*Qui in contractu societatis solum capitale apponit non abdicat se dominium illis sicut in mutuo*" and also "*Si is, qui operas erat appositurus, nondum illas apposuit, aut nondum integras eas apposuit, et capitale totum perivit, nihil teneri restituere ratione operarum, aut usus rei, quae nondum apposuit. Quoniam ea lege censetur contractus celebratus, ut ad alterum sociorum spectet periculum totius capitalis: eo quod ad eundem, si maneat salvum, pertineat totum: ad alterum vero solum adhibere spectet operas, aut usum alicuius rei, quandiu capitale fuerit salvum: eo autem omnino perdito, non amplius teneatur id praestare: quoniam satis est ad id solum esse astrictum: quando quidem totum amittat quodex parte sua apponit*": de Molina, *De Iustitia et de Iure*, *tract.* 2, *disp.* 411, no. 5 and *disp.* 416, no. 7.

28 de Mercado, *Suma de tratos y contratos*, *lib.* 2, *cap.* 9: "*Solo el dinero jamas gana, y si solo alguna vez gana, como en la usura, es contra natura su ganancia nephanda*".

profit.[29] As was the case with regard to the *lucrum cessans* (the loss of profits), the logical consequence of the new conception of capital as a productive element (aforementioned), was that every time someone deprived himself of money, he deprived himself of the possibility of making it yield an advantage in an alternative way.[30]

The simple fact of investing money in a specific economic operation and not in another one justified the remuneration of the capital,[31] in the form of a share in the profits of the partnership. The aspect of the *periculum sortis* (the undertaking of the risk) was especially relevant. The merely monetary partner participated proportionally in the losses of the company, but for the totality in the risk of losing the capital that he had provided, since he remained the owner of the money invested. The interests at stake were all the more important because the risk level in transatlantic expeditions was considerably higher than for commercial ventures within Europe. Once again, a new concept was put forward: the hazard, meaning the undertaking of the risk with regard to the capital, was now an element of the legal relationship, which had to be compensated and which therefore represented an autonomous title of profit. In this way, the contract of partnership, now freed from the suspicion of usury, was analyzed, organized and systematized by the doctors of the Late Scholasticism.

29 Hans Thieme, affirms that "the Second Scholastics tried to change this doctrine by way of a theory of titles of interest" in "Qu'est-ce que nous les juristes, devons à la Seconde Scolastique Espagnole?," in Paolo Grossi (ed.), *La Seconda Scolastica nella formazione del pensiero giuridico moderno* (Milan: Giuffrè, 1973), 7–22, here 7 *seq.*

30 "*Si vero jactura sit interesse, quod ea ratione acquirere omittet, dicitur lucrum cessans. Id quippe quod de novo quis sua industria acquirit, lucrum nuncupatur: quomodo autem ab eo acquirendo desistit, cessare dicitur*": de Molina, *De Iustitia et de Iure, tract.* 2, *disp.* 314, no. 2; "*Lucrum cessans dicitur, quando quis impeditur ab aliquo bono consequendo, seu a lucro, quod illi non erat debitum*": Leonardus Lessius, *De Iustitia et Iure ceterisque virtutibus cardinalibus libri IV* (Leuven: Ioannis Masius, 1605; edition consulted: Paris: Typographia Rolini Theodorici, 1610), *lib.* 2, *cap.* 20, *dub.* 10; "*Suelen esto responder con uno de aquellos titulos de lucro cessante, y daño emergente (conviene a saber) que dexan de ganar en el tiempo que esperan*": de Mercado, *Suma de tratos y contratos, lib.* 4, *cap.* 8.

31 "*Ut pretium pro lucro cessante sine usura accipi possit*": de Molina, *De Iustitia et de Iure, tract.* 2, *disp.* 316, no. 9; "*Quod multo magis locum habet, quando interveniret lucrum cessans ex parte conferentis capitale, qui vel negotiaturus, esset vel aliquid fructiferum empturus, si non dedisset capitale ad societatem, qui titulus secundum se sufficeret ad iustificandum contractum*": Juan de Lugo, *Disputationum de Iustitia et de Iure* (Lyon: Prost, 1642; edition consulted: Lyon: Prost, Borde & Arnaud, 1644), *disp.* 30, *sectio* 4, no. 48; "*De lucro cesante digo que quando tuviesse una aparejada su moneda par emplear en alguna suerte de ropa, o en qualquier negocio y contrato licito*": de Mercado, *Suma de tratos y contratos, lib.* 5, *cap.* 10.

3 Towards a "Capital Society"?

Even though it is certainly true that the efforts of classification and organization of the contract of partnership in Late Scholasticism made it possible for the following generations of authors to take advantage of a solid and comprehensive definition of that contract, it is also true that the purposes and the methodology of those scholars are relevant from an historical perspective. There was not only a desire to establish order, but also an ambition to build a new type of contract of partnership that was centred on the capital and no longer on the partners.

The definition of commercial partnership that we find in the mentioned treatises already contains the key elements, namely the lucrative purpose and the *affectio societatis*, which in later times would be incorporated into civil codes (art. 1832 French *Code civil*, art. 1175 Austrian ABGB, art. 2247 Italian Civil code, art. 1665 Spanish Civil code, etc.).[32] Nowadays, these elements still distinguish an association from a commercial company, according to today's judge-made law.[33] To this can be added that the criteria of distribution of the profits of the partnership, according to the reflections of these doctors, corresponded to a logic of rigorous proportionality with respect to the contributions of the partners: "profits are divided in proportion with what each contributed" Leonard Lessius wrote.[34] That requirement of proportionality obviously implied the invalidity of a *societas leonina*.[35]

All the mentioned jurists took special care in defining the distinction between a contract of commercial partnership on the one hand, in which the

32 *"Societas est conventio duorum, pluriumve, ad conferendum aliquid in usum vel quaestum communem, contracta"*: Lessius, *De Iustitia et Iure, lib.* 2, *cap.* 25 (*"De contractu societatis"*), *dub.* 1 (*"quid sit societas et quibus modis contrahatur"*). The partnership is a strictly consensual contract, *Las Partidas* prescribed that the continuity of the company depended exclusively on the wish of the partners literally qualified as *"affectio societatis"*: Antoni Jordá-Fernández, "Sociedades mercantiles hispànicas: de la tradición jurídica romana al código de comercio de 1829," *Revue historique de droit français et étranger* 3 (2012), 379–419, here 389.

33 For instance, French *Court de Cassation*, Cass. com. 9 November 1981, *Bull. Civ.* IV, no. 385; Cass. com., 1 March 1971, *Bull.civ.* IV, no. 66; Cass. civ., 13 October 1987, *Bull. Joly* 1987; Cass. civ. 24 October 1978, *Bull. Civ.* I, no. 318. And also *Cour d'appel de Paris*, 25 March 1993, *RJDA* 1993, no. 1040; *Cour d'appel de Versailles*, 17 March 2000, no. 97/05761.

34 *"Fiat divisio lucri, secundum proportionem sortis a singulis collatæ"*: Lessius, *De Iustitia et Iure, lib.* 2, *cap.* 25, *dub.* 1, no. 3.

35 Tomás de Mercado affirms that *"contra toda buena ley de compañia es querer la ganan-*

contribution of one or more partners was their sole labour, and the *locatio operis* on the other. This distinction, as Luis de Molina and Juan de Lugo emphasized, was necessary in order to guarantee the substantial justice (so important for scholastics): it was very important to distinguish the contract of business partnership from the *locatio operis*. A remuneration could be correct inside a contract of location of work, but it did not correspond to justice when it was provided in a contract of partnership. However, often, if the party to the contract was a partner, it was considered fair that he received a bigger remuneration than a simple worker.[36]

The decisive element was the predictable or unpredictable character of the *stipendium*, the remuneration due to the one who contributed.[37] When a fixed remuneration was promised, and it was possible to know the amount of this remuneration from the beginning (even if it was indicated in proportional terms, for instance ½ or ¼), there was no participation in the gains and in the losses, and consequently one of the essential elements of the contract of partnership was lacking; on the other hand, when the *stipendium* was established

---

cia y provecho sin peligro de pérdida y daño": *Suma de tratos y contratos*, *lib*. 2, *cap*. 10, but doctrine admitted the possibility of waiving the rigorous proportion between the contribution of the partner and his participation to the losses: Jordá-Fernández, "Sociedades mercantiles hispànicas," 395.

36 "*Multum interest ad iustitiam contractus an sit locatio vel societas: advertit autem Molina quod pars aliquota fructuum assignatur pro stipendio et sit locatio, vel quod ratione operae admittatur ad societatem: tum quia in primo casu contractus non iudicaretur iuxta leges societatis, nec frueretur eius privilegiis: tum etiam quia contingere posset contractum esse iustum in ratione locationis et non esse iustum in ratione societatis; posset enim pars illa fructuum promissa aestimari sufficiens recompensatio laboris in ratione stipendii, quia multi pro illo stipendio locaret operas suas; et tamen non esset sufficiens pars correspondens societati quia ex magno lucro plus illi contingeret si ad missus fuisset, ut socius*": de Lugo, *Disputationum de Iustitia et de Iure*, *disp*. 30, *sectio* 1, no. 2.

37 "*Additur ad communem lucrum, ad hoc enim singuli contribuere debent ut lucrum sit communem, et dividendum pro rata eius partis, quam singuli contribuerunt. Unde non est societas sed locatio quando unus alteri animalia tradit in eius custodiam et curam, assignato ei stipendio pro labore: tunc enim lucrum non est commune, sed solius conductoris, qui pretio assignato conducit operas alterius*": de Lugo, *Disputationum de Iustitia et de Iure*, *disp*. 30, *sectio* 1, no. 1; "*Ratio autem est, quia locator non tenetur nauclero dare occasionem majoris lucri, admittendo eum in societatem, in qua eadem summa, et valor operæ plus lucrari posset, quam in contracto locationis simplicis, sed sibi soli vult reservare occasionem illam maioris lucri, et hoc facere solent mercatores, qui suis factoribus solvunt stipendium operæ iustum, nec volunt cum iis inire contractum societatis ad lucrum*": de Lugo, *Disputationum de Iustitia et de Iure*, *disp*. 30, *sectio* 1, no. 3.

in proportion to the profits of the economic activity, there was a partnership participation.[38]

Moreover, the distinction between a contract of partnership and a loan was crucial for the mentioned jurists, not only in order to rescue the former from the suspicion of usury, but also for more technical reasons. These were strictly connected to the coherence of their system of private law, in which it was necessary to define the owner of the money, the one bearing the risk of losing money, etc. So, one can notice that in their treatises, the doctors of the second Scholasticism took good care in establishing the legal perimeter of the commercial partnership, by underlining the differences not only with the *locatio operis* and the loan, but also with the "commission", the contract of insurance, the *encomienda*,[39] and other contracts which were popular at the time.

After establishing the fundamental distinction from other types of contracts, the treatises *De Iustitia et de Iure* concentrated their attention on a rigorous and analytical definition of all the elements of the commercial partnership. Molina, Lessius and Lugo wrote many pages on the commercial partnership. Their writings express not only a will to systematize and define the contract, but also a tendency to value the element of capital and the remuneration of the risk of losing one's investments, in accordance with a modern concept of the company with share capital, rather than following the medieval concept of a partnership between persons.

What, then, can be said about the contribution of these early-modern legal scholars to the formation of modern company law? It is about understanding whether the construction of the late Scholasticism led to the modern configuration of the joint-stock company with shares: the appreciation of the capital

38 "*Quia re vera est contractus contribuendi in ordine ad commune lucrum postea dividendum*": de Molina, *De Iustitia et de Iure, tract.* 2, *disp.* 411, no. 3. Also Juan de Lugo: "*Quando vero non determinatur sed promittitur sexta, vel octava pars fructuum, magis dubitari poterit, an intenta fuerit societas vel conductio. Si vero stipendii, mercedis aut pensionis mentio facta fuerint saltem virtualis, non videtur iudicanda societas sed conductio industriæ ac operæ; sicut et contra nulla tali mentione facta expressa, aut virtuali præsumitur societas, ut docent Molina disp. 411 n. 3 et alii*": de Lugo, *Disputationum, disp.* 30, *sectio* 1, no. 1.

39 "*Confirmatur hæc omnia, quoniam consuetudine est receptum, postquam aliquis societatem inivit apponendo operas suas, ut cum societatis mercibus in Indias aut in novum Orbem, vel in alia loca transfretaret, accipere merces aliorum (encomiendas nostri vocant) ab uno valoris quingentorum ducatorum, ab alio sexcentorum, et ab aliis majoris, aut minoris valoris, quas in eis locis vendant, pretiumque earum in aliis mercibus reportet: atque ob eam industriam certum ei lucrum persolvitur, vel pars lucri aliquota*": de Molina, *De Iustitia et de Iure, tract.* 2, *disp.* 419, no. 3.

as a title of profit, and the appreciation of its autonomy as opposed to the persons of the partners,[40] would lead us to think that this was the case. As a matter of fact they all represent essential characters of the present-day corporation. Indeed, we have underlined the fact that sixteenth-century commercial partnerships needed funds rather than partners. The trader who wanted to create a trading partnership looked above all for financing to realize it. Thus, the qualities of the active partners (*socii tractantes*) were certainly still essential, but the personal qualities of the partner investors (*socii stantes*) were much less so: the main element was their monetary contribution. We have already seen that the doctrine of the period integrated the fact that the capitalist partners were utterly extraneous to the commercial environment.

However, it is also true that a correct analysis of the reflections of these doctors cannot neglect the importance of the *intuitus personæ*. In the legal system which they had in mind, the superiority of the patrimonial element over the personal element was not firmly established. The approach of Justinian's Institutes persisted: "*qui societatem contrahit certam personam sibi elegit*". In fact, the partnership was admitted independently from the existence of a shared capital: Molina noticed that the existence of a future shared gain was sufficient for the formation of a partnership, a common capital not being essential.[41]

The importance of the *intuitus personæ* had significant consequences regarding the succession of the participation in the partnership and the transfer of the quality of partner. From this point of view, it is significant that generally, at the time, the duration of the partnership was limited to the lifetime of the partners, although one often tried to find expedients to make the partnership continue with the heirs of the dead partner. The problem of the death of a partner was largely discussed by Molina, Lessius and Lugo who strongly

---

40 "*Eorum vero, quæ ex capitali post contractam societatem emendo et negotiando cum eodem capitali acquiruntur, innuit l. si quis societatum, ff. pro socio, solum eum comparare dominium, qui ita negotio ea acquirit; teneri tamen ea communicare ac dividere cum aliis sociis. Covarruvias 3. Var. res. c. 19 n. 5 cum aliis quos citat, id intellligit, quando socius nomine proprio illo modo est negotiatius cum capitali: secus autem quando nomine societatis intendendo agere partes societatis: tunc enim socii omnes, absque particulari traditione facta singulis, comparant dominium et possessionem eorum: id quod plane æquitas efflagitat*": de Molina, *De Iustitia et de Iure, tract.* 2, *disp.* 411, no. 7.

41 "*Circa eandem societatis definitionem observa. Idcirco in ea esse dictum, esse conventionem contribuendi ad commune lucrum: quoniam ad rationem societatis satis est communio in lucro future neque est necessaria communio in capitali* (…)": de Molina, *De Iustitia et de Iure, tract.* 2, *disp.* 411, no. 4.

reaffirmed the Roman principle according to which the death of a partner put an end to the partnership with effect on all the partners.[42]

At the same time, the difficulty in the conceptualization of limited liability within the partnership shows that the elaboration of the company with share capital remained unfinished. Molina paid attention to the case of "*periculum ad eum pertineat qui apponit operas*",[43] but he was still far from the conceptualization of the limited liability of the partners. Actually, if it is true that Molina encouraged such types of pacts, it is also true that he did not go as far as working out a model of a company where the limitation of liability was part of the essence of the company. He rather suggested various possibilities of contractual exemption from the general principle of the community of the gains and the losses, established exclusively on the basis of the contractual autonomy in every specific case.[44] According to Tomás de Mercado, who explicitly considered the liability of the partners towards third parties, it seemed that the general principle was the collective and unlimited liability: all the partners had to pay for the obligations of the partnership, jointly and severally.[45]

However, with regard to unlimited and joint liability for partnerships of all kinds, the contemporary opinion was not unanimous. According to some authorities dealing with the developing law of partnerships, it went too far to affirm the unlimited liability of the partner as a general norm. Actually, with regard to the more specific commercial partnership, it was considered to be a favourable doctrine *more italico* to limit the liability of the partners on the basis

---

42 "*Morte unius sociorum dissolvitur societas*": de Molina, *De Iustitia et de Iure, tract.* 2, *disp.* 414, no. 1; de Lugo, *Disputationum, disputatio* 30, *sectio* 1, no. 8; Lessius, *De Iustitia et de Iure, lib.* 2 *cap.* 25, *dub.* 3. The agreements between the partners for the continuation of the partnership after the death of one among them will be easily admitted at a later point, for example by Robert-Joseph Pothier, *Œvres de R.-J. Pothier contenants les traités de droit français*, M. Dupin Ainé (ed.) (Brussels: Tarlier, 1831), 436, no. 145: "*I think that in our law, although usually the company finishes by the death of one of the partners, and although his heir does not succeed in the rights of the company, nevertheless the agreement that he can succeed is valid*" (my own translation).

43 de Molina, *De Iustitia et de Iure, tract.* 2, *disp.* 417.

44 According to Molina, the natural way for the *socius stans* to protect oneself against possible losses was to insure his capital, and not to limit his liability through a pact with the *tractans*.

45 "*Digo que los compañeros están ygualmente obligados a las deudas con persona y bienes. De modo que como se executa y prende el uno, se puede executar y prender el otro*": Tomas de Mercado, *Suma de tratos y contratos, lib.* 2, *cap.* 10.

of a patrimonial separation between the partners and the company.[46] Once again, it therefore appears that the elaboration of the doctors of the Second Scholasticism represented a turning point. If the distinction of the assets was certainly clear, the limitation of liability was much less solidly established.

4 Conclusion

In concluding, two different tendencies can be discerned. The first was an "impersonal", modern approach to commercial partnerships, while the second may be viewed as a trend in stressing "personal" characteristics, which was still medieval. That ambivalence is a symptom of an unstable balance between traditional and new ways of thinking, between the ancient system and the modern system.

---

46 Carlos Petit, "Ignorancias y otras historias, o sea, responsabilidades limitadas," *Anuario de Historia del Derecho Español* 60 (1990), 497–508, especially 503.

CHAPTER 4

Legal Structure of Early Enterprises—from Commenda-like Arrangements to Chartered Joint-Stock Companies (Early Modern Period)

*Anja Amend-Traut**

1 Introduction

The task and aim of the following chapter is to show lines of development in historical law that did not continue and are not in use today. This is actually a rewarding task, since this approach allows us to be free from the shackles of present-day applicable law which is fixed and which, when taken as point of departure, obscures a comprehensive view on historically relevant contexts and particularities which do not have an equivalent today.[1]

The commercial revolution of the Middle Ages serves as a starting point for the following considerations, because it paved the way for the development which led to the creation of the forerunners of modern joint stock companies.[2] For understanding the genesis of the latter, a whole range of issues that had already been addressed in medieval times needs to be re-examined.[3] Only then will it become clear that for the period under research here, the historic manifestations of enterprises were congruent in some respects and divergent in others, which ultimately resulted in a clustering of depersonalized criteria. Based on the *Code de commerce*, Karl Lehmann in the nineteenth century described how, when looking back from the present to the past, "one component after the other disappears (…) in the centuries until the *montes* and

* I would like to express my sincere thanks to Dr. Daniel Velinov for his valuable suggestions and impulses in the preparation of this chapter.

1 This risk was already pointed out by Albrecht Cordes and Katharina Jahntz, "Aktiengesellschaften vor 1807?," in Walter Bayer and Mathias Habersack (eds.), *Aktienrecht im Wandel. I: Entwicklung des Aktienrechts* (Tübingen: Mohr, 2007), 1–45, here marginal no. 5 *seq*.

2 An overview of the developments of trading companies with further substantiation is provided by Anja Amend-Traut, "Handelsgesellschaften," in Albrecht Cordes, Heiner Lück, Dieter Werkmüller and Christa Bertelsmeier-Kierst (eds.), *Handwörterbuch zur deutschen Rechtsgeschichte* (Berlin: Schmidt, 2012), vol. 2, 703–712.

3 See the chapter by Ulla Kypta in this volume.

 | DOI: 10.1163/9789004351868_006

maonae (...), everything becomes uncertain and volatile—this moment the focus is on this, the next moment on that".[4] It is therefore necessary to outline first the essential features of *commenda*-like arrangements, starting with the so-called *accommendatio* itself and its variants, against the background of the economic requirements.

2 Why Companies? Division of Responsibilities

The transition from luxury goods to bulk commodity trading started in the twelfth century. Enormous quantities of fish, salt, grain, furs and a great deal more were transported over large distances via the Hanseatic trading area to cities located in the south of Germany, from where in particular wine, wax, skins and fabrics were sent to Northern Italy and South-West Europe.[5] Merchants started delegating the sale of their commodities to others and also no longer travelled personally to deliver them. Merchants acting alone and autonomously increasingly less often conducted superregional trade over land and sea. It became a widespread practice to be represented by one or several persons at different locations, in particular in cases of geographically more extensive business activities.

Such a division of labour was already early proven in legal sources. The town charter of Medebach in 1165 stipulated: *Qui pecuniam suam dat alicui concivi suo, ut inde negocietur in Datia vel Rucia vel in alia regione ad utilitatem utriusque, assumere debet concives suos fideles, ut videant et sint testes huius rei* ("Whoever gives his money to one of his fellow citizens, so that it can be traded for mutual benefit in Denmark or in Russia or in another region, shall consult trusting fellow citizens, so that they can see it and be witnesses in this matter").[6] Thus, anyone giving money to a fellow citizen for carrying out mutually beneficial trade with Denmark, Russia or any other place should involve witnesses in this transaction.

---

4 Karl Lehmann, *Die geschichtliche Entwicklung des Aktienrechts bis zum Code de Commerce* (Berlin: Heymann, 1895; repr. Frankfurt am Main: Sauer & Auvermann, 1968), 1 *seq.*

5 As an introduction see Stuart Jenks, "Von den archaischen Grundlagen bis zur Schwelle der Moderne (ca. 1000–1450)," in Michael North (ed.), *Deutsche Wirtschaftsgeschichte. Ein Jahrtausend im Überblick* (Munich: Ugarit, 2005), 15–106, and 478–485, here 68–72.

6 Text according to Johann Suibert Seibertz (ed.), *Urkundenbuch zur Landes- und Rechtsgeschichte des Herzogthums Westfalen*, 4 vols. (Arnsberg, 1839–1875), vol. 1, 74 *seq.* (no. 55). More detailed literature: Stephan Dusil, *Die Soester Stadtrechtsfamilie. Mittelalterliche Quellen und neuzeitliche Historiographie* (Cologne: Böhlau, 2007), 80 *seq.*

Legal-historical research in the later nineteenth and early twentieth century in particular brought extensive source materials of Italian origin to light, such as notarial deeds and town charters.[7] These source records demonstrate that already in the middle of the thirteenth century, associations among several persons for their mutual benefit were fully developed in the form of trading partnerships. This was not only the case in southern Europe but also in the Hanseatic League. For promoting their joint purpose, the partners contributed resources or skills that were available to them, which could be money, goods, services, expertise, or experience.

3 The *Accommendatio* and Its Variants

The financing of maritime trade journeys around the Mediterranean led to the creation of the *accommendatio, commendatio* or *commenda*, which in Genoa was known under the term *societas maris*, and in Venice as *collegantia*.[8] All these arrangements are generally considered to be forerunners of the limited partnership. Fundamental thereto are the works of Levin Goldschmidt, Gustav Lastig and Wilhelm Silberschmidt.[9] The origins may have been in the Arabic caravan trade, and perhaps in the Byzantine Empire; forerunners can even be found in ancient Babylon.[10] In the Hanseatic region, the basic structure of

7 Thus for example stated by Gustav Lastig, *Die Accomendatio, Die Grundform der heutigen Kommanditgesellschaften in ihrer Gestaltung vom XIII. bis XIX. Jahrhundert* (Halle a. d. S.: Buchhandel des Waisenhauses, 1907) with further substantiation, vi *seq*.; Wilhelm Silberschmidt, *Die Commenda in ihrer frühesten Entwicklung bis zum XIII. Jahrhundert. Ein Beitrag zur Geschichte der Commandit- und der stillen Gesellschaft* (Würzburg: Stuber, 1884); Max Weber, *Zur Geschichte der Handelsgesellschaften im Mittelalter: Nach südeuropäischen Quellen* (Stuttgart: Enke, 1889; repr. Amsterdam: Bonset, 1970).

8 Further linguistic variants naming their use can be found in sources such as Lastig, *Accomendatio*, xviii *seq*.

9 Levin Goldschmidt, *De societate en Commandite Specimen* I (PhD thesis, University of Halle, 1851); Lastig, *Accomendatio*; Gustav Lastig, *De Comanda et Collegantia* (Halle a.d. S.: Hendel, 1870); Silberschmidt, *Commenda*; Weber, *Handelsgesellschaften*, 100–106; Following Lastig: Slavomir Condanari-Michler, *Zur frühvenezianischen Collegantia* (Munich: Beck, 1937), 4 *seq*. More recent works include John H. Pryor, *Commerce, Shipping and Naval Warfare in the Medieval Mediterranean* (London, Variorum reprints, 1987); Quentin Van Doosselaere, *Commercial Agreements and Social Dynamics in Medieval Genoa* (Cambridge: CUP, 2009).

10 Abraham L. Udovitch, "At the Origins of the Western Commenda: Islam, Israel, Byzan-

these early trading companies is indicated in the so-called *wedderlegginge*.[11] Apart from the aforementioned company arrangements, which were primarily designed for maritime trade, a *commenda* for trade over land can also be identified. The internal structure of this land *commenda* largely mirrored that of its maritime counterpart, but it seems to have been less common, due to its more modest profitability.[12] The abundance of relevant deeds allows a summary in the form of the following observations:

3.1 *Purpose of the Contract*

The common purpose of the *accommendatio* contract and related forms of company arrangements was to minimise the risks while increasing the profits. These two aims could be reached when a travelling partner could rely on personal experience, which the investor did not have. Thus, the former, on his own responsibility, decided at which port he should call, checked the quality of the goods, which he was to buy, and decided which travel route to take. It was therefore in his hands whether the voyage generated any profit. On the other hand, for lack of his own or sufficient capital, he was entirely dependent upon the investor. Consequently, a mutual interdependency of the parties was characteristic for this form of trade association. The penniless merchant used his expertise while benefiting from the investment of the capital holder, and vice versa.[13]

3.2 *Conclusion of Contract*

The *accommendatio* could be established by simply transferring the entrusted commodities, and was thus a real contract.[14] The transferee took on the obli-

---

tium?," *Speculum* 37 (1962), 198–207; Abraham L. Udovitch, *Partnership und Profit in Medieval Islam* (Princeton: Princeton University Press, 1970), especially 170–248.

11 In this respect, Albrecht Cordes, *Spätmittelalterlicher Gesellschaftshandel im Hanseraum* (Cologne: Böhlau, 1998), 35 *seq.*, and 121–154. Differentiating unilateral and bilateral capital investment, the former named "*sendevegesellschaft*", the latter "*wedderlegginge*", Paul Rehme, *Geschichte des Handelsrechts* (Leipzig: Reisland, 1914), 163.

12 More details in Weber, *Handelsgesellschaften*, 36–43.

13 On the particular significance of the credit function in times when the clerical prohibition of interest generally still applied, albeit not for capital contributions to an entrepreneurial venture, see Van Doosselaere, *Commercial Agreements*, 123 *seq.* A clear distinction with the silent partnership is often difficult to assess in individual cases. For more details, see Anja Amend-Traut, "The Productivity of Capital With (Silent) Participation in Trading Companies. Controversies," in Luisa Brunori and Xavier Prévost (eds.) *L'économie sans travail* (Paris: Classiques Garnier, expected 2018).

14 Silberschmidt, *Commenda*, 95, and 101. On the other hand, according to prevailing opinion the bilateral *accommendatio*—or in this context more precisely *societas*—was a consensual contract, e.g. Silberschmidt, *Commenda*, 95, 101, and 107.

gation to transport and subsequently surrender received goods or profit to the investor.[15] Later it became common practice to fix the contract in writing, either as a private document or as a public deed. Since the fifteenth century, local statutes more frequently prescribed a notarized version. As a consequence of not following this legal obligation, the *accommendator*, i.e. the investor, lost the collateral security of the skipper's property. The investor was thus deprived of the possibility to sue the skipper with regard to the ship, its equipment and cargo.[16]

3.3 *Contractual Relationship*

The *accommendatio* contract between the entrepreneur and the skipper was, in its essential content, designed as a service relationship.[17] Usually, the parties were a merchant granting a loan on the one hand, and a traveller taking out the loan on the other hand. The latter was granted the right to conduct the undertaking with the contributed capital in his own name but on behalf of the investor. The *collegantia* was peculiar in that both parties made investments.[18] The same applied to the *wedderlegginge*.[19] In contrast to family enterprises and the *compagnia*, both of which will be discussed in more detail later, the members of the *accommendatio* were usually not related.

3.3.1 Risk Sharing

While the entrepreneur carried the sole capital risk for loss of the goods, the skipper carried the risk of labour. The latter transported the merchandise to various trading locations. He was responsible for strictly abiding by the contractual scope of action. In case of non-compliance, he was threatened with being held liable for the capital and lost profit. In performing his activities, the travelling partner had to exercise the diligence of a prudent businessperson. This was the case particularly with regard to the invested capital and the merchandise that he had to deliver or take home. He was liable for culpable action. Upon settlement of the *accommendatio*, the investor was entitled and obliged to sell the imported goods.

---

15 This obligation is significantly different from the maritime loan, Condanari-Michler, *Zur frühvenezianischen Collegantia*, 67.

16 Lastig, *Accomendatio*, 128. On the form of contractual set-up also Silberschmidt, *Commenda*, 76–79.

17 Silberschmidt, *Commenda*, 96.

18 Condanari-Michler, *Zur frühvenezianischen Collegantia*, 1, with further substantiation of this difference at 18; Levin Goldschmidt, *Handbuch des Handelsrechts. 1/1: Universalgeschichte des Handelsrechts* (Stuttgart: Enke, 1891; repr. Aalen: Scientia, 1973), 259 *seq.*

19 In this respect, see Cordes, *Spätmittelalterlicher Gesellschaftshandel.*

A distinctive feature of this early form of trading through company arrangements is the limitation of liability, without which it would have been unacceptable for the skipper to take on another person's funds for risky business; likewise, the investor could not have accepted any liability for the uncontrollable actions of his agent above the invested capital. Thus, the risk was shared according to their respective contribution.[20]

Mutual trust was a decisive factor for entering into such temporary ventures. A Venetian deed of 1156 states: (…) *participare debemus sine fraude et malo ingenio* (…) ("(…) we have to participate without fraud and malicious spirit (…)").[21] If, on the other hand, trust had been abused, no new business transaction could be expected. In the twentieth century, modern institutional economics took up this aspect and found that trust was responsible for reducing the transaction costs: "Trust is the most important lubricant of the social system. It is highly efficient; a lot of effort is saved if you can fairly rely upon the word of other people."[22]

3.3.2 Duration

The *accommendatio* relationship was usually concluded only for the duration of a business trip or transaction. This granted the investor the option of entering into a new *accommendatio* after the successful completion of the previous one, or to refrain from doing so. In addition, the *wedderlegginge* known in the Hanseatic region was limited in time.[23] However, because of its arrangement as a service agreement, the contractual relationship could also end before the end of the journey or contractually agreed term, namely if the travelling contract partner had become insolvent, had to declare bankruptcy, or had died.[24] In contrast to the *accommendatio*, the term of the later limited partnership was usually not limited beforehand.

---

20 Thus also Condanari-Michler, *Zur frühvenezianischen Collegantia*, 81, and 86, for the *collegantia*.

21 Quoted from Silberschmidt, *Commenda*, 41.

22 Kenneth Joseph Arrow, *Wo Organisation endet—Management an den Grenzen des Machbaren* (Wiesbaden,: Gabler 1980), 49 *seq.*, quoted from Rudolf Richter and Eirik G. Furubotn, *Neue Institutionenökonomik. Eine Einführung und kritische Würdigung* (Tübingen: Mohr, 1999), 240. A fundamental contribution to the economic performance of institutions can be found in Douglass C. North, *Institutions, Institutional Change and Economic Performance* (Cambridge: CUP, 1990).

23 In this respect, see Cordes, *Spätmittelalterlicher Gesellschaftshandel.*

24 Sources evidencing the individual aspects are presented in Lastig, *Accomendatio*, 129–132, 142 *seq.*

3.4 *Capital Contribution and Distribution of Profits*

Given that both contracting parties contributed capital to the *wedderlegginge*, both participated in the profits. The financial contribution of the Hanseatic lender usually amounted to two thirds: that of the borrower at one third, plus his personal labour during the business venture.[25] Italian notarial deeds, on the other hand, contain numerous examples of quarterly participations. One deed from Amalfi in the year 1254 provides an example: (...) *et ego inde tollere debeam mihi ipsa quartam partem pro labore et fatica mea sine omni occassione* ("(...) and I shall be entitled to the fourth part for my work and effort without any empediment").[26] After the successful completion of a venture, the granted loan was first repaid, and the profits shared. Generally, the lender received three quarters of the profit, the borrower one quarter. Other allocation keys are also evidenced, albeit more rarely.[27] In any case, the participation in profits was the decisive incentive for the travelling merchant to treat the investor's interests as if they were his own.

The mentioned division of profits was later modified when the travelling partner either worked for multiple investors, or when he contributed more personal capital. The corresponding shift of the service characteristics to a commercial focus entailed a change to the respective positions of the parties to the contract: the entrepreneur lost his dominant role and reduced his capital risk. Conversely, the skipper gained more influence and assumed a part of the capital risk, which was reflected accordingly in the distribution of profit.

Although the fundamental structure of the Genoese *societas maris* was similar to the *accommendatio* contract, it differed in one crucial respect. There, the travelling merchant contributed one third of the capital before the start of the trading voyage, but received half of the generated profit. In case of losses, he lost only his invested capital and was otherwise exempt from liability. Thus, his earning prospects were larger than the risk of loss.[28]

Both the handover of the imported goods and the payment of the profit shares necessarily required a rendering of accounts, which the travelling contract partner was obliged to provide directly after his return or after the expiry of a later deadline, either based on the contract or statutory law.[29] After all, a formalized rendering of accounts guaranteed legal certainty for the transaction and strengthened the trust basis for future *accommendatio* contracts, too.

---

25 In this respect see Cordes, *Spätmittelalterlicher Gesellschaftshandel*.

26 According to Silberschmidt, *Commenda*, 41.

27 Silberschmidt, *Commenda*, 96.

28 For an overall view on the *societas maris* see Silberschmidt, *Commenda*, 106–112.

29 Sources evidencing the individual aspects in Lastig, *Accomendatio*, 144–148.

3.5 *Interim Result*

The heyday of the regionally very differently structured *accommendatio* continued until about the end of the thirteenth century. This medieval form of personal association was ideal at a time when the skills and possibilities of the various market participants differed strongly and when no alternative instruments for financing and organizing foreign trade were available.

It is also evident that medieval trade was structured very similarly in many places. The described core elements of profit participation, limitation of liability and limited duration are found both North and South of the Alps, with some but overall rather marginal individual particularities. In view of this widespread practice, at first glance, it seems doubtful that the respective variants could develop independently from one another. On the other hand, there was a common commercial need, which might have determined these structures. Obviously, however, these essential elements did not meet the new challenges resulting from the discovery of the sea passage to India and the ensuring shift of trade flows between Asia and Europe on the one hand, and within Europe on the other hand.

4 Permanent Multiple Member Companies

First, confraternity-like coalitions and family enterprises were formed, but also corporate associations not bound by family ties, where several persons permanently joined in common commercial activities.[30]

Owing to intensive recent research particularly about the trading companies located in the south of Germany, we are particularly well informed about the dissemination and operation of family enterprises.[31] A role model for these

30 As regards the manifestations of companies derived from medieval confraternities, which were set up for economic reasons as particularly observable for the Hanseatic region, only a few differences from family enterprises can be identified. These companies were not solely composed of family members and were obviously established for an indefinite period of time, for example the *Greveradenkompanie*. In this regard, see Antjekathrin Graßmann, "Die Greveradenkompanie. Zu den führenden Kaufleutegesellschaften in Lübeck um die Wende zum 16. Jahrhundert," in Stuart Jenks and Michael North (eds.), *Der hansische Sonderweg? Beiträge zur Sozial- und Wirtschaftsgeschichte der Hanse* (Cologne: Böhlau, 1993), 109–134, here in particular 115–117, and 124 *seq*.

31 For an overview see Mechthild Isenmann, *Die Familie—ein Unternehmen. Frühe Familiengesellschaften zwischen Kontinuität und Konflikt* (Bonn: Unternehmen Medien, 2011) with further substantiation. In more detail, see Walter Bauernfeind, "Marktinformationen und Personalentwicklung einer Nürnberger Handelsgesellschaft im 16. Jahrhundert—Das

familial associations has probably been the *compagnia* emerging in Northern Italy since the twelfth century, which already showed the characteristic feature that its partners were often connected very closely or even by family relations.[32] Often marriages were arranged in order to merge traditional family enterprises for further increasing their economic power through extending the network of branches.[33] One of the best-known family enterprises of the fifteenth century, the Medici from Florence, had family-run branches in many important Italian trading cities, e.g. Venice, Pisa, Milan, and beyond its national borders, e.g. in London and Bruges.[34] At first, family ties held a promise of having reliable partners amidst the uncertainties of business,[35] but this was of course no guarantee.[36] The *compagnia*, which was widespread in Northern Italy, usually—and

Briefarchiv von Anthoni und Linhart Tucher in der Zeit von 1508 bis 1566," in Angelika Westermann and Stefanie von Welser (eds.), *Beschaffungs- und Absatzmärkte oberdeutscher Firmen im Zeitalter der Welser und Fugger* (Husum: Matthiesen, 2011), 23–60; Frank Göttmann, "Die Bedeutung des textilen Verlagswesens und die Konstanz-Memminger Handelsgesellschaft Grimmel Mitte des 16. Jahrhunderts," in Angelika Westermann and Stefanie von Welser (eds.), *Beschaffungs- und Absatzmärkte oberdeutscher Firmen im Zeitalter der Welser und Fugger* (Husum: Matthiesen, 2011), 143–158; Mark Häberlein, *Die Fugger. Geschichte einer Augsburger Familie (1367–1650)* (Stuttgart: Kohlhammer, 2006); Mechthild Isenmann and Eberhard Isenmann, "Das Innenverhältnis einer spätmittelalterlichen Handelsgesellschaft und die Ausweitung interner Konflikte—Hans Arzt und Gesellschaft, Anton Paumgartner und die Reichsstadt Nürnberg (1447–1471)," *VSWG* 101 (2014), 432–487; Christian Kuhn, "Handelspraxis als Gegenstand familiärer Kontinuitätsdiskurse. Der Generationenwechsel nach dem Nürnberger Kaufmann Leonhart II. Tucher (1487–1568) in der historischen Darstellung und in Briefen," in Mark Häberlein and Christof Jeggle (eds.), *Praktiken des Handels. Geschäfte und soziale Beziehungen europäischer Kaufleute in Mittelalter und früher Neuzeit* (Konstanz: UVK, 2010), 309–333.

32 The "family" however, under certain circumstances, included domestic servants, Weber, *Handelsgesellschaften*, 48 *seq.*

33 Isenmann, *Familie*, 14.

34 Raymond De Roover, *The Rise and Decline of the Medici Bank* (Cambridge (Ma.): Harvard University Press, 1963).

35 De Roover, *Medici Bank*, 148.

36 This is evidenced by the many internal conflicts within enterprises, which were the subject matter of lawsuits that often ended before the Imperial Chamber Court. Examples for this are the Fuggers and the Brentanos. In respect of the former, Britta Schneider, *Fugger contra Fugger. Die Augsburger Handelsgesellschaft zwischen Kontinuität und Konflikt (1560–1597/98)* (Augsburg: Wissner, 2016), with regard to the latter Anja Amend-Traut, "Brüder unter sich—die Handelsgesellschaft Brentano vor Gericht. Elemente privater Konfliktlösung im Reichskammergerichtsprozess," in Albrecht Cordes and Serge Dauchy (eds.), *Eine Grenze in Bewegung: Öffentliche und private Justiz im Handels- und Seerecht. Justice priveé et justice publique en matières commerciales et maritimes* (Munich: Oldenbourg, 2013), 91–116.

contrary to the *accommendatio*—still concentrated on trade in goods handled via land routes. This did no longer occur later with regard to the related term of *compagnie*.[37]

A typical factor of the contracts of family enterprises and other partnerships since the late fifteenth century was that they usually did not end upon the completion of a particular transaction. Particularly with regard to the duration of Italian enterprises, these were set up for a predetermined period of time, which, as a rule, extended over three to five years. Contracts of family enterprises from the South German region, on the other hand, did not provide for any specific duration; rather, they contained detailed stipulations on the continued existence of the enterprise in case one of the members died.[38] The enterprises were organized in a form comparable to today's general partnership, where all contract partners shared in the contribution as well as in the profits and losses, and where all partners were involved in the management of the business. The profit share was proportionate to the invested capital. In case of loss, the partnership capital and each partner with his private assets were liable towards third parties.[39] As an alternative, there were also the forerunners of today's limited partnership, in which on the one hand the managing partners were fully and personally liable, and on the other hand the limited partners were liable only for the amount of their investment and they usually cooperated without any influence in decisions on trade.[40] In both models, individual cases show silent partners next to working partners, who merely acted as investors and who in family enterprises often were female family members who invested their dowry or inheritance against a specific interest rate.[41] Moreover, it was regularly provided that an agent concluded the contracts relating to the enterprise *pro societate*, i.e. in the name of the firm, which in the event of a legal dispute generally meant that each member could sue and be sued.[42]

37 A special form of land route contract is the *societas terrae*, with features similar to those of the *accommendatio*. In a case of loss, the lender carried the sole risk, and in case of profit, the parties shared the earnings. The invested amounts, however, could vary.

38 Thus, for example, in the Fugger family. In this respect, see Schneider, *Fugger contra Fugger*.

39 As one of many Weber, *Handelsgesellschaften*, 89.

40 Such limited liability of the limited partners is found already in the Nuremberg city law reformation of 1564, ch. 18 s. 1,4, and in the Frankfurt city law reformation of 1578, ch. 33, s. 12. In more detail, see Goldschmidt, *De societate*, 12.

41 Isenmann, *Familie*, 14 *seq*; Amend-Traut, *(Silent) participation*.

42 Thus e.g. Weber, *Handelsgesellschaften*, 87, on Italian statutes of the fourteenth century.

Participants in business and legal transactions usually did not have any insight into the internal structure of these family enterprises. This held substantial potential for conflicts when claims against such enterprises were asserted in court and a decision had to be taken on the issue of liability. In the Empire in the fifteenth and sixteenth century, public registers of company statutes, such as the later company or trade registers, which could have ensured transparency, and thus public trust and protection of trade, were non-existent, as was a consistent company law.[43] However, the emerging inter-continental and long-distance trading companies with their huge financial challenges, for which investors were sought and in which trading partners could engage, did particularly require publicity and legal certainty. Besides, the unlimited liability of partners most probably also rendered the previous models of enterprises unsuitable for the new, large-scale and particularly risky oversees expeditions. An additional circumstance was that maritime trading followed its own rules; it was incompatible with the trading companies in Southern Germany, which traditionally focused on overland business.

5 New Challenges—Overseas Expeditions and Other Large-Scale Ventures

The aforementioned discovery of the sea passage to India was probably the major reason for the further development of trading associations up to the time

43 The only register for companies, which can be found for the Middle Ages is the so-called *Niederstadtbuch* of the city of Lübeck: Albrecht Cordes (ed.), *Societates. Das Verzeichnis der Handelsgesellschaften im Lübecker Niederstadtbuch* 1311–1361 (Cologne: Böhlau, 2003). In Frankfurt, such registers existed from the seventeenth century on. See Anja Amend-Traut, *Wechselverbindlichkeiten vor dem Reichskammergericht: Praktiziertes Zivilrecht in der Frühen Neuzeit* (Cologne: Böhlau, 2009), 113. In Italy, the Florence Merchant Court, the so called *Mercancia*, registered trading companies latest since the 14th century, for this see Luca Boschetto, "Writing the Vernacular at the Merchant Court of Florence," in William Robins (ed.), *Textual Cultures of Medieval Italy. Essays from the 41st Conference on Editorial Problems* (Toronto: University of Toronto Press, 2011), 217–262; Gustav Lastig, *Florentiner Handelsregister des Mittelalters* (Halle a.d. S.: Hendel, 1883). For English law, see William Holdsworth, *A History of English Law*, 16 vols. (Oxford: Clarendon Press, 1925; repr. London: Methuen, 1966), vol. 8, 192. The first statutory regulation on trading companies in the Empire was probably section 30 of the Nuremberg New Reformation of 1479 on the general partnership. The text is reproduced in Gerhard Köbler (ed.), *Reformation der Stadt Nürnberg* (Gießen: Arbeiten zur Rechts- und Sprachwissenschaft, 1984). On the significance Amend-Traut, *Handelsgesellschaften*.

of the early corporations.[44] In particular, the two trading companies specifically established for the innovative overseas trade at the beginning of the seventeenth century, the *Verenigde Oost-indische Compagnie* (VOC)[45] and the English East India Company,[46] intensified the European maritime trade with Asia. In addition, the *montes*, which were corporative associations of state creditors that were used for financing war, have been identified as the precursors of the early joint stock companies.[47]

Comparable to the *accommendatio* ventures, the economic function of the aforementioned trading companies lay in the pre-financing of particularly cost-intensive transactions of a longer duration. Oversees trading expeditions usually took months, if not years, before any capital reflux or even profit could at best be expected. There are also obvious parallels to mining, where modern expertise and substantial capital resources were required.[48] The risk involved in overseas trade was considerably larger than had been the case in medieval

44 Johan Matthijs de Jongh, *Tussen societas en universitas. De beursvennootchap en haar aandeelhouders in historisch perspectief* (Dordrecht: Kluwer, 2014), which focusses on the tension between the individual interests of the investors and the public importance of the consolidated investments.

45 Femme S. Gaastra, *De geschiedenis van de VOC* (Zutphen, 1991); Paul Frentrop, *A History of corporate Governance: 1606–2002* (Zutphen: Walburg, 2003), 49–114; Femme S. Gaastra, "Die Vereinigte Ostindische Compagnie der Niederlande—ein Abriß ihrer Geschichte," in Eberhard Schmitt, Thomas Schleich and Thomas Beck (eds.), *Kaufleute als Kolonialherren. Die Handelswelt der Niederländer vom Kap der Guten Hoffnung bis Nagasaki 1600–1800* (Bamberg: C.C. Buchners, 1988), 1–89; Anneli Partenheimer-Bein, "Vereinigte Ostindische Kompanie (VOC) der Niederlande," in Hermann Hiery (ed.), *Lexikon zur Überseegeschichte* (Stuttgart: Steiner, 2015), 839 *seq.*

46 Wilhelm Hartung, *Geschichte und Rechtsstellung der Compagnie in Europa. Eine Untersuchung am Beispiel der englischen East-India Company, der niederländischen Vereenigten Oostindischen Compagnie und der preußischen Seehandlung* (PhD-thesis, University of Bonn, 2000).

47 Lehmann, *Die geschichtliche Entwicklung des Aktienrechts*, 5 *seq.*

48 A very early example is probably the so-called "*Innerberger Hauptgewerkschaft*", which was established on 30 August 1625 as a "company sharing profits and losses". It came into existence by investments of 19 water-powered smelting furnace operations of Innerberg and 39 hammer mills on the banks of the Enns and its tributaries. The "*Innerberger Hauptgewerkschaft*" is deemed to be the precursor of VOEST Alpine. Its "statutes" were published in the form of the "Capitulation of 20 October 1625". In this respect: Anton Teuscher, *Die Capitulation der Innerberger Hauptgewerkschaft und die erste Fusion der alpinen Eisenwirtschaft 1625* (Graz: Akademische Druck- und Verlags-Anstalt, 1973); Anton von Pantz, *Die Innerberger Hauptgewerkschaft 1625–1783* (Graz: Styria, 1906). The opportunity is taken here to thank Mr. Theodor Bühler, Winterthur, for this information.

sea trade. Both the investment requirement and the profit margin had been smaller, but the income—albeit reduced by losses caused by weather and wars—had been consistent. With the need for larger contributions, the capital became increasingly more self-contained in the form of separate estates, which were primarily linked to the company and no longer to the investors personally—the first step towards a concept of legal person. The individual investor could not prematurely reclaim his capital investment that was bound in the company's assets. For liquidating his capital investment, he needed to sell his participations or shares to interested parties.[49] This separation of the capital from its provider was the very step that enabled the emergence of secondary markets of investment securities but also the fact that efforts across generations—colonization, later the canal and railway construction—could be realized.

While the agreements of the medieval associations described above usually give no reasons for the chosen organizational form of the enterprise, the contract works of the newly emerging trading companies are more telling in this respect. The contract of the Swedish Australian or *Süder-Compagny*, for example, describes the motives

> as to why [trade] is organized under a company and cannot be launched with many individually: Amongst them is not least the fact that a united force, in the event of need, is the most convenient way of offering resistance to the enemy. It will also be much harder for the enemy to encroach on such a unified structure than on one that is divided. As a body, its members stand by one another more faithfully than in a case of separate accounts being held, since in the latter case each one seeks to maintain their own capital even if detrimental to the others. Because economic concerns begin at home. Moreover, the expenses incurred by this structure are then not so onerous and are also more easily borne by trade; and lastly it is a better means of increasing merchant trade as opposed to when it is divided, since in the latter case no one wants to do anything for the other but instead envies, damages and obstructs the other.[50]

---

49 The shares of VOC were in high demand and they traded at a very high price. In 1678, they had increased to more than 400% above par, i.e. above their nominal value, Gaastra, "Die Vereinigte Ostindische Compagnie," 9.

50 The privilege from the "extensive report on the manifest = or contract letter of the Australian or Süder = Company in the Kingdom of Sweden" of 14 June 1626, fol. 4, is found in Johann Marquardt, *Tractatus politico-juridicus de iure mercatorum et commerciorum singulari,* (…) (Frankfurt am Main: Götzius, 1662), 371 (*lib.* 3, *cap.* 1., no. 83). According to

5.1 *Change in External Conditions*

Progress benefited from the improving cartography[51] and the means of communication,[52] but primarily from the change in social structures in general and the further development of commercial know-how in particular; along with the establishment of professional investors and merchant bankers and the spreading of hedging and credit instruments such as the bill of exchange or maritime insurance, the need for associations such as the *accomandatio* dwindled away.[53] Thus, as early as the fourteenth century, new economically and legally progressive regulations made it possible for project-related associations, i.e. an *accommendatio* intended for just a single sea voyage, to be renounced in favour of lasting corporate structures.[54] It proved useful to spread the high risks by investments in many individual ventures.[55] The establishment of banks, such as for example the Medici Bank in 1397, enabled on the one hand the accumulation of capital, and on the other hand the use of funds for capital-intensive ventures over longer periods, which was also done, for example, by of bills of exchange because of its prolonging effect.[56] Large-scale professional investors

E. Duyker (ed.), *Mirror of the Australian Navigation by Jacob Le Maire: A Facsimile of the 'Spieghel der Australische Navigatie ...' Being an Account of the Voyage of Jacob Le Maire and Willem Schouten 1615–1616 published in Amsterdam in 1622* (Sydney: Hordern House, 1999), 11–30, the foundation of this "*Australischen oder Zuid Companie*" goes back to the Dutch sailor Isaac Le Maire in the year 1614.

51 Gaastra, "Die Vereinigte Ostindische Compagnie," 4.

52 Sven Schmidt, "Kommunikationsrevolution oder Zweite Kommerzielle Revolution? Die Neuen Geschäftsmedien des 16. Jahrhunderts und ihr Einfluss auf die Praktiken des frühneuzeitlichen Börsenhandels am Beispiel der Nürnberger Preiscourants (1586–1640)," in Mark Häberlein and Christof Jeggle (eds.), *Praktiken des Handels. Geschäfte und soziale Beziehungen europäischer Kaufleute in Mittelalter und früher Neuzeit* (Konstanz: UVK, 2010), 245–282; Clé Lesger, "Der Buchdruck und der Aufstieg Amsterdams als Nachrichtenzentrum um 1600," in Mark Häberlein and Christof Jeggle (eds.), *Praktiken des Handels. Geschäfte und soziale Beziehungen europäischer Kaufleute in Mittelalter und früher Neuzeit* (Konstanz: UVK, 2010), 283–308. In summary: Michael North, "Von der atlantischen Handelsexpansion bis zu den Agrarreformen," in Michael North (ed.), *Deutsche Wirtschaftsgeschichte* (Munich: Ugarit, 2005), 112–196, here 119 *seq.*

53 Van Doosselaere, *Commercial Agreements*, 67, 210.

54 Ron Harris, "The institutional dynamics of Early Modern Eurasian Trade. The Commenda and the Corporation," *Journal of Economic Behaviour and Organisation* 71 (2009), 606–622, and at http://ssrn.com/abstract=1294095 (consulted on 17 January 2017), 1–48, here 29–34, which examines why the companies emerging since the seventeenth century were a purely European phenomenon.

55 More details e.g. De Roover, *Medici Bank*, 142–148.

56 De Roover, *Medici Bank*, 108–141.

were no longer willing to pass on a relatively large share in the profits. The establishment of marine insurance made it possible to dispense with spreading the risk over several *accommendatio* contracts.[57] Finally, the introduction of double-entry bookkeeping also contributed to the possibility of maintaining and profitably operating long-term business relations over longer distances.[58]

5.2 *Deviation of Intra-company Parameters*

What then remained as a continuing element, what was changed, and what were the innovations in the early *Compagnien*? The term *Compagnie*, which was derived through Old French from the Medieval Latin word for bread cooperative (*companium*), covers the large trading companies that have emerged since the seventeenth century.[59] All variants in the Netherlands,[60] England,[61] Germany,[62] and other Central European countries[63] had a common denominator: their special relationship with the authorities. Such a relationship was on the one hand marked by the fact that the sovereigns themselves held economic participations in the company's business transactions and that they requested private investors also to subscribe for shares. On the other hand, the large colonial trading companies served the purpose of developing new empires far

57 Regarding maritime insurance Karin Nehlsen-von Stryk, *Die venezianische Seeversicherung im 15. Jahrhundert* (Ebelsbach: Gremer, 1986).

58 De Roover, *Medici Bank*, 97–100; on overall innovations in the fourteenth century De Roover, "The Organization of Trade," in Michael Moïssey Postan, Edwin E. Rich and Edward Miller (eds.), *The Cambridge Economic History of Europe. III: Economic Organization and Policies in the Middle Ages* (Cambridge: CUP, 1963), 42–118, here 44, and 90–99.

59 See "Kompanie," in *Deutsches Rechtswörterbuch. Wörterbuch der älteren deutschen Rechtssprache*, vol. 7 (Weimar: Böhlau, 1974–1983; repr. Stuttgart: Böhlau, 1998), 1193 *seq.*

60 Gaastra, "Die Vereinigte Ostindische Compagnie," 5 *seq.*

61 Holdsworth, *A History of English Law*, 8, 199–201.

62 Katharina Jahntz, *Privilegierte Handelscompagnien in Brandenburg und Preußen. Ein Beitrag zur Geschichte des Gesellschaftsrechts* (PhD thesis 2005; Berlin: Duncker & Humblot, 2006); Sven Klosa, *Die Brandenburgische-Africanische Compagnie in Emden. Eine Handelscompagnie des ausgehenden 17. Jahrhunderts zwischen Protektionismus und unternehmerischer Freiheit* (PhD thesis 2010; Frankfurt am Main: Lang, 2011); Anja Amend-Traut, "Der Reichshofrat und die Kapitalgesellschaften. Die Bemühungen um eine Handelscompanie zwischen den Hansestädten und Spanien," in Anja Amend-Traut, Albrecht Cordes, Wolfgang Sellert (eds.), *Geld, Handel, Wirtschaft. Höchste Gerichte im Alten Reich als Spruchkörper und Institution* (Berlin: De Gruyter, 2013), 61–89.

63 Regarding the Portuguese companies, see Jorun Poettering, "Handelskompanien, portugiesische," in Hermann Hiery (ed.), *Lexikon zur Überseegeschichte* (Stuttgart: Steiner, 2015), 324–325.

from home. For this purpose, the *Compagnien* were endowed with sovereignty over their own personnel and the right to maintain their own armed forces and erect fortifications.[64] Privileges and monopolies were tried and tested as means of protecting and promoting the companies in the spirit of mercantilistic economic policy, not only for the sake of such economic policy, but also and primarily in the sovereigns' own interest. For the lack of any general statutory regulations for companies during the *Ancien Régime*, these privileges were the legal foundations of the companies, which were usually issued in the form of so-called *Octrois, Charters* or *Lettres Patentes*.[65] They usually granted the companies the right to exclusive trade.[66]

In contrast to their medieval predecessors, but also like the family enterprises and other companies since the end of the fifteenth century, the early privileged trading companies were not subject to fixed term contracts for endowing individual trade expeditions, but in most cases they were long-term associations of persons. None of their predecessors, however, had any special status granted by the sovereign setting it apart from general law.

In detail, the privileged companies were differently structured. The English regulated companies[67] did not run the business themselves, but rather through their cartel-like associated members. In contrast, the so-called joint stock companies[68] operated their trading business themselves without any members appearing externally. The latter can therefore be seen as the forerunners of the later joint-stock companies.[69] Apart from individual examples such as the

---

64 Thus, for example, VOC, Gaastra, "Die Vereinigte Ostindische Compagnie," 6; Partenheimer-Bein, "Vereinigte Ostindische Kompanie (VOC) der Niederlande," 839; or the early Portuguese enterprises, Poettering, "Handelskompanien, portugiesische," 325. On the jurisdiction of the *Brandenburgisch-Africanischen Compagnie*, see Klosa, *Die Brandenburgische-Africanische Compagnie in Emden*, 80–82.

65 In more detail, Helmut Coing, *Europäisches Privatrecht. 1: Älteres Gemeines Recht (1500 to 1800)* (Frankfurt am Main: Klostermann, 1985), 526; Rudolf Gmür, "Die Emder Handelscompagnien des 17. und 18. Jahrhunderts," in Wolfgang Hefermehl, Rudolf Gmür and Hans Brox (eds.), *Festschrift für Harry Westermann zum 65. Geburtstag* (Karlsruhe: Gieseking, 1974), 167–197, here 180–185.

66 According to Johann Marquard, *Tractatus*, 359 (*lib*. 3, *cap*. 1, no. 11), approval by authorities was mandatory. Critical comment Gmür, "Emder Handelscompagnien," 182 *seq*. As to the *Oktrois* of the VOC, more details in Gaastra, *Geschiedenis*, 20–23.

67 Holdsworth, *A History of English Law*, 8, 199–205.

68 Holdsworth, *A History of English Law*, 8, 206–219; for details on the differentiation of these variants see Gmür, *Emder Handelscompagnien*, 168–170.

69 Zu den Aktiengesellschaften zusammenfassend Albrecht Cordes, "Aktiengesellschaften," in Albrecht Cordes, Heiner Lück, Dieter Werkmüller and Christa Bertelsmeier-Kierst

Dutch VOC, where the entrepreneurial organization was from the outset structured independently, several companies held a midway position between the two described types, and thus marked a development towards a separate legal personality. Members participating with their capital contributions, who were associated in a long-term enterprise, made short-term business transactions on their own behalf. Thus, smaller associations for individual transactions were occasionally formed within the company. In contrast to the long-term invested capital in joint stock, these investments were short-term, i.e. in a terminable stock. Thus, just as with the medieval associations, the latter constituted a close relationship between the investor as a person and his capital investment. This was different in the joint stock companies, where the shareholder on the one hand and the company on the other hand were largely independent from each other.

5.3 *Liability*

One is inclined to think that with regard to uncertain ventures, the liability of shareholders/partners was limited. Silberschmidt had already noticed for the *accommendatio* that in view of the considerable risks which a sea voyage entailed for body and life, it would have been unfair to impose all financial risks on the *Commendatar* (i.e. the traveller).[70] In fact, the overseas trading companies show a separation between the liability of the company and the liability of its externally acting directors, who often had higher participation than the other investors. However, according to the sources analyzed so far, a limitation of liability was explicitly provided only in the English joint stock companies,[71] and the VOC,[72] but otherwise was not provided for without an exception or in clear terms.[73] In addition, the contemporary literature of the eighteenth and nineteenth century classified the participation instruments—which had

(eds.), *Handwörterbuch zur deutschen Rechtsgeschichte* (Berlin: Schmidt, 2008), vol. 1, 132–134.

70 Silberschmidt, *Commenda*, 112.

71 Holdsworth, *A History of English Law*, 8, 203.

72 Partenheimer-Bein, "Vereinigte Ostindische Kompanie (VOC) der Niederlande," 839. This has been criticized in Oscar C. Gelderblom, Abe de Jong and Joost P.B. Jonker, "The formative years of the modern corporation: the Dutch East India Company VOC, 1602–1623," *Journal of Economic History* 73 (2013), 1050–1076; with regard to source material evaluated for the first time the authors recently assume a personal liability of at least the directors (*Direktoren*), see 1063.

73 See Jahntz, *Privilegierte Handelscompagnien in Brandenburg und Preußen*, 87, who could not prove any express limitations for the trading companies in Brandenburg and Prussia, and Lehmann, *Die geschichtliche Entwicklung des Aktienrechts*, 23. In contrast see

already been called *Aktie/Actie* (share) since the fifteenth century[74]—not so much as a debenture, and in its consequence, a limitation of liability,[75] but rather as a membership right.[76] Solely, some *Octroi* drafts of unrealized companies provided for an explicit limitation of liability of the shareholders to their one-time contribution.[77]

5.4 *Independence between Company and Shareholders*

A corporate form more separate to the acting persons, especially when secured by contracts involving authorities, allowed for both a larger continuity in corporate management and the transferability of the shares, and also facilitated legal actions against third parties as well as against members.[78] Also, apart from the active participation in legal actions, legal transactions were easier if the company had an independent existence in its own right and could therefore be sued directly, in particular as a debtor. These aspects increased the effectiveness and practicability of the companies. Even though the capacity to sue and be sued, and the procedural capacity, usually did not explicitly follow from the *Octroi*, individual regulations allow this conclusion. Thus, for example, the *Octroi* of the *Brandenburgisch-Africanischen Compagnie* states that if the Compagnie was "*in* corpere [my emphasis] *von Jemand wollte besprochen*", i.e. sued, the Elector could handle the matter personally.[79]

Markus Söhnchen, *Die historische Entwicklung der rechtlichen Gründungsvoraussetzungen von Handels- und Aktiengesellschaften* (Berlin: Duncker & Humblot, 2005), 109 *seq*.

74 Substantiations: "Actie," in *Deutsches Rechtswörterbuch. Wörterbuch der älteren deutschen Rechtssprache*, vol. 1 (Weimar: Böhlau, 1914, also 1932; repr. Stuttgart: Böhlau, 1998), 473 *seq*.

75 Friedrich Georg August Lobethan, *Grundsätze des Handlungs-Rechts mit besonderer Rücksicht auf das Verlagsrecht des Buchhändlers und das Eigenthumsrecht des Schriftstellers* (Leipzig: Reinicke, 1795), s. 41; Carl Günther Ludovici, "Actien," in *Eröffnete Akademie der Kaufleute, oder vollständiges Kaufmanns-Lexicon*, vols. 1–5 (Leipzig: Breitkopf, 1767–1768), here vol. 1, 220–229.

76 Georg Arnold Heise, *Heise's Handelsrecht, nach dem Original-Manuscript* (Frankfurt: Sauerländer, 1858), s. 27, mentions a membership right, at 68, but presumes a limitation of liability, see 69; Johann Christoph Nehring and Christian Gottlieb Riccius, "Actie," in *Historisch-Politisch- und Juristisches Wörter-Buch oder Lexicon* (Gotha: Mevius, 1756), 10.

77 More details on this range of topics with further substantiation Cordes and Jahntz, "Aktiengesellschaften vor 1807?," recital 39.

78 In this respect, see also Holdsworth, *A History of English Law*, 8, 202.

79 Klosa, *Die Brandenburgische-Africanische Compagnie in Emden*, 83.

6 Summary and Outlook

The different forms of joint economic activities in the Middle Ages and in the first half of the Early Modern Age indicate rough lines of development that were congruent with the technical skills and business requirements of merchants. While at first, individual and thus manageable transactions brought the participants together, these were later largely replaced by continuous associations. After all, larger-scale investments could best be managed by modern hedging and credit forms and a larger risk could be minimized through many investors. Even if the different early companies show one or several aspects of a legal entity, these can at best be considered to be general forerunners of joint stock companies.

As demonstrated in the overview, the number of handed down and analyzed contracts of privileged trading companies is modest. The present findings in this respect can possibly be extended in the future based on court files. Further research promises the revelation of fundamental uniformities in legal structures, and may allow conclusions on a prototype or several—e.g. regionally different—base models, as, has already been discovered for the Fugger contracts.[80] Court files, especially those of the two supreme courts in the Old Empire, often contain draft contracts, but particularly company statutes that were in force. These do not only allow conclusions on the structure and internal affairs of companies, but also provide information on the significance of trading companies within the overall economic system of the Old Empire.[81] They are thus as important for the history of private law as they are for economic history.

80 Schneider, *Fugger contra Fugger*.

81 In summary, see Anja Amend-Traut, *Die Spruchpraxis der höchsten Reichsgerichte im Römisch-Deutschen Reich und ihre Bedeutung für die Privatrechtsgeschichte* (Wetzlar: Gesellschaft für Reichskammergerichtsforschung, 2008), 17 *seq.*; Anja Amend-Traut, "Zivilverfahren vor dem Reichskammergericht. Rückblick und Perspektiven," in Friedrich Battenberg and Bernd Schildt (eds.), *Das Reichskammergericht im Spiegel seiner Prozessakten. Bilanz und Perspektiven der Forschung* (Cologne: Böhlau, 2010), 125–155, here 130, and 146–148. More details Anja Amend-Traut, *Brentano, Fugger und Konsorten—Handelsgesellschaften vor dem Reichskammergericht* (Wetzlar: Gesellschaft für Reichskammergerichtsforschung, 2009); Anja Amend-Traut, "The Aulic Council and incorporated companies. Efforts to establish a trading company between the Hanseatic Cities and Spain," in *Annales Universitatis Scientiarum Budapestinensis De Rolando Eötvös Nominatae, Sectio Iuridica* 53 (2012), 203–238; in the German language Anja Amend-Traut, "Der Reichshofrat und die Kapitalgesellschaften"; Anja Amend-Traut, "Brüder unter sich".

Apart from the legal-historical approach that was pursued in this chapter, with its focus on corporate contracts and its contents, silent participations[82] and commission trade has to be considered for an overall view of the developments in early modern company trading. There are qualified indications that the large trading companies and their numerous smaller imitations overall played a significantly smaller role in practice than commission trade did. A Europe-wide view shows that this latter form of organization is the one that can be called representative. It is true that no formal contracts on commission trade have been handed down, i.e. on the dealings between the commission agent and the principal, in which the purchase object and the commission were stipulated. However, it was very wide-spread: accounting books of merchants,[83] but also commercial expert opinions, so-called *Parere*,[84] and commercial handbooks,[85] all provide significant information in this regard. In the sixteenth century, large enterprises working on a commission basis, i.e. by charging minor commissions for arranging bills of exchange or commodity transactions, started to spread. Commission agents, who in contrast to "factors"

82 Amend-Traut, *(Silent) participation.*

83 For Antwerp: Wilfrid Brulez, *De Firma Della Faille en de internationale handel van Vlaamse firma's in de 16de eeuw* (Brussels: Academy Palace, 1959); Florence Edler, "The Van der Molen, Commission Merchants of Antwerp. Trade With Italy, 1538–1544," in James Lea Cate and Eugene N. Anderson (eds.), *Medieval and Historiographical Essays in Honor of James Westfall Thompson* (Chicago: University of Chicago Press, 1938), 78–145; Jeroen Puttevils, *Merchants and Trading in the Sixteenth Century. The Golden Age of Antwerp* (London: Pickering & Chatto, 2015). For London: Henry Roseveare, *Markets and Merchants of the late Seventeenth Century: The Marescoe-David Letters, 1668–1680* (Oxford: OUP, 1987). For Florence: Richard A. Goldthwaite, *The Economy of Renaissance Florence* (Baltimore: John Hopkins University Press, 2009). For the entire Italian and Portuguese area: Francesca Trivellato, *The Familiarity of Strangers. The Sephardic Diaspora, Livorno, and Cross-cultural Trade in the Early Modern Period* (New Haven: Yale University Press, 2009). For the Hanse: Ortwin Pelc, "Lübecker Kommissionshandel um 1700. Die Handelsgeschäfte zwischen Peter Tesdorpf und dem Magdeburger Kaufmann Valentin Haeseler," in Michael Hundt and Jan Lokers (eds.), *Hanse und Stadt. Akteure, Strukturen und Entwicklungen im regionalen und europäischen Raum. Festschrift für Rolf Hammel-Kiesow zum 65. Geburtstag* (Lübeck: Schmidt-Römhild, 2014), 471–483.

84 In this respect, reference is made to the project financed by the German Research Association and headed by the author, "Die Nürnberger Handelsgerichtsbarkeit. Handelsgerichtliche Gutachten in der Frühen Neuzeit," which has been running since 2015, http://www.jura.uni-wuerzburg.de/lehrstuehle/amend_traut/die_nuernberger_handelsgerichtsbarkeit/ (consulted on 17 January 2017).

85 Jaques Savary, *Le parfait négociant* (ed.) Édouard Richard, 2 vols. (Geneva: Droz, 2011), here vol. 1, 886–923.

were not employed by companies, were independent and at the same time did not carry any risk for the success of the transaction in their activities as agent. Moreover, the use of commission agents for small local enterprises with little financial resources allowed for access to international markets; long-distance trade thus became "democratized".[86]

However, a stronger emphasis on the commission trade for the Early Modern Age results in still not conclusively answered questions, for example regarding whether and if they are applicable when the use of "factors" (*Faktoreiwesen*) lost the significance it had held in the time of the large-scale family enterprises such as the Fugger family, to name but one.[87]

All aspects only briefly indicated here show that more case studies are required to be able to provide a full picture of early modern company trading.

---

86 Brulez, *De firma Della Faille*, 354, and 367–374; Puttevils, *Merchants and Trading*, 100. Since the 16th century commission trade was labelled "commission" in its present meaning: Alfred Schirmer, *Wörterbuch der deutschen Kaufmannssprache auf geschichtlichen Grundlagen*, (Straßburg: Trübner, 1911; repr. Berlin: de Gruyter, 1991), art. "Kommission," 102.

87 Some historical aspects of the commission trade can be found in Goldschmidt, *Universalgeschichte des Handelsrechts*, 331 *seq*.

CHAPTER 5

Delving for Diversity in Early Modern Company Law: Mining Companies in Seventeenth-Century Liège*

Bram Van Hofstraeten

1 Introduction

At a very early stage, and due to the richness of its natural resources, the Prince-Bishopric of Liège developed both a significant metallurgical industry, as well as a uniquely organized exploitation of its collieries. While the former is generally applauded as the "principal field of industrial expansion in Liège",[1] the British historian John U. Nef described the Liège mining activities "to be more important than anywhere in Great Britain",[2] at least until the sixteenth century. Due to the necessary acquisition of rather expensive mining concessions, extensive infrastructural demands, as well as the considerable labour forces they required, both the transformation of iron as well as the extraction of coal belonged to the most capital-intensive industries in the Low Countries during the *Ancien Régime*. In order to address these needs, such activities had by the fourteenth century led to the creation of private partnerships as an effective means of cost reduction and capital growth.[3] During the sixteenth and seven-

---

* This chapter embodies the results of a first, exploratory examination of industrial private partnerships in early modern Liège. A more exhaustive examination, also comprising the eighteenth century, will be executed in the near future (2017–2021) within the framework of the author's NWO VIDI research project entitled "What's in a Name? Challenging Early Modern Ideal-Types of Private Partnerships in the Low Countries (17th–18th Centuries)".

1 Bruno Demoulin and Jean-Louis Kupper, *Histoire de la Principauté de Liège. De l'an mille à la Révolution* (Toulouse: Privat, 2002), 92.

2 John U. Nef, *The Rise of the British Coal Industry* (London: Cass, 1966), vol. 1, 13–14.

3 Horst Kranz, *Lütticher Steinkohlenbergbau im Mittelalter. Aufstieg, Bergrecht. Unternehmer, Umwelt, Technik* (Herzogenrath: Shaker, 2000), 328–329. In the area around Aachen, such partnerships can be identified from the fifteenth century onwards. See Friedrich Schunder, *Geschichte des Aachener Steinkohlenbergbaus* (Essen: Glückauf, 1968), 93. In addition to the aforementioned financial motivations to create private partnerships, there existed numerous other goals which incited early modern individuals to establish partnerships such as advancing a marriage, rendering the possessions of under-aged children profitable, introduc-

 | DOI: 10.1163/9789004351868_007

teenth centuries, new industries like glassmaking and the extraction of alum, sulphur and lead called for similar action.[4] Finally, in the eighteenth century, the need for capital grew even more exponentially with the introduction of the Newcomen steam engines from the 1720s onwards, followed by the Watt steam engines from the 1770s onwards.[5]

Whereas the mining activities and the metallurgical industries of Liège have already been the object of numerous appraisable historical studies,[6] the organizational and legal features of their enterprises has barely received scholarly attention so far.[7] This major lacuna in the history of company law and corporate practices in the Low Countries is most deplorable because of the

---

ing one's children to the world of commerce, and nurturing their professional development as a merchant-to-be, generating a pension-like income for older people and physically incapacitated merchants, etc. (See Bram Van Hofstraeten, "Limited Partnerships in Early Modern Antwerp (1480–1620)," *Forum Iuris Historiae*, 5 November 2015, http://www.forhistiur.de/en/2015-11-van-hofstraeten/ (consulted on 17 January 2017)).

4 Jean Lejeune, *La formation du capitalisme moderne dans la principauté de Liége au XVIe siècle* (Liège-Paris, 1939), pp. 226–267.

5 René Leboutte, "L'exploitation charbonnière dans le Pays de Liège sous l'Ancien Régime," in Ekkehard Westermann (ed.), *Vom Bergbau- zum Industrierevier* (Stuttgart: Steiner, 1995), 379–403, here 381–383.

6 Georges Hansotte, *La métallurgie et le commerce internationale du fer dans les Pays-Bas autrichiens et la Principauté de Liège pendant la seconde moitié du XVIIIe siècle* (Brussels: Academy Palace, 1980); Georges Hansotte, "La métallurgie wallonne au XVIe et dans la première moitié du XVIIe siècle. Essai de synthèse," *Bulletin de l'institut archéologique liégeoise* 84 (1972), 21–42; Kranz, *Lütticher Steinkohlenbergbau*; René Leboutte, "La métallurgie dans la région liégeoise du XVe siècle à l'aube du XIXe siècle," in Hans-Walter Hermann and Paul Wynants (eds.), *Wandlungen der Eisenindustrie vom 16. Jhdt bis 1960. Mutations de la sidérurgie du XVIe siècle à 1960* (Namur: CERUNA, 1997), 57–83; René Leboutte, "L'exploitation charbonnière dans le Pays de Liège sous l'Ancien Régime," *Vierteljahrschrift für Sozial- und Wirtschaftsgeschichte* 115 (1995), 379–403; Eugène Polain, "La vie à Liège sous Ernest de Bavière (1581–1612)," *Bulletin de l'institut archéologique liégeois* 61 (1937), 46–130; Jean Yernaux, *La métallurgie liégeoise et son expansion au XVIIe siècle* (Liège: Thone, 1939).

7 Kranz, *Lütticher Steinkohlenbergbau*, 328–334; Lejeune, *La formation du capitalisme moderne*, 226–251; Paul Van Hoegaerden, *Des anciennes coutumes de houillerie au pays de Liége* (Liège: De Thier, 1886). From a broader European perspective, the following studies constitute useful reference material: Klaus Kammerer, *Das Unternehmensrecht süddeutscher Handelsgesellschaften in der Montanindustrie des 15. und 16. Jahrhunderts* (PhD thesis, University of Tübingen, 1977), 232–332; Nef, *The Rise*, 2, 43–78; Marcel Rouff, *Les mines de charbon en France au XVIIIe siècle (1744–1791)* (Paris: Rieder & Cie, 1922), 243–277; Bernhard Willms, "Der Anteil der Reichsstadt Aachen an der Kohlengewinnung im Wurmrevier," *Zeitschrift des Aachener Geschichtsvereins* 45 (1923), 144–157.

fact that the industrial nature of the Liège economy in particular—in opposition to the prime devotion to commercial activities in other cities in the Low Countries—as well as its exceptionally capital-intensive demands may have called for differently organized companies and field-specific corporate practices in order to turn the extraction and transformation of commodities into a profitable enterprise. This chapter will address this lacuna in a provisional, exploratory manner. By means of an analysis of notarized partnership agreements, recorded in seventeenth-century Liège, the present contribution aims to identify and describe potential idiosyncrasies regarding the operational and legal features of private partnerships in Liège, and in particular with regard to mining companies. In doing so, it will become apparent that a specific line of industry may call for and actually engender substantially distinctive corporate practices, both from an organizational as well as from a legal point of view.

In order to identify such potential idiosyncrasies, I primarily made use of notarized partnership agreements and partnership-related notarial deeds produced by those notaries who were active in the city of Liège in the course of the seventeenth century.[8] Earlier studies on early modern company law and private partnerships have already proven the suitability of notarial protocol

8 As far as early modern jurisdiction on private partnerships is concerned, the archives of the Liège bench of aldermen hardly contain case files in which corporate practices were at the heart of the dispute. See Sébastien Dubois, *Inventaire des archives de la Souveraine Justice des Échevins de Liège. Dossiers de procès civils (1e série, n° 1–1600) (1529) 1578–1794* (Brussels: Archives of the Realm, 2013). This can be explained by the fact that early modern entrepreneurs generally preferred arbitration over litigation, on the one hand, and because of the existence of the *Cour des Voir-Jurés de charbonnage*, a special court for disputes regarding mining activities, on the other hand. Unfortunately, only very few documents of the latter institution survived the bombing of the Liège state archives in 1944. See Sébastien Dubois, Bruno Demoulin and Jean-Louis Kupper, *Les institutions publiques de la principauté de Liège (980–1794)* (Brussels: Archives of the Realm, 2012), vol. 1, 565–572. With regard to municipal legislation on and recorded compilations of mining practices, much more data has survived. See Kranz, *Lütticher Steinkohlenbergbau*, 189–194. From the fourteenth century onwards, local customs regarding mining activities were recorded continuously. The most significant compilation of such practices can be found in chapter 22 of the so-called *Paix de St.-Jacques* of 1487. Together with the recorded customs of 1318/1330, the latter document has been edited and translated into German by Horst Kranz: Horst Kranz, *Quellen zum Lütticher Steinkohlenbergbau im Mittelalter. Urkunden—Register- und Rechnungseintrage—Bergrecht* (Herzogenrath: Shaker, 2000), 361–382. Other additional regulations, stated by the Liège aldermen, can be found in: Louis Crahay and Stanislas Bormans (eds.), *Coutumes du Pays de Liège*, vol. 3 (Brussels: Gobbaerts, 1884). However, these collections hardly addressed the specific legal features of private partnerships designed for extraction activities.

books in identifying and reconstructing corporate practices.[9] From a chronological point of view, the aforementioned focus on the seventeenth century is justified by the fact that older protocol books of Liège notaries are too scarce and too fragmented. This would change from the 1610s onwards. Moreover, the large number of registers produced after 1610 caused me to opt for a sample-based approach. This sample consists of a synchronic cross-section through the seventeenth century whereby all protocol books of all notaries active in Liège during the years 1651–1655 were analyzed in an exhaustive manner, i.e. by scanning all notarial deeds in search of partnership agreements or company-related deeds. In total, 47 notaries, whose registers are still being preserved, had been active in Liège between 1651 and 1655.[10] During these five years they produced about 13,900 notarial deeds. Again, finding partnership agreements in such a quantity of documents proved to be utterly time-consuming and akin to looking for a needle in a haystack. Still, five notarial deeds, by means of which a private partnership was created, could be identified and located.[11] This number represents a success ratio of 0.036 per cent, or one notarized partnership agreement per 2,780 notarial deeds.[12] In addition, the research sample could

9 As far as the Low Countries are concerned, see Bram Van Hofstraeten, "Historiographical Opportunities of Notarized Partnership Agreements Recorded in the Early Modern Low Countries," in Heikki Pihlajamäki, Albrecht Cordes, Serge Dauchy and Dave De ruysscher (eds.), *Understanding the Sources of Commercial law* (Leiden: Brill, forthcoming); Bram Van Hofstraeten, "Private Partnerships in Seventeenth-Century Maastricht," in Bram Van Hofstraeten and Wim Decock (eds.), *Companies and Company law in Late Medieval and Early Modern Europe* (Leuven: Peeters, 2016), 115–148.

10 On the basis of references to various other notaries in the preserved protocol books, it can safely be concluded that many more notaries, whose registers did not survive, had been active in the city during the period under review. The annex to this chapter provides an alphabetical overview of those 47 notaries whose registers have been preserved and analyzed. See also: Bruno Dumont, *Guide des fonds et collections des Archives de l'État à Liège. III: Archives publiques locales—Archives ecclésiastiques—Notariat* (Brussels: Archives of the Realm, 2012), 686–712.

11 Liège, State Archives (henceforth LSA), *Notariat* (henceforth N), *Notaire J. Pompony*, 13 January 1651 (Mathieu de Trooz, Laurent Truiller alias Collard, Henry Brocart, Jean Fil, Jean Jacques, Fassin Pirchon, Henry Jean-Jacques, Hubert Lorket); LSA, N, *Notaire Th. Pauwea*, 1651, fols. 508^{r}–510^{v} (Pierre Simonis Junior, Aert Wilsens); LSA, N, *Notaire J. Housson*, 1652, fol. 92^{r} (Thomas Doultre le Pont, Cornelis Véris); LSA, N, *Notaire G. Lien*, 1654, fols. 380^{r}–381^{r} (Jérome du Jardin, Christian du Mortier); LSA, N, *Notaire J. Sauveur*, 1655, fols. 95^{r}–95^{v} and 101^{r}–101^{v} (Joris Mathys/Matthieu, Gille Heine).

12 Likewise, identifying notarized partnership agreements proved to be less difficult in Liège than that it was in Maastricht, where the success ratio was 0.028 per cent, i.e.

be expanded by means of references to seventeenth-century notarized partnership agreements in the available literature, on the one hand, and a specific case file preserved in the Maastricht archives on the other hand.[13] Another contract was identified by coincidence, while a last agreement could be located through a cross reference in the Liège notarial archives.[14] In sum, the present data set amounted to sixteen partnership agreements, supplemented with various notarial deeds which concerned private partnerships "in action". Finally, one should realize that these documents merely constitute a tip of the iceberg, for privately-drafted and oral agreements were still a very common practice in the early modern Low Countries. In Liège too, the bench of aldermen recognized the validity of oral contracts.[15] For obvious reasons, one is unable to incorporate such agreements in a study on corporate practices. Therefore, cautiousness is recommended with regard to the conclusions drawn in this article.

---

one partnership agreement for every 3,578 notarial deeds. See Van Hofstraeten, "Private Partnerships," 118. Still, notarized partnership agreements were much less frequently used in Liège than in Antwerp. With regard to the sixteenth century, for example, one was able to identify one partnership agreement per 583 notarial acts, whereas the number of notarized partnership agreements in Antwerp during the French period (1794–1814) amounted to 65 or one contract per 1,116 notarial acts. See Van Hofstraeten, "Private Partnerships," 126–127; Fred Stevens, *Revolutie en notariaat. Antwerpen 1794–1814* (Leuven: Van Gorcum, 1994), 197–198, and 281.

13 Based on Lejeune, *La formation du capitalisme moderne*: LSA, N, *Notaire Lapide*, 1576, fols. 19^r–20^v (Guillaume Stevartz, Anthoine Vaez, Jean Henry); LSA, N, *Notaire Hadin*, 1603, fols. 54^v–55^r (Wilhelm Levrixht, Gilet Servais); LSA, N, *Notaire Hadin*, 1605, fols. 81^v–83^r (Thomas de Sclessin, Thomas de Fossez, Laurent Butbacht, Giel de Noirivaulx, Bastin de Noirivaulx, Hubert Oems, Wilhelm Levrixht Senior, Wilhelm Levrixht Junior, Jean Craisier). Based on Yernaux, *La métallurgie liégeoise*: LSA, N, *Notaire H. Oupie*, 1641, fol. 25^v (Charles de Noirfalize, Jacob Beckers); LSA, N, *Notaire J. Libert*, 1646, fols. 70^r–71^r (Jan Selis, Jean Grisart); LSA, N, *Notaire G. Lien*, 1663, fols. 356^v–357^v (Godefroid-Evrard Nottemans, Bertrand Mariotte); LSA, N, *Notaire G. Lien*, 1663, fols. 452^r–453^v (André Grégoire, Robert Potty); LSA, N, *Notaire Lohier*, 1703, 6th of October (Jean-Guillaume de Requilé, Étienne de Barme). Based on the Maastricht archives: Regionaal Historisch Centrum Limburg (henceforth RHCL), Indivieze Raad Maastricht (henceforth IRM), *Procesdossiers*, 1428.

14 LSA, N, *Notaire F. Rouveroy*, 1650, fols. 106^v–107^v (Nicolas Goffar, Jean Mercenier, Marie le Franck); LSA, N, *Notaire J. Waseige*, 1700, January (Nicolas Briquer, Guilliaume Bouduin).

15 See their response to a *quaeritur* in 1697: Crahay and Bormans, *Coutumes du Pays de Liège*, 3, 369.

2 The Object of Private Partnerships in Early Modern Liège

In general, economic and legal historians associate the use of private partnerships with merchants and artisans in the first place. The Liège partnership agreements, however, show that the legal institution of a private partnership not only met the needs of early modern trade and craftsmanship, but that it also served as an efficient instrument within the economic field of mining, i.e. the extraction of natural resources.[16] Taking into account Max Weber's distinctive definitions of trade, craftsmanship and mining, it becomes possible to distribute the Liège private partnerships, whose notarized agreements could be identified, over these three categories, whereby craftsmanship proved to be the most prominent one.[17] Likewise, Weber's categorization serves as a useful tool in order to identify potential idiosyncrasies with regard to private partnerships which had been created for different economic activities.

Out of 16 contracts, seven created companies which involved craftsmanship exclusively. In at least five of these partnership agreements, the melting of iron was to be the main activity of the enterprise being established.[18] In 1646, for example, Jan Selis, who operated a smelting works in the village of Chaisne, allowed Jean Grisart, a Sancheyde resident, to become a partner in the same iron foundry for a fixed term of six years and in exchange for an annual financial contribution of 400 fl. *brabants*.[19] Profits and losses were to be divided and borne equally. In addition, Grisart, as the master-smith of the iron foundry, was to receive six *pattars* for every *millier* of iron that would be melted, while

16 Recently, while studying private partnerships in seventeenth-century Maastricht, an additional field of application has become apparent, namely the frequent use of notarized partnership agreements by tax farmers. See Van Hofstraeten, "Private Partnerships," 125–130.

17 According to Weber, the terms "industrial work", "industry" and "production" refer to "the transformation of raw materials". Consequently, extractive operations and mining activities are not covered by the terminology. If the transformation of raw materials no longer serves the needs of a household exclusively, and it is being executed in order to sell the final products to third parties, then one should speak of "craftsmanship" or "craft work". See Max Weber, *General Economic History* (New York: Greenberg, 1927), 115–116.

18 LSA, N, *Notaire H. Oupie*, 1641, fol. 25^{v} (Charles de Noirfalize, Jacob Beckers); LSA, N, *Notaire J. Libert*, 1646, fols. 70^{r}–71^{r} (Jan Selis, Jean Grisart); LSA, N, *Notaire J. Sauveur*, 1655, fols. 95^{r}–95^{v} and 101^{r}–101^{v} (Joris Mathys/Matthieu, Gille Heine); LSA, N, *Notaire G. Lien*, 1663, fols. 356^{v}–357^{v} (Godefroid-Evrard Nottemans, Bertrand Mariotte); LSA, N, *Notaire G. Lien*, 1663, fols. 452^{r}–453^{v} (André Grégoire, Robert Potty).

19 LSA, N, *Notaire J. Libert*, 1646, fols. 70^{r}–71^{r} (Jan Selis, Jean Grisart).

Selis, responsible for the shipment of the iron products at his own expense, was to receive 12 *pattars* per *millier* of iron. Furthermore, the contract stated that the costs of repair works concerning the foundry itself, as well as the expenses of the fossil fuels (coal) required to melt the iron, were to be borne by both partners equally. Moreover, each partner was allowed to leave the enterprise after three years as long as he gave due notice, i.e. three months in advance. Finally, it was agreed upon that no partner was allowed to take his part of the profit without the consent of the other partner. In addition to such smelting works, two other partnership agreements established artisanal companies which respectively centred around the production of beer and tapestries.[20]

Four other partnership agreements established commercial companies which were primarily dealing with the purchase and sale of goods.[21] As far as two of these trading enterprises are concerned, textiles were the chief merchandise, while two other commercial businesses described their trading goods merely as "all kinds of merchandise". So, two Liège merchants, Jérôme du Jardin and Christian du Mortier, entered into a private partnership on 18 August 1654 in order to trade in wool for five years.[22] It was agreed that du Mortier would be responsible for the cash register as well as for the accounts of the company, and that he was to render the accounts once a year. For these accounting efforts, du Mortier would receive a salary of two per cent of his share in the company's profits. Additionally, du Mortier would be solely responsible for the recovery of goods debts, as well as the payment of bad debts and company-related expenses. Furthermore, the contract stipulated that none of the constituting partners were allowed to undertake trading activities in wool on a personal basis during their membership of the enterprise. Ignoring this agreement would result in a fine of 200 *pattacons* for the benefit of the poor of the city. In order to start up the business, both partners were expected to provide 5,900 fl. *brabants* each. So far, du Jardin had already advanced a sum of 1,600 fl. *brabants* to du Mortier, on which amount du Jardin would receive an interest of 6.25 per cent from du Mortier until the latter had reimbursed the amount to du

---

20 LSA, N, *Notaire J. Housson*, 1652, fol. 92^r (Thomas Doultre le Pont, Cornelis Véris); LSA, N, *Notaire J. Waseige*, 1700, January (Nicolas Briquer, Guilliaume Bouduin).

21 RHCL, IRM, *Procesdossiers*, 1428 (Christiaan van Raije, Benoit des Andrianes); LSA, N, *Notaire F. Rouveroy*, 1650, fols. 106^v–107^v and 170^r–171^r (Nicolas Goffar, Jean Mercenier, Marie le Franck); LSA, N, *Notaire Th. Pauwea*, 1651, fols. 508^r–510^v (Pierre Simonis Junior, Aert Wilsens); LSA, N, *Notaire G. Lien*, 1654, fols. 380^r–381^r (Jérome du Jardin, Christian du Mortier).

22 LSA, N, *Notaire G. Lien*, 1654, fols. 380^r–381^r.

Jardin. Finally, it was agreed that the heirs of a partner, in case of the premature death of one of the constituting partners, were allowed to leave the partnership if they wished to do so.

A third category consists of four partnership agreements by means of which companies involved in mining activities, more specifically the extraction of coal and sulphur, were founded.[23] This category not only contains those enterprises which were primarily devoted to the actual extraction of natural resources, but also those partnerships that were created in light of the construction and maintenance of so-called *areines* or drainage canals which were indispensable in order to prevent the collieries from flooding. By the end of October 1603, Wilhem Levrixht, a Liège merchant, and Gilet Servais from Engis concluded a partnership in order to start up mining activities "at common expenses" in Warfusée, situated north of Engis and west of Liège.[24] Both partners hoped to find some veins of *kis*, i.e. sulphurous pyrites from which sulphur could be extracted. It was agreed that all the investments that would be necessary in order to launch the mining activities were to be provided for by Wilhem Levrixht. Half of these expenses were to be reimbursed to Levrixht at the expense of Gilet's share in the profits as soon as the mine became profitable. The agreement also stated that in case of an unsuccessful exploration of the terrain, meaning that no minerals could be found, Gilet Servais was still obliged to reimburse half of the expenses already made by Wilhem Levrixht.

In addition to these strictly artisanal or exclusively commercial companies, one partnership agreement established a company which embraced not only trade and craftsmanship but also mining activities. It was founded in 1703 and it brought together Jean-Guillaume de Réquilé and his brother-in-law, Etienne de Barme.[25] On 6 October they entered into a partnership "both for themselves as well as their wives, children and heirs" on "iron, mines (with regard to whatever

23 LSA, N, *Notaire Lapide*, 1576, fols. 19^r–20^v (Guillaume Stevartz, Anthoine Vaez, Jean Henry); LSA, N, *Notaire Hadin*, 1603, fols. 54^v–55^r (Wilhelm Levrixht, Gilet Servais); LSA, N, *Notaire Hadin*, 1605, fols. 81^v–83^r (Thomas de Sclessin, Thomas de Fossez, Laurent Butbacht, Giel de Noirivaulx, Bastin de Noirivaulx, Hubert Oems, Wilhelm Levrixht Senior, Wilhelm Levrixht Junior, Jean Craisier); LSA, N, *Notaire J. Pompony*, 13 January 1651 (Mathieu de Trooz, Laurent Truiller alias Collard, Henry Brocart, Jean Fil, Jean Jacques, Fassin Pirchon, Henry Jean-Jacques, Hubert Lorket).

24 LSA, N, *Notaire Hadin*, 1603, fols. 54^v–55^r (Wilhelm Levrixht, Gilet Servais).

25 LSA, N, *Notaire Lohier*, 1703, 6th of October (Jean-Guillaume de Requilé, Etienne de Barme). As regards the history of this entrepreneurial family and its enterprises, see Yernaux, *La métallurgie liégeoise*.

kind of mineral), coal, salt, wood and grain". Inputs, profits and losses were to be divided and borne equally, and none of the partners were allowed to undertake private activities during the existence of the enterprise. The accounts of the partnership were to be inspected every month, while once a year "an overall account" was to be produced. Sales on credit were restricted to amounts of up to 100 *ecus* unless there existed common consent among the partners, and the enterprise was to last for at least fifteen years. If one of the constituting partners were to die during the existence of the partnership, then his wife, children or heirs were to respect the partnership agreement and continue the partnership. In so doing, they were allowed to assign a person to act on their behalf as a partner of the company. Despite the predetermined duration of fifteen years, constituting partners could leave the partnership on the condition that they had warned the other contracting party two years in advance. Finally, it was stated that all disputes arising with regard to the content of the agreement were to be resolved by means of arbitration instead of litigation.

From an overall perspective, the Liège data set presents us with a fairly diversified image of the use of private partnerships in the early modern period. The application of the legal instrument appears to be rather evenly distributed over the three main fields of contemporary economic life: trade, craftsmanship and mining.[26] In opposition to earlier observations regarding the use of private partnerships in the neighbouring city of Maastricht, no partnership agreements, by means of which tax farming companies were established, could be identified in the Liège notarial archives.[27] So, thanks to the richness of its soil, the city of Liège manages to distinguish itself, as far as the use of private partnerships is concerned, from an exclusively commercially and artisanally-oriented city like Antwerp where trade and craftsmanship appeared to be the main fields of application with regard to private partnerships.[28] Likewise, the city of Liège becomes an ideal test case in order to determine whether a specific economic field of application, different from trade and crafts work, also gave rise to distinctive, field-specific corporate practices. In addition, idiosyncrasies with regard to organizational and legal features of private partnerships may have arisen merely on the basis of a city's geographical location. Therefore, I will first analyze and describe those Liège partnership agreements establish-

26 The fact that craftsmanship was the object of more partnership agreements in opposition to trading and mining activities is to be explained by the fact that many of these partnership agreements were delivered by a study by Jean Yernaux on the history of metallurgy in Liège. See Yernaux, *La métallurgie liégeoise*.

27 Van Hofstraeten, "Private Partnerships", 125–130.

28 Ib.

ing commercial and artisanal enterprises, and compare them to the already available information on early modern private partnerships in the Low Countries.

3 Commercial and Artisanal Companies

From an overall perspective, the Liège partnership agreements establishing artisanal and commercial companies demonstrate a large conformity, with regards to contract design, with the agreements that were being notarized in other cities of the Low Countries during the early modern period.[29] As one can observe in sixteenth-century Antwerp and seventeenth-century Maastricht, Rotterdam and Amsterdam, partnership agreements in Liège start off with an introduction in which the date, the line of industry or type of trading goods, the identity of the contracting parties, and their mutual commitment to form a private partnership are expressed. The middle part of the Liège contracts also presents us with constituting elements that are similar to the ones that can be observed in partnership agreements produced in the rest of the early modern Low Countries: the intended duration of the agreement, the respective contributions of the contracting parties to the working capital of the company, the distribution of profits and losses, arrangements on cost management, regulations on bookkeeping as well as the intermediate settlement of the accounts, non-competition clauses, clauses on how to deal with unforeseen circumstances (death, illness, captivity or withdrawal of one of the partners), the respective capacities of the partners to act on behalf of the company as well as limitations thereupon, the division of operational tasks, etc.

Illustrative in this matter is the partnership agreement, concluded in 1651, between the Liège merchant, Pierre Simonis Junior, and his brother-in-law, Aert Wilsens.[30] On 21 December, both parties established "for their greatest benefit and usefulness" and "irrevocably" a six-year trading partnership in cloth, silk, "and all other goods which they may consider to be suitable in light of their greatest usefulness and benefit". The working capital consisted of 10,000 fl. *brabants* in total, whereby each party was to provide 5,000 fl. *brabants*, supplemented by all the merchandise which was currently present in the house *La Tête d'Or* owned by Pierre Simonis Senior. Half of these goods already belonged to Pierre Simonis Junior while the other half had been sold

29 See Van Hofstraeten, "Historiographical Opportunities".

30 LSA, N, *Notaire Th. Pauwea*, 1651, fols. 508^{r}–510^{v}.

to Aert Wilsens by Pierre Simonis Senior.[31] Although no longer a partner, the latter remained the owner of the house which he rented out to the partnership, and it was agreed that all the company's accounts and books were to remain in the aforementioned house. Profits and losses would be divided equally. Pierre Simonis Junior would be responsible for the cash register and the ledger, while Aert Wilsens was to keep the journal of the company. Every year, both partners would gather in order to execute an intermediate settlement of the accounts. As regards cost management, the contract contains several clauses on potential expenses regarding a maid, a servant, merchants staying over, chandeliers to light the store, etc. As far as the personal household costs of the contracting parties were concerned, both men were allowed to withdraw cash from the company "as much as they need". From an operational view, Pierre Simonis Junior was obliged to be in the store every day, while Aert Wilsens was assigned to be the one who would be travelling on behalf of the company. However, his capacity to act personally was limited to textile goods. If Aert wanted to buy non-textile goods on behalf of the company, then the explicit consent of Pierre was required. Finally, unforeseen circumstances were anticipated in the contract: if one of them were to die during the existence of the company, the partnership would continue to exist with the deceased's successor(s). If one of the partners were to fall ill or be arrested while travelling on behalf of the company, the expenses to remedy such unfortunate situations were to be borne by the partnership. Finally, all transactions on behalf of the company were to occur while making use of the name *Pierre Simonis et Aert Wilsens*. A more exceptional clause allowed both partners to leave the city for two or three weeks twice a year "for health reasons in order to get some fresh air", and for five or six days for personal business.

So, partnership agreements establishing commercial and artisanal companies were designed in a similar way in Liège as was customary in the rest of the early modern Low Countries. In addition to contract design, such conformity is also demonstrated by more content-related elements. For example, the large majority of partnerships were created for a limited duration, ranging from one to fifteen years, with an average duration of five to six years.[32] Moreover, the number of contracting parties constituted no idiosyncrasy either. Most of the partnerships consisted of two or three partners who were all actively involved in the execution of the partnership's activities.[33] Likewise, eleven out of twelve

---

31 Pierre Simonis Senior had left the partnership due to his old age and ceded his part to Aert Wilsens. See LSA, N, *Notaire Th. Pauwea*, 1651, fol. 505^r.

32 Van Hofstraeten, "Private Partnerships," 121 and 130–131.

33 Ib., 121 and 130–131.

partnership agreements could be interpreted as contracts establishing a general partnership of which all contracting parties were considered to be jointly and severally liable. In one case, one might assume the existence of a silent partner whose liability might have been limited to the extent of his initial contribution to the company's working capital. On 20 May 1650, a Liège schoolmaster, Nicolas Goffar, concluded a partnership agreement with Jean Mercenier and his wife, Marie le Franck, for an undetermined period of time. Goffar entrusted 300 fl. *brabants* "in proper gold" to Jean and Marie, who were to fructify these assets by means of trading activities which were to be executed by them alone. It was agreed that they would hand over fifty per cent of the company's profits to Goffar every six months, or pay him an annual interest of ten per cent. Clearly, Goffar was merely a passive capital provider, and therefore one might presume that his external liability was limited to the 300 fl. *brabants* which he had invested in the trading partnership. Still, as in most partnership agreements produced in the early modern Low Countries, explicit clauses on external liability remain absent. Consequently, a call for cautiousness is required if one wants to categorize such partnerships with passive capital providers as limited partnerships.[34] It is clear, as illustrated by the aforementioned examples, that the internal organization of the company and "their greatest benefit and usefulness" constituted the contracting parties' main concerns while drafting the agreement.

Finally, the Liège partnership agreements for trade and craftsmanship do not surprise us with regards to the familiarity between their contracting parties. Most of them were primarily recorded on behalf of contracting parties without family ties, while only one-fourth of the contracts gathered related partners, more specifically brothers-in-law.[35] Likewise, the Liège observations are in line with those made about notarized partnership agreements in sixteenth-century Antwerp and seventeenth-century Maastricht.[36]

Despite the observed conformity between Liège partnership agreements and those notarized in the rest of the early modern Low Countries, the former do give proof of some specific features that distinguish them from the latter. First of all, the geographical origin of the constituting partners is much more local than can been seen in contracting parties in sixteenth-century

---

34 Nevertheless, there are good reasons to do so anyway. See Van Hofstraeten, "Limited Partnerships".

35 LSA, N, *Notaire Th. Pauwea*, 1651, fols. 508^r–510^v (Pierre Simonis Junior, Aert Wilsens); LSA, N, *Notaire G. Lien*, 1663, fols. 356^v–357^v (Godefroid-Evrard Nottemans, Bertrand Mariotte); LSA, N, *Notaire Lohier*, 1703, 6 October (Jean-Guillaume de Requilé, Etienne de Barme).

36 Van Hofstraeten, "Private Partnerships," 121, and 125–126.

Antwerp. In seventeenth-century Liège, partners generally originated from the city itself and its surroundings: Prayon, Engis, Polleur, Chaisne, Sancheyde, Fléron, Malmedy, and Huy. Obviously, this dissimilarity is to be explained by the much more international character of the early modern Antwerp market.

Secondly, there is an almost complete absence of so-called renunciation clauses in the Liège contracts. In Antwerp and Maastricht, 35 to 45 per cent of the notarized partnership agreements contained a renunciation clause, whereby partners renounced explicitly all legal instruments, both *beneficia* (e.g. *senatus consultum Velleianum*, *Authentica si qua mulier*, *senatus consultum Macedonianum*, ...) as well as written and customary rules that contracting parties might have recourse to in order to disregard the content of the agreement. In Liège, however, such a renunciation clause can only be observed in one contract.[37] At the end of their agreement, Wilhem Levrixht and Gilet Servais renounced "all privileges and legal exceptions" which were contrary to the content of the contract. The absence of such clauses could be interpreted as a sign of a growing confidence in local legislation, its corresponding jurisdictions, and their speediness in resolving disagreements. Nevertheless, such an interpretation is countered by the observance that a quarter of the Liège partnership agreements contained a so-called arbitration clause, i.e. a clause stipulating the parties' preference for arbitration over litigation in order to resolve conflicts. Such clauses barely existed in the contracts notarized in Antwerp and Maastricht.[38] So, in order to avoid litigation, four contracts stated explicitly that, if disputes were to arise on the interpretation of the constituting clauses, the warring parties were to have recourse to arbitration.[39] When Jean-Guillaume de Requilé and his brother-in-law, Etienne de Barme, concluded a fifteen-year partnership in 1703, by means of which they were to execute not only trading and industrial but also mining activities, they decided that as soon as doubts, ambiguities or difficulties might arise regarding the content of the partnership agreement, they would report these concerns to three arbiters: Councillor Rickman, Mayor of Louvrex and Jean-Guillaume Clerx, a local merchant-banker.[40]

---

37 LSA, N, *Notaire Hadin*, 1603, fols. 54ᵛ–55ʳ (Wilhelm Levrixht, Gilet Servais).

38 Van Hofstraeten, "Historiographical Opportunities".

39 LSA, N, *Notaire Hadin*, 1605, fols. 81ᵛ–83ʳ (Thomas de Sclessin, Thomas de Fossez, Laurent Butbacht, Giel de Noirivaulx, Bastin de Noirivaulx, Hubert Oems, Wilhelm Levrixht Senior, Wilhelm Levrixht Junior, Jean Craisier); LSA, N, *Notaire Th. Pauwea*, 1651, fols. 508ʳ–510ᵛ (Pierre Simonis Junior, Aert Wilsens); LSA, N, *Notaire G. Lien*, 1663, fols. 356ᵛ–357ᵛ (Godefroid-Evrard Nottemans, Bertrand Mariotte); LSA, N, *Notaire Lohier*, 1703, 6 October (Jean-Guillaume de Requilé, Etienne de Barme).

40 LSA, N, *Notaire Hadin*, 1605, fols. 81ᵛ–83ʳ (Thomas de Sclessin, Thomas de Fossez, Lau-

If one of these three men were to die during the existence of the company, the two remaining arbiters were to choose a replacement. The fact that the identities of the arbiters was already agreed upon is rather exceptional. Most often, contracting parties merely pointed out that each contracting party could choose an arbiter, and if these arbiters were to fail to reconcile the conflicting parties, they were allowed to choose an extra *superarbiter*.[41] Whereas arbitration clauses in, for example, early modern Amsterdam and Rotterdam partnership agreements also expressed the condition that the arbiters had to judge "by equity" instead of by the law, such specification is not to be found in the Liège documents.[42] Finally, none of the observed arbitration clauses allowed for an appeal or a *reductio ad arbitrium boni viri* against the arbiters' final decision, and sometimes it was agreed that the one who was unwilling to abide by the arbiters' decision had to pay a fine. For example, the aforementioned de Requilé and de Barme agreed that any of them who ignored the judgment of the arbiter had to pay 1,000 *écus* to the one who did abide by the arbiters' ruling.

So, whereas Liège partnership agreements establishing commercial and artisanal enterprises mainly demonstrate a large degree of conformity with contract design as it was applied in the rest of the early modern Low Countries, these contracts did give proof of some particular idiosyncrasies, more specifically a more local recruitment area, the absence of renunciation clauses and a more significant presence of arbitration clauses. These idiosyncrasies did not only occur in partnership agreements creating commercial and artisanal companies, both also in those contracts establishing mining enterprises.

---

rent Butbacht, Giel de Noirivaulx, Bastin de Noirivaulx, Hubert Oems, Wilhelm Levrixht Senior, Wilhelm Levrixht Junior, Jean Craisier); LSA, N, *Notaire Th. Pauwea*, 1651, fols. 508^{r}–510^{v} (Pierre Simonis Junior, Aert Wilsens); LSA, N, *Notaire G. Lien*, 1663, fols. 356^{v}–357^{v} (Godefroid-Evrard Nottemans, Bertrand Mariotte); LSA, N, *Notaire Lohier*, 1703, 6 October (Jean-Guillaume de Requilé, Etienne de Barme).

41 LSA, N, *Notaire Hadin*, 1605, fols. 81^{v}–83^{r} (Thomas de Sclessin, Thomas de Fossez, Laurent Butbacht, Giel de Noirivaulx, Bastin de Noirivaulx, Hubert Oems, Wilhelm Levrixht Senior, Wilhelm Levrixht Junior, Jean Craisier); LSA, N, *Notaire Th. Pauwea*, 1651, fols. 508^{r}–510^{v} (Pierre Simonis Junior, Aert Wilsens); LSA, N, *Notaire G. Lien*, 1663, fols. 356^{v}–357^{v} (Godefroid-Evrard Nottemans, Bertrand Mariotte).

42 Simon Van Brakel, "Een tiental vennootschapsacten uit de 17de eeuw," *Bijdragen en mededeelingen van het Historisch Genootschap* 37 (1916), 182–231; Simon Van Brakel, "Ontbrekende schakels in de ontwikkeling van ons vennootschapsrecht," in Sybrandus Johannes Fockema Andreae, Robert Fruin et al. (eds.), *Rechtshistorische opstellen aangeboden aan Mr. S.J. Fockema Andreae, hoogleraar aan de Rijksuniversiteit te Leiden* (Haarlem: Bohn, 1914), 153–194.

4 Mining Companies

In addition to commercial and artisanal companies, the Liège research sample contained four partnership agreements which established enterprises whose chief line of industry was related to mining activities.[43] As far as the extraction of natural resources is concerned, Liège distinguished itself from all other coal producing regions in Europe at the time. In the latter, the extraction of coal belonged to the *droits de régale* or regalia of the sovereign.[44] In Liège, however, the owner of the surface was at the same time the owner of all commodities that were stored underneath it: *Qui possède le comble possède le fond*. During the early modern period, the most significant landowners in Liège were local ecclesiastical institutions as well as the Prince-Bishopric itself. In order to exploit the hidden riches of their lands, they sold exploitation concessions to Liège entrepreneurs and merchants, who generally had to organize themselves into private partnerships in order to finance the concession itself as well as the subsequent exploitation activities.

In our research sample, two enterprises involved the extraction of *marcasites* and *kisses*, i.e. sulphurous pyrites from which sulphur was to be extracted, while another was organized around the construction and maintenance of so-called *areines* or drainage canals which were necessary for a proper exploitation of the surrounding collieries. Finally, a fourth contract involved the extraction of coal, but the agreement itself had a particular *raison d'être*. It embodies the conclusion of a conflict between the partners or *maîtres et comparchonniers* of the mine entitled *La Blanche Plombière* in Prayon, on the one hand, and the *maîtres et comparchonniers* of the mine *La Rochette* in the neighbouring locality of Rochette, on the other hand. The conflict had its origins in 1586, and concerned the disputed frontier between both territories.[45] After twenty years of quarrelling, both companies decided to resolve their conflict amicably "in order to avoid numerous disputes", and created together a separate partnership

43 LSA, N, *Notaire Lapide*, 1576, fols. 19ʳ–20ᵛ (Guillaume Stevartz, Anthoine Vaez, Jean Henry); LSA, N, *Notaire Hadin*, 1603, fols. 54ᵛ–55ʳ (Wilhelm Levrixht, Gilet Servais); LSA, N, *Notaire Hadin*, 1605, fols. 81ᵛ–83ʳ (Thomas de Sclessin, Thomas de Fossez, Laurent Butbacht, Giel de Noirivaulx, Bastin de Noirivaulx, Hubert Oems, Wilhelm Levrixht Senior, Wilhelm Levrixht Junior, Jean Craisier); LSA, N, *Notaire J. Pompony*, 13 January 1651 (Mathieu de Trooz, Laurent Truiller alias Collard, Henry Brocart, Jean Fil, Jean Jacques, Fassin Pirchon, Henry Jean-Jacques, Hubert Lorket).

44 Kranz, *Lütticher Steinkohlenbergbau*, 195–204.

45 More details on the conflict can be found in Lejeune, *La formation du capitalisme moderne*, 158 and 165.

with regard to the exploitation of the disputed area around the border between both mines in particular.

As regards contract design, these partnership agreements differ considerably from those creating commercial and artisanal enterprises. None of the four examples at our disposal possess clauses on bookkeeping, a partner leaving prematurely, the unforeseen death of a partner, the obligation of intermediate settlements of the accounts, competitive restrictions, etc. Mostly, a clause on the intended duration of the partnership is missing too, for mining companies generally existed for as long as they were profitable. Moreover, local statutes even obliged them to continue to extract as long as minerals could be found.[46]

From an overall perspective, partnership agreements establishing mining companies are merely concerned with the internal, operational organization of the company, the respective contributions of the partners for the bearing of the costs, and the eventual distribution of profits or losses.[47] In June 1576, for example, Antoine Vaez, Jean Henry and Guillaume Stevartz established a partnership in order to distil and refine sulphur.[48] Vaez and Stevartz possessed the mining rights with regard to the Sasserote mine in the land of Franchimont, which was to provide the sulphurous pyrites from which the sulphur would be extracted by means of a distillation process that requires specific expertise and an appropriate furnace. The latter requirements were provided for by Stevartz, whereas Vaez and Henry would deliver all necessary financial means. It was agreed that the company would last for "as long as one can find sufficient amounts of sulphur", while all the pyrites leaving the Sasserotte mine were to be processed for the benefit of the three constituting partners equally. Since Stevartz provided for and would be operating the furnace, he would receive an additional salary of 3 fl. 10 *aidants liégeois*. For every additional furnace of the same size that Stevartz might erect in the future, he would receive one *philippus daler* per day. All the other instruments that would be

---

46 See the 1487 *Paix de Saint-Jacques*, article 3. See Matthias Guillaume de Louvrex, *Recueil contenant les édits, règlemens, privilèges, concordats et traitez du païs de Liège & comté de Looz* (Liège: Procureur, 1730), 232–233.

47 Unfortunately, the extant partnership agreements do not allow for a proper division of the established enterprises into, for example, general partnerships and limited partnerships. With regard to eighteenth-century mining companies in France, Marcel Rouff did manage to provide such a subdivision. Here, the limited partnership (*société en commandite*) proved to be the most widespread, whereas a general partnership (*société en nom collectif*) was also used frequently to create extraction enterprises. See Rouff, *Les mines de charbon*, 263–277.

48 LSA, N, *Notaire Lapide*, 1576, fols. 19^r–20^v (Guillaume Stevartz, Anthoine Vaez, Jean Henry).

required were to be bought at the expense of the company. In addition to his standard share in the profits and his personal salary, Stevartz was also granted the right to extract all other kinds of minerals and employ the *kisses* for the distillation of vitriol. Moreover, all other minerals that would be extracted from the mine by Stevartz would become his exclusive property, except for the sulphurous pyrites. Antoine Vaez, in turn, would receive 12 *patars de brabant* as a compensation for those extraordinary expenses already made by him for the benefit of the enterprise. Henry would receive 7 *patars de brabant* for his role in the transport of the *kisses* from the mine in Franchimont to the furnace in Prayon. The example clearly demonstrates the contracting parties' prime concern with the internal, financial and operational organization of the company.

In addition to the observed distinctions with regard to contract design, the Liège mining companies allow for the observance of various other distinctive or field-specific corporate practices. First of all, there is the frequency and speediness by means of which shares or *parchons* in a mining company changed hands. Whereas the personal nature of a private partnership is generally considered to be one of its quintessential features, early modern mining companies—in opposition to commercial and artisanal enterprises—seem to defy this qualification. The ease by means of which shares in a mining company were being transferred (sale, rent, lease) from one person to another is striking.[49] Between 1651 and 1655, numerous transfers, which were recorded by a notary, could be identified.[50] On 5 January 1653, for example, Henry le

---

49 The transfer of *parchons* in mining companies was already a widespread practice in medieval Liège. See Kranz, *Lütticher Steinkohlenbergbau*, 329–334. Kranz emphasizes the role of the *terrageurs* or concession providers in the transfer process (both sale and lease), who were to approve every change in the composition of the partnership.

50 Here, one may not ignore the transfer of such shares by means of privately-drafted or oral agreements, whose exact significance, for obvious reasons, could not be incorporated in our assessment. The transfer of shares also occurred with regard to commercial and artisanal enterprises, albeit to a much lesser extent. In 1651, for example, Godefroid Selijs leased his half share in the smelting works called *Dieupart*, which he owned and managed together with his brother, to the same brother, Hubert Selijs. The latter was to pay an annual rent of 300 fl. *brabants* "in circulation in Liège". The reason for his withdrawal was that Godefroid had become too busy after the passing of his mother-in-law. It was also agreed that Godefroid, together with his children, wife and father-in-law (Pierre Coune) would continue to reside in the house attached to the smelting works and that they were allowed to consume the fruits of the adjacent garden during the months between July and November exclusively. All legal disputes that might arise during the lease, and which concerned the smelting works, would be the sole responsibility of the leaseholder, i.e.

Charlier sold half of his share in the colliery called *La Fosse delle Courte* to his brother, Michiel le Charlier.[51] The contract does not express the selling price, but it is stated that Michiel was to pay half of the price that Henry had paid for the share when he acquired it on 20 November 1651.[52] The example not only demonstrates the transfer of a share, it also illustrates the further subdivision of *parchons* in mining companies, a practice very common in Liège.[53] In addition to companies devoted to actual extraction activities, the sale of *parchons* was also a well-established practice regarding those partnerships that were concerned with the exploitation of the *areines* or drainage canals.[54] For example, in 1652, Henry Jean-Jacques, who had acquired a 1/8 share in the partnership established with regard to the exploitation of the *De Venta* drainage canal near Fléron one year earlier,[55] sold this share to his cousin, Mathieu Thomas Jacques, for 600 fl. *liègeois* and half a cask of beer.[56] It was agreed that 400 fl. *liégeois* were to be paid within the next three weeks and the remaining 200 fl. *liégeois* before Whitsuntide. Together, the aforementioned examples, where shares were held

---

Hubert Selijs. (LSA, N, *Notaire G. Lien*, 1651, fol. 142r.) See also LSA, N, *Notaire Th. Pauwea*, 1651, fols. 505r–506r, where the aforementioned Pierre Simonis Senior, who was retiring "because of his old age", cedes to his son-in-law, Aert Wilsens, his half share in the trading company he had been operating with his son, Pierre Simonis Junior.

51 LSA, N, *Notaire J. Pompony*, 5 January 1653.

52 Additional examples can be found at: LSA, N, *Notaire R. Gangelt*, 1655, fols. 402r–402v, where Magdaleine, daughter of Henry de Rocourt, transferred a share to her cousin, the Liège notary Jacques Ruffin; LSA, N, *Notaire Th. Pauwea*, 1655, fol. 433r, where Pier Warmier, a Liège merchant, transferred his share in a mining company to a fellow citizen named Johan de Coupille.

53 In principle, shares in a mining company were unlimitedly divisible. See Kranz, *Lütticher Steinkohlenbergbau*, 334. Another example can be found at: LSA, N, *Notaire R. Castro*, 1653, fol. 341r, where Leonard Zutman, a Liège wine merchant, ceded one-third of his share to his German cousin, Anthoine Etten. The remaining two-thirds remained in his possession.

54 Various examples can be found at: LSA, N, *Notaire J. Pompony*, 5 February 1651, where Jehenne, widow of Anthoine Pirchon, sold a one-fourth "*part, droict, claim et action*" that she possessed in three drainage canals called *La Grande Voine, La Voine aux Houilles* and *Le Frouxhin*, "*aux environs de fond dit Mironcroist*", next to Bellaire (Beyne-Heusay) "*dans les sarts*" belonging to Georis Mordant and various other persons for 15 fl. *liégeois*, already paid by Fassin Pirchon, her son; LSA, N, *Notaire J. Pompony*, 11 March 1651, where Laurent Truiller dit Collard sold a one-eighth *parchon* in a drainage canal and a one-tenth share in another drainage canal to Henry Michiel Lange for 34 fl. *brabants*. On the same day, Henry Michiel Lange acquired two other shares.

55 LSA, N, *Notaire J. Pompony*, 13 January 1651 (Mathieu de Trooz, Laurent Truiller alias Collard, Henry Brocart, Jean Fil, Jean Jacques, Fassin Pirchon, Henry Jean-Jacques, Hubert Lorket).

56 LSA, N, *Notaire J. Pompony*, 30 January 1652.

in possession for only one year approximately, illustrate the high turnover of shares in mining companies, as was the case in early modern Britain too.[57]

Although not formalized in local legislation, the available source material seems to suggest that it was a fairly well-established practice that the transfer of a share in a mining company always required the common consent of the other partners or *maîtres et comparchoniers*, who enjoyed the benefit of the right to acquire the shares in preference to third persons or non-*comparchonniers*. In 1675, for example, eight *maîtres et comparchonniers* of the mine called *La Picxherette* appeared before the Liège notary, P. Moullin, in order to record that, in light of their future common activities, these partners would always have a right of pre-emption as soon as one of them aspired to sell his share in the company: "the masters are preferable above all others without having to pay certain expenses or start up specific legal proceedings".[58] In addition, it was agreed that whoever wanted to sell his share was obliged to inform his fellow-partners about his intentions in advance, so that no one could become a partner in the mining company without their common consent.[59] The preference of the other partners over strangers when a *parchon* was being sold was also incorporated in the partnership agreement that Mathieu de Trooz, a miller in Fléron, concluded in 1651 with ten extra partners in order to exploit the nearby drainage canal called *De Venta*.[60] The partnership agreement is utterly succinct and, in

57 Nef, *The Rise*, 2, 60. With regard to British collieries, Nef noticed that parts in mining companies changed hands very frequently. He could hardly observe a same list of partners with regard to a specific mine within a period of two years.

58 LSA, N, *Notaire P. Moullin*, 1675, fol. 92r. As regards medieval mining activities in Liège, Kranz too noticed the right of pre-emption of the co-partners. If a partner had sold his share to a stranger, without having offered the same share first to his co-partners, the stranger-buyer was obliged to transfer the share to the *maîtres et comparchonniers* in exchange for the same price by means of which he had previously acquired the *parchon*. See Kranz, *Lütticher Steinkohlenbergbau*, 333. See also Schunder, *Geschichte*, 62; Willms, "Der Anteil der Reichsstadt Aachen," 146.

59 LSA, N, *Notaire P. Moullin*, 1675, fol. 92r. The requirement of common consent experienced a growing importance from the fifteenth century onwards. See Kranz, *Lütticher Steinkohlenbergbau*, 331. John Nef, however, stressed that such requirement was by no means a universal rule in Europe. See Nef, *The Rise*, 2, 60. With regard to eighteenth-century France, Marcel Rouff also observed partnership agreements in which the requirement of common consent as well as the right of pre-emption of the co-partners were safeguarded "*pour prévenir la multiplication des voix délibératives de la société*". See Rouff, *Les mines de charbon*, 265. See also Willms, "Der Anteil der Reichsstadt Aachen," 145.

60 LSA, N, *Notaire J. Pompony*, 13 January 1651 (Mathieu de Trooz, Laurent Truiller alias Collard, Henry Brocart, Jean Fil, Jean Jacques, Fassin Pirchon, Henry Jean-Jacques, Hubert Lorket).

addition to the division of the 24 *parchons* among the respective partners, it merely stated that "none of the partners were allowed to transfer his share(s) to a person unfamiliar to the other partners", and that in case of a sale of a share to such third parties, the original partners had a right of "post-emption": they could buy the share(s) themselves for a "just price" in a period of six weeks after the first buyer had presented himself to the company.

The core business of commercial companies consists of selling and buying merchandise. Since the buying of goods, and thus creating debts on behalf of the company, was generally executed by one of the constituting partners individually, the question of the external liability of the other partners with regard to such debts becomes highly relevant. Such liability could be held jointly and severally, on the one hand, or limited to the initial contribution of a (silent) partner to the company's working capital, on the other hand. In a mining company, the situation was quite different, at least at first sight. Here, partners were primarily occupied with the sale of the resources that they had extracted, whereas they hardly concluded contracts by means of which a debt towards a third party came into being. This might explain the absence of clauses on external liability in the extant partnership agreements establishing early modern mining companies. However, such a nonappearance proved to be a general characteristic of the majority of early modern partnership agreements recorded in the Low Countries.[61] So, the explanation does not persist. The truth is that the *maîtres et comparchonniers* of a mining company did have obligations to live up to, and that they could indeed be held liable in a several and joint manner.[62]

First of all, mining companies had to pay the so-called *cens d'areine* for their use of the drainage canals often operated by a third party. The *cens* could vary from one to three per cent of the total amount of minerals extracted by the mining company. Secondly, salaries had to be paid, to the miners on the one hand, but also to the so-called *ouvriers trayeurs*, who counted the number of panniers leaving the mine in order to determine, for example, the *cens d'areine*. Thirdly, the *maîtres et comparchonniers* were obliged to give their workers so-called *bottées*, i.e. a free amount of extracted minerals to be handed over on a weekly basis. If a miner had stayed underground for one to four days, he was to receive one pannier of minerals; if he had stayed underground for four or more days, he received two panniers. Finally, debts could arise

61 Van Hofstraeten, "Historiographical Opportunities"; Van Hofstraeten, "Private Partnerships," 131.

62 As regards these obligations, see Kranz, *Lütticher Steinkohlenbergbau*, 220–238.

through the acquisition of materials that were required for the construction or expansion of the colliery. These obligations were standard for those individuals or mining companies that were operating on and in a territory of which they themselves were the owner. Mostly, however, the land was leased from a grantor or concession provider. In that case, additional obligations were to be fulfilled. Firstly, there is the so-called *terrage* or price of the concession. In general, this price consisted of a part of the extracted minerals (two to twenty per cent) and had to be paid in kind or in cash. Secondly, there was the *droit de dommage*, and the *droit de double dommage*. The former implied the concessionaire's obligation to restore the land in its original condition, after the closure of the colliery, and compensate all damages (to roads, lands, vineyards, etc.) caused by the prior exploitation of the mine.[63] The latter consisted of a similar obligation but particularly with regard to indirect damages to neighbouring terrains.

The idea that the constituting partners of a mining company could be held jointly and severally liable for such obligations is attested in two rare clauses which Horst Kranz identified in two fourteenth-century concession contracts, while studying the history of collieries in medieval Liège.[64] The first contract was concluded in 1378 between the Augustinian abbey of Saint-Gilles and four concessionaires (Gilon Berbis, Hanes Rabar, Gilles Barailhe, and Jamar Caltru) and stated explicitly that the concessionaires' liability was *in solidum* and *ad infinitum* (i.e. jointly and severally): "And in order to provide us with more security regarding this, the aforementioned entrepreneurs are indebted to us, each one of them for the entirety while none of them is allowed to refuse [to vouch for] another one".[65] Here, the liability relates to the payment of the concession or *terrage*. A similar clause could be found in an agreement by

63 It seems that such *droit de dommaige* was paid in advance before one started with the erection of a mine or the construction of a drainage canal. On 13 January, i.e. the same day that Mathieu de Trooz accepted Laurent Truiller, Henry Brocart, Jean Fil, Jean Jacques, Fassin Prichon, Henry Jean-Jacques and Hubert Lorket as partners in order to exploit the drainage canal called *De Venta*, these *maîtres et comparchonniers* contracted with one of them, Henry Jean-Jacques, regarding the use ("*faire burres, voynes et pairis*") of a terrain owned by the latter. It was agreed that Henry would receive six *dallers* for every "*verge grande*", i.e. twenty "*verges petites*" or twenty times 21,7945 m^2, that the company would make use of. It is stipulated that this contribution also included the so-called *droit de dommaige*. See LSA, N, *Notaire J. Pompony*, 1651, 13 January.

64 Kranz, *Lütticher Steinkohlenbergbau*, 332.

65 Kranz, *Lütticher Steinkohlenbergbau*, 332; Kranz, *Quellen*, 210–213: "*Et por nos* [i.e. the concession provider] *faire de chu plus segur, li ovrirs* [i.e. the concessionaires] *deseur dis en sont dette envers nos et chascon d'eaux por le tout* [i.e. *ad infinitum*], *sens escuseir l'unc por l'autre* [i.e. *in solidum*]".

means of which Johan Borleis and Libier Colignon bought the right to collect the *terrage*, with regard to the mining activities on a terrain called *Sour le male Chavée*, which belonged to the Liège cathedral chapter of Saint-Lambert: "And with regard to everything that has been said, we incur a debt towards the lords of Saint-Lambert, each one of us for this and the entirety while no one is allowed to refuse [to vouch for] another one".[66]

In addition to a joint and several liability of the partners with regard to the *terrage*, the *Cour des Voir-Jurés du Charbonnage* also confirmed a similar extent of liability with regard to the payment of the *droit de dommage*, while responding to a *quaeritur* addressed to them: "the *maîtres et comparchonniers* of a mine are liable jointly and severally regarding the damages caused to the terrain of the concession provider".[67] Moreover, a former partner continued to be liable even if he had sold his *parchon* in the mining company, and also if a partner had not been a partner for a long time or was not yet a partner at the time that the damage was caused. A second *quaeritur*, addressed in 1709 to the aldermen of the Liège city council, involved the liability of the partners with regard to merchants-suppliers, on the one hand, and workers or miners, on the other hand.[68] Here, the external liability distinguishes itself significantly from the external liability of members of a commercial or artisanal enterprise in the early modern Low Countries, for in Liège it was limited in time. The aldermen's response to the 1709 *quaeritur* stated that a merchant-supplier, who had delivered materials to a mining company and who had already been indemnified partly by one of the partners, was allowed to address himself to the other partners for the payment of the rest of the debt, but only within a period of six months after the creation of the debt. Afterwards, the company was liberated. As far as workers or miners and the payment of their salaries were concerned, this term was limited to six weeks. Afterwards, the other partners could no longer be held accountable and the miner/worker at hand could only undertake action against the original partner-debtor, who had been assigned initially to pay the worker's wage. Together with the significant transferability of mining shares, this particular interpretation of external liability constitutes one of the most important idiosyncrasies of early modern corporate practices regarding mining companies in Liège.

---

66 Cited after: Kranz, *Quellen*, 245–246: *"Et de tout ce que dit est, faysons nos propres debtes, cescun de nos par li et par le tout, sens escuseir l'unc de nos pour l'autre, envers les dis saingnours de Saint Lambert, (...)".*

67 The *quaeritur* and the reponse by the court can be found in de Louvrex, *Recueil*, 266–267.

68 The *quaeritur* and response can be found in de Louvrex, *Recueil*, 268–270.

Finally, mining companies distinguish and characterize themselves by means of the social background of their constituting partners. In addition to the more obvious professional category of merchants, Horst Kranz observed a substantial participation by the local clergy (priests and canons) as well as nobility.[69] Because of their need for fossil fuels while executing their profession, brewers and bakers too constituted a significant part among late medieval *maîtres et comparchonniers* in Liège.[70] Finally, the medieval source material demonstrated the weighty presence of women as shareholders.[71] Whereas the latter observation can be confirmed by means of the early modern notarial deeds regarding the transfer of mining shares, the continuous participation of clerics in extraction companies is demonstrated by the present research sample of seventeenth-century partnership agreements. For example, one of the *maîtres et comparchonniers* of the aforementioned sulphur company named *La Rochette* was Jean Crassier, a canon of the collegiate church of Saint-Denis in Liège.[72] The uninterrupted involvement of the nobility can be illustrated by a notarial deed in which Philippe de Wanzoulle, lord of Grosfays and Nedercanne, appears as a shareholder in "certain red lands existing on the plateau of Engis".[73]

In addition to the aforementioned categories, numerous local aldermen from the thirteenth century onwards played an important role as *maîtres et comparchonniers* in the development of the Liège collieries.[74] Their participation in mining enterprises was to some extent still restricted by the end of the fifteenth century. Article 13 of the *Paix de St.-Jacques* stated that aldermen were not allowed to acquire a *parchon* in a mine or drainage canal "from that day onwards".[75] However, they could retain those parts, which they had acquired

69 Kranz, *Lütticher Steinkohlenbergbau*, 336–338.

70 Ib., 343–344.

71 Ib., 341–342.

72 LSA, N, *Notaire Hadin*, 1605, fols. 81^{v}–83^{r} (Thomas de Sclessin, Thomas de Fossez, Laurent Butbacht, Giel de Noirivaulx, Bastin de Noirivaulx, Hubert Oems, Wilhelm Levrixht Senior, Wilhelm Levrixht Junior, Jean Craisier); Lejeune, *La formation du capitalisme moderne*, 164–165.

73 LSA, N, *Notaire Th. Pauwea*, 1651, fols. 448^{r-v}. In the Aachener Reich, however, mining activities were mainly executed by persons with a more modest social background or "*kleine Leute*", and were avoided by the higher social strata. This is to be explained by the city's efforts to keep the price of coal relatively low, so that potential profits remained modest as well and mining activities lost their attraction. See Schunder, *Geschichte*, 105–106.

74 Kranz, *Lütticher Steinkohlenbergbau*, 336–341.

75 de Louvrex, *Recueil*, 235.

before "the date of today", as well as the ones that they would inherit. If the aldermen did not comply with this regulation, they were to lose the *parchon* at hand and undertake a pilgrimage to Santiago de Compostela. Unfortunately, the phrases "from that day onwards" and "the date of today" cause interpretative difficulties. It remains unclear whether it refers to the day on which they had become an alderman, or the day on which the *Paix de St.-Jacques* had been promulgated.[76]

5 Conclusion

The present article aspired to delve for diversity in early modern corporate practices within the geographical area currently corresponding to the Low Countries, i.e. present-day Belgium and the Netherlands. In so doing, it made use of sixteen partnership agreements that had been notarized in the city of Liège during the years between 1651 and 1655. As hypothesized earlier, the research sample at hand gave proof of various minor as well as major idiosyncrasies regarding the use of private partnerships, the way their contracts were designed, and the interpretation of some of their legal features.

A major difference, in comparison to the use of private partnerships in the rest of the early modern Low Countries, has to be attributed to the richness of the Liège soil. Whereas private partnerships were generally an instrument in the hands of entrepreneurs primarily active in trade, craftsmanship and tax farming, the Liège underground caused a significant application of private partnerships as a legal instrument in order to facilitate the exploitation of collieries and drainage canals. In opposition to sixteenth-century Antwerp and seventeenth-century Maastricht, where only merchants and artisans manifested themselves as partners, in Liège no social category stayed on the sidelines regarding the establishment of (mining) companies.[77]

The participation of most social classes in mining activities may partly be explained by the ease and speediness by means of which so-called *parchons* or shares in a mining enterprise were being transferred. Despite the fact that the transferability of mining shares was hampered to some extent by a right of preference for the constituting partners over third parties, as well as the requirement of the former's consent regarding the transfer, the Liège source

76 In addition, it was forbidden to buy or purchase "disputed shares," i.e. *parchons* that were the object of a legal dispute. See de Louvrex, *Recueil*, 235.

77 See Lejeune, *La formation du capitalisme moderne*, 251–254.

material illustrated a high frequency of transfers and a large turnover of mining shares. Likewise, corporate practices regarding mining companies distinguished themselves considerably from those governing commercial and artisanal enterprises.

The observed diversity in corporate practices becomes even greater if one assesses the way in which the external liability of the partners of a mining enterprise was interpreted in early modern Liège. First of all, such partners were considered to be jointly and severally liable not only during the membership of a mining company, but also after they had sold or transferred their share to a third person. Such extended external liability was, however, compensated by a restriction of the liability in time. Merchant-suppliers only had six months to address themselves to one of the partners for the payment of their bills. Afterwards, the company was liberated. As far as the payment of the workers' wages was concerned, the other partners could only be held accountable for six weeks. Afterwards, the miners could only address themselves to that partner to whom the payment of their salary had been assigned initially. Such an exceptional interpretation of the partners' external liability towards third parties is clearly one of the most significant idiosyncrasies of early modern corporate practices in Liège. The observation not only proves that different lines of industry may call for and even engender diversified elaborations of early modern company law, but it also urges legal historians to further explore and examine such idiosyncrasies.

Annex: Liège Notaries (1651–1655)[78]

B. Bechet: 1651–1655; L. de Bellevaux: 1651–1655; R. Castro: 1651–1655; H. Collette: 1652–1655; S. Dambleve: 1651–1655; M. Delbrouck: 1651–1655; A. Dellehessalle: 1655; F. Delooz: 1652; G. Delrée: 1651–1655; H. Delymborgh: 1653; P. Dengis: 1652–1655; J. Deparfondry: 1651–1655; R. Deroufosse: 1651–1655; H. Detignee: 1651–1655; N. Dodeur: 1652–1653; V. Donnea: 1651–1655; H.J. Dor: 1653–1655; G. Douffet: 1651–1655; G. Dufresne: 1651–1655; A. Etten: 1651–1655; L. Fabri: 1653; Ch. Frerart: 1651–1652; R. Gangelt: 1651–1655; M. Herck: 1655; M. Heussen: 1655; E. and J. Housson: 1652–1655; J. Julinet: 1654–1655; J. Lefebvre: 1651–1655; J. Libert: 1651–1653; G. Lien: 1651–1655; M. Louvrix: 1651–1655; G. Milemans: 1651–1655;

78 The protocol registers of the notaries active in Liège between 1651 and 1655 are preserved at the Liège State Archives (Belgium). See also Bruno Dumont, *Guide des fonds et collections des Archives de l'Etat à Liège. III: Archives publiques locales—Archives ecclésiastiques—Notariat* (Brussels: Archives of the Realm, 2012), 686–712.

L. Moers: 1651–1655; H. Ouillus: 1651–1655; H. Oupie: 1651–1652; Th. Pauwea: 1651–1655; J. Pollain: 1654–1655; J. Pompony: 1651–1655; J. Prion: 1651–1655; J.G. Rochart: 1651–1655; F. Rouveroy: 1651–1652; J. Ruffin: 1651–1655; J. Sauveur: 1651–1655; F. Servadon: 1651–1655; G. Servadon: 1651–1655; G. Warnotte: 1652–1655.

CHAPTER 6

Incorporation and Limited Liability in Seventeenth-Century England: The Case of the East India Company

Stefania Gialdroni

1 Introduction

In 1599 the promoters of the East India Company stated, in their petition for a charter to the Privy Council, that their reason for adopting the joint-stock organization was that "a trade so far remote cannot be managed but by a joint and united stock".[1] This assumption is confirmed by the list of the principal English joint-stock companies of the sixteenth and seventeenth centuries, which were all engaged in long-distance trade: the Russia Company, Levant Company (until 1605), New River Company, Royal Fishery, Royal African and Hudson's Bay Company. These companies not only needed a great initial capital outlay but they had to face semi-political and semi-military functions in non-European countries. On 31 December 1600,[2] 219 members were incorporated by Queen Elizabeth I under the title "The Governor and Company of Merchants of London Trading into the East Indies", obtaining, for fifteen years, the monopoly of the trade "to the *East-Indies*" as well as "in the Countries and Parts of *Asia* and *Africa*", with the exception of such territories and ports under the control of any

1 Kitri N. Chaudhuri, *The English East India Company. The Study of an Early Joint-Stock Company 1600–1640* (London: Taylor & Francis, 1965), 26. Despite the explicit petition of the London merchants, contemporary scholars have questioned the efficiency of chartered companies in developing long-distance trade: S.R.H. Jones and Simian P. Ville, "Efficient Transactors or Rent-Seeking Monopolists? The Rationale for Early Chartered Trading Companies," *The Journal of Economic History* 56/4 (1996), 898–915. See also Ann M. Carlos and Stephen Nicholas, "Theory and History: Seventeenth Century Joint-Stock Chartered Trading Companies," *The Journal of Economic History* 56/4 (1996), 916–924. For a very recent history of the East India Company, see otherwise Emily Erikson, *Between Monopoly and Free Trade. The English East India Company, 1600–1757* (Princeton: Princeton University Press, 2014).

2 43 Elizabeth I, 31 December 1600, in John Shaw (ed.), *Charters Relating to the East India Company from 1600 to 1761. Reprinted from a Former Collection with Some Additions and a Preface* (Madras: Government Press, 1887), 1–15.

 | DOI: 10.1163/9789004351868_008

Christian prince, in order to avoid unnecessary conflicts with the Spanish and the Portuguese.[3] The main aim was to import spices (pepper, cinnamon, nutmeg, cardamom and mace) from what is now known as the Malay Archipelago, challenging the Portuguese and Dutch competitors.

Though the East India Company managed to obtain exceptional profits by means of separate and short-term joint-stocks[4] until 1657 (when the capital became permanent)[5] it was, from the very beginning, both a joint-stock and a corporation, in a period in which there was no necessary connection between the two, as these concepts "coalesced" only in the nineteenth century.[6] Furthermore, the legal ideas now connected to the joint-stock company, i.e. transferable shares and limited liability were, in the early history of the East India Company, not present or very uncertain. Shares began to be transferred to outsiders at the end of the seventeenth century.[7] Otherwise, the limited liability of the East India Company members at that time is still such a controversial issue that it deserves an in-depth analysis.

As the case of what we now call "limited liability" (a terminology which is completely absent in the seventeenth century sources of the East India Company) clearly demonstrates, great legal "inventions" usually do not arise from the mind of a single jurist, and cannot be isolated from the social and economic context in which they develop. They are rather prepared by hundreds of "obscure men" who, adding new elements to already widespread commercial practices, change both the economic substance and the legal format.[8]

---

3 Chaudhuri, *The English East India Company*, 28.

4 See for example Stefania Gialdroni, *East India Company. Una storia giuridica (1600–1708)* (Bologna: Il Mulino, 2011), 42–45.

5 Ib., 190.

6 C.A. Cooke, *Corporation, Trust and Company. An Essay in Legal History* (Manchester: Manchester University Press, 1950), 18.

7 The guild-like organization of the East India Company limited privileges to the members and their sons aged twenty-one, who had to take a corporal oath. From 1615 onwards, general conditions of admission were stated: entrance-fees were still demanded but membership became based on the mere holding of shares. However, shares could not be sold to outsiders and the transfer of the shares could not be registered in the company's book "until the purchaser had bought his place in the company. By 1693 the patents expressly incorporate all shareholders and specify forms for the transfer of shares": Cooke, *Corporation, Trust, and Company*, 59. See also Larry Neal, "Capital Markets before 1750," in Joel Mokyr (ed.), *The Oxford Encyclopedia of Economic History*, vol. 1 (Oxford: OUP, 2003), 325–326.

8 Massimo Montanari, *Impresa e responsabilità. Sviluppo storico e disciplina positiva* (Milano: Giuffrè, 1990), 121.

2 Joint-Stock Companies: A Matter of Law?

It has been stated that "the historical analysis (…) supports the view that in the evolution of the joint-stock company, law does not matter".[9] This assumption is based on the observation that at the time of the development of English lucrative long-distance trade and despite the 1720 Bubble Act,[10] joint-stock companies proved to be successful, even though the legal system was "relatively weak and undeveloped".[11] From this point of view, the development of joint-stock companies can be understood only by means of cultural factors and social norms established long before the success of regulated and joint-stock companies,[12] which created a ""path-dependency"[13] of co-operation and trust which fostered investment in joint-stock companies and the development of stock exchanges".[14] In synthesis, the ""law in the books" presents a misleading impression which over-emphasizes the importance of statutory developments".[15]

In his *Industrializing English Law*, Ron Harris[16] underlines how most of the works devoted to the relationship between legal and economic development in early-modern and modern England can be reduced to two paradigms or ideal types. According to the first one, law evolves autonomously, thanks to internal dynamics, while the second one considers it functional to economic develop-

9 Phillip Lipton, "The Evolution of the Joint Stock Company to 1800. A Study of Institutional Change," in *Workplace and Corporate Law Research Group of the Monash University*, working paper no. 15 (2009), 46, available at: http://www.buseco.monash.edu.au/blt/wclrg/workpaper-15.pdf (consulted on 17 January 2017).

10 6 George I c. 18. See Ron Harris, "The Bubble Act: Its Passage and its Effects on Business Organization," *The Journal of Economic History* 54/3 (1994), 610–627.

11 Lipton, "The Evolution of the Joint Stock Company," 46.

12 To deepen the link between merchant guilds and regulated/joint-stock companies see Stefania Gialdroni, "A Commercial Soul in a Corporate Body. From the Medieval Merchant Guilds to the East India Company," in Bram Van Hofstraeten and Wim Decock (eds.), *Companies and Company Law in Late Medieval and Early Modern Europe* (Leuven: Peeters, 2016), 149–170.

13 For the use of the expression see Paul A. David, "Why are Institutions the "Carriers of History"? Path Dependence and the Evolution of Conventions, Organizations and Institutions," *Structural Change and Economic Dynamics* 5/2 (1994), 205–220.

14 Lipton, "The Evolution of the Joint Stock Company," 42.

15 Ib., 2.

16 Ron Harris, *Industrializing English Law. Entrepreneurship and Business Organization, 1720–1844* (Cambridge: CUP, 2000), 3–8.

ment and to the rise of the middle class.[17] The first paradigm states that the English legal context had been, for a long time, unresponsive to the new economic needs, determining a delay in the progress of joint-stock companies in England until the nineteenth century. This interpretation was very widespread until recent times, being based on the assumption that common law is inherently isolated and traditional, a judge-made law founded on stable customs and enforced by a class of jurists educated outside the universities, who considered themselves to be autonomous from an intellectual point of view.

On the contrary, according to the second interpretation, economy and law developed in parallel and only the success of the railway industry (1830–1840) determined a widespread diffusion of joint-stock companies, which were in that period freed from the ties of Crown/Parliament charters and also (finally) obtained general limited liability. Harris proposes another interpretation, however. If the "law-in-the-books" was indeed autonomous, the "law-in-action" was rather functional. If judges and lawmakers imposed *their* norms, a law made by businessmen and lawyers, often acting at the boundaries of legality, trembled at the bottom. To a certain extent, this kind of reasoning can also be applied to the commercial companies of the Elizabethan Era, and in particular to the East India Company, in the sense that a law imposed "from above" was cleverly "manipulated" in order to answer the needs coming "from below". During the reign of Queen Elizabeth, in fact, the "manipulation" of the incorporation charters, used mostly for boroughs and municipalities (besides ecclesiastical entities), had two consequences: the crystallization of the (definitive) features of corporations and the introduction of a new (very verbose) incorporation formulary, which was still used under the reign of Queen Victoria, almost three hundred years later.[18] What was "manipulated" here was the legal format of the medieval mercantile guild.

The aim of the guild was to control commerce in the city by means of an organized community of merchants, which was recognized as an entity entitled with specific privileges. The members were considered to be a brotherhood. As a gigantic guild, the East India Company was recognized as an entity, entitled with privileges. The company was defined, at the beginning of the century, as a fellowship. As was the case for many guilds, a Governor (usually called Alderman in the guilds) and twenty-four Committees led the East India Company.

---

17 See also Cooke, *Corporation, Trust and Company*, 9.

18 E.g. the formula "We of Our especial grace, certain knowledge and mere motion": Cecil T. Carr, *Select Charters of Trading Companies* (London: Quaritch, 1913), xiii–xiv. See the incorporation charter of the British South Africa Company: George Cawston and A.H. Keane, *The Early Chartered Companies* (A.D. *1296–1858*) (London: Arnold, 1896), 305 *seq.*

What was new in the Elizabethan period was the incorporation *strictu sensu*, the creation of a *corpus corporatum et politicum de se in re, facto et nomine* (e.g. in the case of the *societas mercatorum* of Hull, of the Levant Company and of the East India Company). Until the fifteenth century, in fact, municipal and guild charters did not contain creative words, and no corporation or body politic was founded: they rather granted, or simply recognized, privileges.[19] Thus, during the Elizabethan Period, traditional institutions were re-defined in a clever compromise between past and present and this was applied to commercial organizations.

3 Corporations: Literature, Case Law and East India Company Documents Compared

> The corporation is, first of all, an organ of government, ecclesiastical and municipal, which controls the activities of its members, exercises jurisdiction over them and negotiates on their behalf with other corporations.[20]

Despite the diffusion of ecclesiastical, municipal and commercial corporations in seventeenth-century England, only two (rather obscure) treatises were devoted to the analysis of what a corporation was, and none of them concentrated on business corporations. The first one, by William Sheppard, a lawyer active under Cromwell's Protectorate and therefore condemned to a quick *damnatio memoriae* at the time of Restoration,[21] was entitled *Of Corporations, Fraternities and Guilds* (1659), the second one was published anonymously *c.* forty years later under the title *The Law of Corporations*.[22] Both works confirm

---

19 Friedrich Pollock and Frederic W. Maitland, *The History of English Law Before the Time of Edward I*, vol. 1 (Cambridge: CUP, 1898), 669.

20 Cooke, *Corporation, Trust and Company*, 17.

21 Nancy L. Matthews, *William Sheppard, Cromwell's Law Reformer* (Cambridge: CUP, 1984), 133 *seq*.

22 W. Sheppard, *Of Corporations, Fraternities and Guilds. The Learning of the Law Touching Bodies-Politique is Unfolded, Shewing the Use and Necessity of that Invention, the Antiquity, Various Kinds, Order and Government of the Same* (London: Twyford, Dring and Place, 1659), section 1, 1: "A corporation, or an incorporation (which is all one) is a body, in fiction of law; or, a body politick that indureth in perpetuall succession". In the treatise published anonymously in 1702 (*The Law of Corporations, Containing the Laws and Customes of all the Corporations and Inferior Courts of Record in England. Treating of the Essentials of, and Incidents to, a Corporation* (London: Atkins, 1702)) the definition is almost identical: "A

the fact that these are the only two books related to the topic published during the whole seventeenth century. Sheppard stated in fact that he was the first writer to address the topic while the unknown author of the 1702 treatise did not remember any "treatise designedly written on this subject, except a little duodecimo by Mr. Sheppard".[23] Within Sheppard's long list of *bodies politick* (as opposed to *bodies naturall*, i.e. individuals), those devoted to commercial activities were simply quoted even though, at that time, business corporations were numerous and successful. Sheppard was one of the four clerks appointed by Cromwell to write towns' and boroughs' incorporation charters. If he was therefore comprehensibly concentrated on corporations other than commercial companies, it is however strange that he did not mention the East India Company at all (incorporated almost sixty years before), nor any other company devoted to the transoceanic trade. He seemed furthermore a little bit confused when, citing the merchants' companies, he wrote "these (...) are called guilds, fraternities, companies, companies corporate, companies incorporate, brotherhoods, fellowships, and bodies corporate".[24]

The anonymous author of the 1702 treatise did not add much, even though he at least thought it necessary to insert a chapter, albeit very short, entitled "Incorporation of Companies".[25] In those few lines all the attention of the author was devoted to the description of some concrete cases and to the criticism of monopoly, which had to be considered always "unreasonable and unwarrantable".[26]

The scholar who expects to find some useful information about the history of limited liability in those treatises will therefore be disappointed. In the framework of a legal system in which the importance of treatises cannot be compared to the role they played on the continent in the same period, they do not add really meaningful information to the list of the features of a corporation contained in the famous "Case of the Sutton's Hospital" (1612), described by Sir Edward Coke.[27] That report clarified "what things are of the essence of a corporation":

corporation or incorporation is a body framed by policy or fiction of law, and it's therefore called a body politick", chapter 1, 1.

23 *The Law of Corporations*, preface.

24 Sheppard, *Of Corporations*, section 1, 5. He quoted only three London companies as examples of companies that were corporations: Sheppard, *Of Corporations*, section 4, 15.

25 *The Law of Corporations*, 294–297 (chap. 22).

26 Ib., 294–297 (chap. 22).

27 Sutton's Hospital Case, 10 Coke Report 23a, 77 ER 960. Sir Edward Coke was at that time Chief Justice of the Court of Common Pleas.

> 1. Lawful authority of incorporation; and that may be by four means, scil. by the Common Law, as the King himself, &c. by authority of Parliament; by the King's Charter (as in this case); and by prescription. The 2. which is of the essence of the Incorporation, are persons to be incorporated, and that in two manners, persons natural, or bodies incorporate and political. 3. A name by which they are incorporated; as in this case Governors of the Lands, &c. 4. Of a place, for without a place no Incorporation can be made; (...) 5. By words sufficient in Law, but not restrained to any certain, legal, and prescript form of words.

Coke's Report is the most quoted in Sheppard's treatise (fifteen quotations).

One hundred and fifty years later, William Blackstone, in his *Commentaries on the Laws of England*, listed, in a more systematic way, the five features of a corporation: "to have perpetual succession", "to sue or be sued", "to purchase lands, and hold them", "to have a common seal" and "to make by-laws or private statutes".[28] All these features were already present in the four charters which can be considered fundamental to the early history of the East India Company: the incorporation charter granted by Queen Elizabeth in 1600,[29] which granted privileges (and in particular the monopoly of the East-India trade) for fifteen years; the 1609 James I's charter, by which those privileges became perpetual;[30] the 1661 Charles II's charter, which confirmed the privileges of the company after the interruption of the Protectorate;[31] and finally the charter granted in 1693 by William and Mary.[32] The fundamental charter granted by Oliver Cromwell in 1657, which created a new and united capital stock, has unfortunately been lost.

In all the above mentioned sources, the problem of limited liability was not considered at all, apart from, perhaps, for the following (not very clear) quotation by Sheppard:

> A corporation may have, enjoy, and retain, lands, goods, and chattels, and have debts by bonds, and take and hold, and make use of engagements, as a body naturall may do, with this difference. That all that which the

---

28 William Blackstone, *Commentaries on the Laws of England*, vol. 1 (Oxford: Clarendon Press, 1765), chapter 18.

29 See footnote 2.

30 7 James I, 31 May 1609, in Shaw, *Charters Relating to the East India Company*, 16–31, here 19.

31 13 Charles II, 3 April 1661, in Shaw, *Charters Relating to the East India Company*, 32–46.

32 5 William and Mary, 7 October 1693, in Shaw, *Charters Relating to the East India Company*, 103–112, here 103.

> corporation hath, doth go in succession to the whole corporation: But if any engagement be to one of the members, or he have any private estate, this will go to his heirs, and executors.[33]

If we analyze the documents of the East India Company, the framework does not change: neither the charters, nor the court minutes,[34] nor that interesting and strangely neglected document entitled *The Lawes or Standing orders of the East-India Company* dated 1621[35] mention the issue of the members' liability. Guido Rossi was probably right in stating that limited liability was certainly not the main feature of the *società per azioni* (companies limited by shares) at the moment of their first development, as it was rather a kind of "indirect consequence" of their discipline, at the beginning not particularly relevant, even though it would become essential for their diffusion and success.[36] According to Rossi, this fact is "well known", but the historiographical analysis leads us to opposite conclusions.

4 Limited Liability: Towards a New Narrative?

If separate corporate personality has been defined as "the cornerstone of modern company law",[37] and limited liability the "invention of an anonymous genius",[38] it is also widely accepted that the complete separation between the

33 Sheppard, *Of Corporations*, section 9, 113.

34 For the period 1513–1634: William Noël Sainsbury (ed.), *Calendar of State Papers, Colonial Series, East Indies, China and Japan*, 4 vols. (London: Eyre and Spottiswoode, 1862–1892). For the period 1635–1679: Ethel Bruce Sainsbury and William Foster (eds.), *A Calendar of the Court Minutes etc. of the East India Company*, 11 vols. (Oxford: Clarendon Press, 1907–1938).

35 *The Lawes or Standing Orders of the East-India Company* (London: s.n., 1621; repr. Farnborough: Gregg International Publishers, 1968).

36 Guido Rossi, "Dalla Compagnia delle Indie al Sarbanes-Oxley Act," *Rivista delle Società* 5–6 (2006), 890–905, here 893. See also Carlos Petit Calvo, "Ignorancias y otras historias, o sea, responsabilidades limitadas," *Anuario de historia del derecho español* 60 (1990), 497–508.

37 Paddy Ireland, Ian Grigg-Spall and Dave Kelly, "The Conceptual Foundations of Modern Company Law," *Journal of Law and Society* 14/1 (1987), 149–365, here 149.

38 "The economic historian of the future may assign to the nameless inventor of the principle of limited liability, as applied to trading corporations, a place of honour with Watt and Stephenson, and other pioneers of the Industrial Revolution": *The Economist*, 18 December 1926, in Paul Halpern, Michael Trebilcock and Stuart Turnbull, "An Economic Analysis of

business company and its members, as a direct consequence of the legal act of incorporation, dates back—in the United Kingdom—only to the second half of the nineteenth century. If general limited liability was in fact introduced in 1855–1856,[39] it was only in the year 1896—the year of the famous Salomon v. Salomon and Co. Ltd case[40]—that perfect limited liability was recognized by a British tribunal. This is quite recent, if we consider the long history of corporations and joint-stock companies in the United Kingdom, which underwent an accelerated development during the Tudor and Stuart Period. It is on the basis of this long history that many scholars have argued that limited liability, i.e. the complete separation of the company's capital from the personal assets of the shareholders, was introduced in England long before the nineteenth century.

Some recent articles refer to the "standard" or "traditional narrative" of the corporation form of business organization[41] or even to the "narrative" of the historical development of joint-stock companies.[42] The idea that narration is the means by which law is communicated and thus justified and explained is nowadays more and more accepted and widespread,[43] and it is therefore unsurprising to find this terminology used by historians dealing with law. What the historian usually does, in fact, is to organize the past into stories, and a story needs a beginning and an end.[44] According to this definition, it is very hard to provide a narrative of the limited liability principle in the seventeenth century as it has no precise beginning nor end. In reality, the expression is not even used

---

Limited Liability in Corporation Law," *University of Toronto Law Journal* 30:2 (1980), 117–150, here 118.

39 Limited Liability Act (18 & 19 Vict., c. 133, 1855) and Joint Stock Companies Act (19 & 20 Vict., c. 47, 1856). See H.A. Shannon, "The Coming of General Limited Liability," in E.M. Carus-Wilson (ed.), *Essays in Economic History* (London: Arnold, 1954), 372–379.

40 Salomon v. Salomon and Co. Ltd [1897] AC 22. See in particular: G.R. Rubin, "Aron Salomon and his circle," in J.N. Adams (ed.), *Essays for Clive Schmitthoff* (Abingdon: Professional Books, 1983), 99–120.

41 Joshua Getzler and Mike Macnair, "The Firm as an Entity before the Companies Acts," in Paul Brand, Kevin Costello and W.N. Osborough (eds.), *Adventures of the Law. Proceedings of the Sixteenth British Legal History Conference* (Dublin: Four Courts, 2005), 267–288. Available at http://ssrn.com/abstract=941231 (consulted on 17 January 2017).

42 Lipton, *The Evolution of the Joint Stock Company*, 1.

43 Greta Olson, "Narration and Narrative in Legal Discourse," in Peter Hühn et al. (eds.), *The Living Handbook of Narratology* (Hamburg: Hamburg University, 2015), available at: http://www.lhn.uni-hamburg.de/article/narration-and-narrative-legal-discourse (consulted on 17 January 2017).

44 J. David Velleman, "Narrative Explanation," *The Philosophical Review* 112/1 (2003), 1–25, here 20.

in the sources. But it is possible to try to provide a narrative of the shareholders' responsibility in the East India Company in the seventeenth century, from its incorporation (1600) to a judicial case which involved the East India Company in the year 1700 (Harvey v. East India Company).[45]

According to Ron Harris, the confusion that still characterizes the topic of limited liability in its historical development is due not only to the rather ambiguous and inconsistent definitions provided by both contemporaries and historians, but also to the fact that both lawyers and historians, when discussing limited liability, refer to different things: "the debts of shareholders to the corporation, those of shareholders to third parties, and those of the corporation to third parties".[46] The main advantage of limited liability, as we understand it today, is that shareholders are not liable for the obligations of the corporations beyond their capital investment. Unfortunately, the lack of sources related to the topic provides only very fragmentary information and many a question remains completely unanswered (e.g. if the shareholders were liable only up to the nominal value of the shares held, or if one shareholder could be asked to pay the entire debt, etc.). Harris' conclusion is that "limited liability in this period should not even be viewed as a continuum, but rather as a matrix with several dimensions".[47] However, even the few sources at our disposal can tell us something about the first, uncertain steps towards a separation between capital investment and the shareholders' personal assets. It is the story of a problem (who pays the debts?), rather than of its solution (the emerging of limited liability in the eighteenth century and the introduction of general limited liability in the nineteenth century).

5 Limited Liability as a Direct Consequence of Incorporation

It is possible to identify three theses with reference to the early history of what we now call "limited liability". According to the first one, limited liability has always been, as it is today, a direct consequence of incorporation.[48] This statement has been applied by scholars to the East India Company. Quite recently, for example, Francesco Galgano wrote that the East India Company

45 See footnote 67.

46 Harris, *Industrializing English Law*, 128.

47 Ib., 128.

48 Or *indirect* consequence, if we refer to Guido Rossi's statement. Nevertheless, we find the expression "direct consequence" less ambiguous.

was born thanks to the incentive of incorporation, which implied limited liability for all members.[49] This assumption relies on a very widespread and well-established historiographical orientation, which dates back at least to William Holdsworth's "History of English law", where he asserted that the principle of the limited liability of the members of a corporation "gradually gained recognition during the fifteenth century"[50] and that it certainly applied to business corporations by the late seventeenth century.[51] Many scholars followed the idea of the early establishment of the principle, saying that "if profits were made, the dividends could be disbursed, but if losses were incurred, investors would only be liable up to the nominal value of their paid-in capital"[52] and that "a member, having paid his capital, had no further liability".[53] Therefore, limited liability has been regarded as an essential attribute of corporateness, such as the power to sue, or the possession of a seal, an attribute that could be taken for granted without specific statement in the charter. More cautiously, Ron Harris writes, referring to the early history of the East India Company, that even though limited liability as we understand it today had not yet emerged:

> It was clear, by virtue of the East India Company's corporate legal personality, separate from the individual legal personalities of its members, that the debts of the company were not identical to the debts of its members, as a group or individually.[54]

Also, the scholars who sustain that the aim of limited liability was to protect the company from its members' debts rather than its members from the company's debts, support the same theory of the "direct consequence".[55]

---

49 Francesco Galgano, *La forza del numero e la legge della ragione. Storia del principio di maggioranza* (Bologna: Il Mulino, 2007), 104.

50 William Holdsworth, *A History of English Law*, vol. 3 (London: Methuen, 1923), 482.

51 Ib., vol. 8 (London: Methuen, 1925), 203–205.

52 Nick Robins, *The Corporation that Changed the World. How the East India Company Shaped the Modern Multinational* (London: Pluto Press, 2006), 24.

53 Shannon, "The Coming of General Limited Liability," 358.

54 Ron Harris, "The Formation of the East India Company as a Cooperation-Enhancing Institution" (2005), http://papers.ssrn.com/sol3/papers.cfm?abstract_id=874406 (consulted on 17 January 2017), 24–25.

55 Paul L. Davies and L.C.B. Gower, *Gower's Principles of Modern Company Law* (London: Sweet & Maxwell, 1997), 21–22: "But, although it [limited liability] was recognised, it appears at first to have been valued mainly because it avoided the risk of the company's property being seized in payment of the members' separate debts", And also: "Another factor suggestive of strong entity shielding in the joint stock companies is that courts

Many scholars assert otherwise that particular agreements were often signed in order to limit the liability of the company's members. But does this not mean that the general rule did not foresee a limitation of liability? Is this not a proof of the weakness of the theory of the direct consequence?[56] Furthermore, there are cases in which it seems that many commercial companies acted without taking into account the advantages of limited liability.[57] A rather strange "distraction", which opens the doors to the supporters of the theory of "unlimited liability".[58]

---

consistently referred to those companies as "incorporated", a term implying at the time both perpetual existence and that the entity rather than its members owned the joint property": Henry Hansmann, Reiner Kraakman and Richard Squire, "Law and the Rise of the Firm," *Yale Law & Economics Research Paper* no. 326 (2006), available at: http://ssrn.com/abstract=873507, 39, footnote 123. The other evidence should be that shares were tradable, but, for the East India Company, they could be sold to outsiders only at the very end of the seventeenth century (see above, footnote 7). Often not quoted, although very important, is the introduction of limited liability in various joint-stock companies (East India, African e Fishery Companies) by a precise act dated 1662, a means by which Charles II wanted to confirm the exclusion of non-traders from the bankruptcy procedures: 13 & 14 Car. II, c. 24, cit. in William Robert Scott, *The Constitution and Finance of English, Scottish and Irish Joint-Stock Companies to 1720*, vol. 1 (Cambridge: CUP, 1910–1912), 270. William Robert Scott was the Adam Smith Professor of Political Economy at the University of Glasgow from 1915 to 1940. His book *The Constitution and Finance of English, Scottish and Irish Joint-Stock Companies to 1720*, analyzes in detail the development of the joint-stock system in the context of the general economic conditions of Great Britain up to the Bubble Act. See the review of the second volume of the book by Theodora Keith: *The Scottish Historical Review* 8/31 (1911), 286–290.

56 Leonard W. Hein, "The British Business Company. Its Origins and its Control," *The University of Toronto Law Journal* 15:1 (1963), 134–154, here 148. Scott gives two examples: the Mosquito Islands Company and the Million Bank. See also Scott, *The Constitution and Finance*, 1, 270 and 344.

57 K.G. Davies, "Joint-Stock Investment in the Later Seventeenth Century," *The Economic History Review* 4/3 (1952), 283–301, here 293.

58 Leonard W. Hein, for example, in noticing that the principle of limited liability developed during a very long period of time, was open to the hypothesis of the responsibility of the members' for the company's debts. According to Hein, when the East India Company business was still organized on the basis of the so called "separate voyages", adventurers simply invested a certain amount of money and at the end of the voyage they divided what they obtained from the sale of the goods and, sometimes, from the sale of the ship itself. The only debts that could remain unpaid were, in theory, only the captain's and crew's wages. For those debts, or for the losses deriving by a ruinous voyage or any other debts, the adventurers were to be considered personally responsible. Hein, "The British Business Company".

6 Unlimited Liability as One of the Main Features of Modern Business Corporations

Supporters of the opposite theory of the unlimited liability of the shareholders of business corporations in their early history are equally numerous and combative.[59] What's more, they can count on the support of Thomas Hobbes, according to whom:

> If a Body Politique of Merchants, contract a debt to a stranger by the act of their Representative Assembly, every member is liable by himself for the whole. For a stranger can take no notice of their private Lawes, but considereth them as so many particular men, obliged every one to the whole payment, till payment made by one dischargeth all the rest.[60]

It is not unusual to read that "early English law knew nothing of limited liability"[61] or that among the "obvious facts" to keep in mind when referring to early commercial companies there is the *absence* of limited liability,[62] or that, more ambiguously, there is no case decided before the nineteenth century "which is inconsistent with the theory that members of a corporation are thus liable, though very possibly that idea became contrary to the general understanding".[63] In 1824 one could still read, in *The Times*, editorials such as this:

> Nothing can be so unjust as for a few persons abounding in wealth to offer a portion of their excess for the information of a company, to play with that excess—to lend the importance of their whole name and credit to the society, and then should the funds prove insufficient to answer all demands, to retire into security of their unhazarded fortune, and leave the bait to the devoured by the poor deceived fish.[64]

---

59 See for example Armand Budington DuBois, *The English Business Company After the Bubble Act, 1720–1800* (New York, 1938), 94.

60 Thomas Hobbes, *Leviathan* (London: Crooke, 1651), chap. 22.

61 Oscar Handlin and Mary F. Handlin, "Origins of American Business Corporation," *The Journal of Economic History* 5 (1945), 1–23, here 11.

62 Davies, "Joint-Stock Investment," 293.

63 Samuel Williston, "History of the Law of Business Corporations Before 1800. II. (Concluded)," *Harvard Law Review* 2 (1888), 149–166, here 162.

64 *The Times*, 25 May 1824, 3. The anonymous author also asked: "The companies being incorporated, may sue or be sued through their treasurer: but in case of a verdict obtained,

An answer to the question of limited liability has been often found in the case of Dr. Salmon v. The Hamborough Company, decided by the House of Lords in 1671[65] (see below). Nevertheless, this famous case cannot completely exclude limited liability. It rather traces a "third path", that of indirect personal responsibility.

7 A "Third Path": The Indirect Responsibility of the Company's Members

The silence of the seventeenth century sources with reference to the liability regime of business corporations brings us apparently only to two conclusions: limited liability was an obvious consequence of incorporation or, on the contrary, liability was not limited at all. But there is a third possibility, the one that was adopted by the *genus* corporation and therefore also by the *species* joint-stock company in England at the time of the chartered companies. It can be defined as "indirect responsibility".

There are two judicial cases that are commonly quoted by the supporters of limited liability in the joint-stock companies: Edmunds v. Brown and Tillard (1668)[66] and the above mentioned Dr. Salmon v. The Hamborough Company. In the first case, the limited liability of the members of an already dissolved company was stated; in the second one, the House of Lords overturned the decision of the Court of Chancery (favourable to limited liability) introducing, by means of compulsory levitations, the "third path" of personal indirect responsibility. A third, less quoted, case, Harvey v. East India Company (1700),[67] not only confirmed the latter decision but directly involving the East India Company, closes this overview of limited liability in seventeenth century England with a case against the "Honourable Company".

7.1 *Edmunds v. Brown and Tillard (1668)*[68]

In the case of Edmunds v. Brown and Tillard, the plaintiff sued two members of the Company of Woodmongers who, as officers of the company, had signed

or of claims existing against them, what or whose property is to be answerable for the demand?".

65 1 Chancery Cases 204, 22 ER 763.

66 1 Levinz 237, 83 ER 385.

67 2 Vernon's Chancery Cases 395, 23 ER 856.

68 See, also for the following cases: Justus Meyer, *Haftungsbeschränkung im Recht der Handelsgesellschaften* (Berlin: Springer, 2000), 234.

a bond. The King's Bench clearly stated that, as the company was already dissolved, the defendants were not personally liable: "A corporation seal a bond, and particular persons sign it, the corporation is dissolved, the particular persons not chargeable".

The object of the claim was a debt of £500. The defendants opposed a *non est factum*,[69] "a plea that an agreement mentioned in the statement of case was not the act of the defendant",[70] commonly used to demonstrate that a supposed debtor was not at all the author of a certain document or that the document was fake, or that the debtor was illiterate and that he was deceived about the content of a certain text. It was proved, in fact, that the defendants could not be attacked "in their own rights", as the company's debts were not the shareholders' debts. Nevertheless, the decision referred to the case of a dissolved company, whereas it was necessary to clarify whether the principle was also applied during the life of a company, and in particular during the very long life, two hundred and fifty-eight years, of the East India Company. Only three years later, the House of Lords called into question the principle in a decision that remained for a long period a point of reference on business corporations both in the UK and in the USA.[71]

7.2 *Dr. Salmon v. The Hamborough Company (1671)*

In 1656 the Court of Chancery stated that, in a suit brought by a creditor (Dr. Salomon) against a corporation (the Hamborough Company), this latter was not obliged to appear in court because "they having nothing by which they may be distrained". But the House of Lords, the court of last resort, stated on the contrary, almost fifteen years later, that the members of the company had to pay the company's debts.[72] In particular, if the debt had been proved, a decree had to be issued establishing a deadline of ninety days for the payment. Failure to meet this request would have forced the Governor, the Deputy-Governor

69 Frederic Jesup Stimson, *Glossary of Technical Terms, Phrases and Maxims of the Common Law* (Boston: Little, Brown and Cie., 1881), 213. See John H. Baker, *An Introduction to English Legal History* (London: Dayton, 2002), 324.

70 Elizabeth A. Martin and Jonathan Law (eds.), "Non est factum," in *Oxford Dictionary of Law* (Oxford: OUP, 2006).

71 According to Samuel Williston this decision continued to be followed in the US until the first half of the nineteenth century: Williston, *History of the Law of Business Corporations*, 162.

72 Harris underlines that in this case the incorporation charter gave the company power to levy on its members. Otherwise, "a degree of limitation of liability existed": Harris, *Industrializing English Law*, 128, footnote 39.

and the twenty-four Assistants (or a number sufficient to reach the quorum) to oblige the shareholders to pay leviations in order to pay the company's debts. If they did not succeed, the court would have acted directly:

> Then and from thenceforth every Person of the said Company, upon such a Leviation, shall be made to be liable in his Capacity to pay his quota or Proportion assessed. And the Lord Chancellor or Lord Keeper is to order or decree, that such Process shall issue against any such Member so refusing or delaying to pay his quota or Proportion, as is usual against Persons charged by the Decree of the said Court, for any Duty in their several Capacities.

Twenty-nine years after this decision, in the case of Harvey v. East India Company, the principle was still remembered: "In the case between Dr. Salmon and the Hamborough Company, the members in their private persons were made liable, the Company having no goods".

7.3 *Harvey v. East India Company* (1700)

Harvey v. East India Company was discussed in 1700 and concerned the fulfilment of an obligation of £3,700. As a general rule, for the process to be duly conducted, the defendant had to be present or, as an alternative, he could be "outlawed". The only way to duly conduct a trial against a corporation which refused to appear before the bar was a kind of equity process called *distringas*.[73] On the basis of the fact that a decree ordering the fulfilment of the obligation had already been issued against the East India Company, it was now time to enforce it without any need to hear the defendant another time. In synthesis: "private members of a company made liable to the company's debts, where the company had no goods".

8 Conclusion

It seems therefore that, at least until the eighteenth century, there was no complete separation between the corporation and the personal assets of its members, unless limited liability had been explicitly stated in the incorporation charter or by means of specific agreements. The only clearly stated "limitation"

73 See Stimson, *Glossary of Technical Terms*, 116; Baker, *An Introduction to English Legal History*, 64.

consisted of the fact that the shareholders were not directly sued, but instead their assets could be attacked by means of a sentence, as they could be obliged to pay at least a part of the corporate debts, i.e. more than the amount of the subscribed capital, by means of leviations.

The assumption that law is a mere body of rules deriving from statutes and court decisions, and the connected idea that the ultimate source of law is the will of the lawmaker (i.e. the state), have been widely criticized starting at least from Harold Berman's masterpiece *Law and Revolution*. Law is rather "a process, an enterprise, in which rules have meaning only in the context of institutions and procedures, values and ways of thought".[74] Nevertheless, if we accept the idea of a "narrative of shareholders' responsibility", then, in the case of the East India Company, this story can only be reconstructed using charters, court minutes and court decisions. It is the story of a group of merchants of London who wanted to take advantage of the long-distance trade with Asia, who had the main aim of obtaining from the Crown the monopoly of this trade—together with the authorization to carry ingots and weapons—who wanted to start as soon as possible (and before the Dutch competitors), relying, for their internal organization, on structures they knew well: the guilds or other chartered companies such as the Levant Company.[75] Monopoly was the central issue for business corporations. As Thomas Hobbes noticed, in fact: "the End of their Incorporating, is to make their gain the greater; which is done two ways: by sole buying, and sole selling, both at home and abroad".[76] But what kind of "narrative" can we find where there is no reference to this issue? Maybe this silence tells a story too. It is possible that trust and co-operation based on "informal social sanctions, social norms and fear of loss of reputation and future business"[77] were sufficient for facing even the problems related to the adventurers' liability or that "it was clear, by virtue of the East India Company's corporate legal personality (...) that the debts of the company were not identical to the debts of its members".[78] Or maybe it simply demonstrates that law, and especially commercial law, is a process which is continuously adapting to new needs, the result of the work of hundreds and thousands of

74 Harold J. Berman, *Law and Revolution. The Formation of the Western Legal Tradition* (Cambridge (Ma.): Harvard University Press, 1983), 10.

75 At least twenty-one adventurers listed in the first charter of the East India Company were already adventurers of the Levant Company.

76 Hobbes, *Leviathan*, chapter 22.

77 Lipton, "The Evolution of the Joint Stock Company," 38; see also Harris, "The Formation of the East India Company," 33.

78 Harris, "The Formation of the East India Company," 24–25.

"obscure men", and that it was only when joint-stock companies reached the general public that the need for a law providing general rules was felt, also substituting uncertain rules and practices by then outdated.

CHAPTER 7

From Commercial Guilds to Commercial Law: Spanish Company Regulations (1737–1848)

Carlos Petit

1 Introduction

> A partnership is the union of two or more men, made with the intention of acquiring something in common, by uniting themselves together. Great advantage arises from such union, where it is formed between good and honest men; for then they mutually assist one another, as if they were brothers.

This definition, contained in the *Partidas* (5,10,1),[1] brilliantly captures the essence of the old commercial company; from the ancient community of heirs (*consortium ercto non cito*) contemplated by Roman law to the general partnership articulated by modern law, it can be asserted that the family has constituted the model for for-profit associations. For instance, the so-called partners' *ayuntamiento*—from the verb *ayuntar*, which, according to Sebastián de Covarrubias in *Tesoro de la lengua castellana o española*, 1611, 93, means *quando dos cosas distintas se allegan la una con la otra* ("when two different things ally themselves with each other")—can also be found in the *Partidas* (4,2,1), where marriage is defined as an *ayuntamiento de marido e de muger, fecho con tal entencion de beuir siempre en vno, e de non se departir; guardando lealtad cada vno dellos al otro*.[2] The similarity between the two definitions is obvious: an identical interpersonal situation (*ayuntamiento*), the existence of a shared objective (*entencion*), and the same moral premise (*lealtad*). In Latin,

1 "*Compañía es ayuntamiento de dos hombres o de mas, que es fecho con entencion de ganar algo de so vno, ayutandose los unos con los otros. E nasce ende gran pro, quando se face entre algunos omes buenos, e leales: ca se acorren los vnos a los toros, bien assi como si fuesen hermanos*": Louis Moreau Lislet and Henry Carleton (trans.), *The Laws of the Seven Partidas which are still in force in the State of Louisiana* (New Orleans, 1820), vol. 2, 765.

2 "Marriage is the union of husband and wife, made with the intention of always living together and never separating, each observing mutual fidelity towards the other.": Lislet and Carleton, *The Laws of the Seven Partidas*, vol. 1, 453.

 | DOI: 10.1163/9789004351868_009

the rare term *affectio* (and not *consensus*, which was the standard term in contract law) was employed to express the love that existed between the partners (*affectio societatis*, cf. D. 17,2,31; *voluntad de fincar en ella*, according to the *Partidas*, 5,10,11), and which was akin to the love between spouses (*affectio maritalis*, cf. D. 34,1,32,12). Were that noble sentiment to disappear, the only option was divorce, or for the commercial company, the dissolution of the company.

2 Family and Partnership

The family mould into which partnerships were inserted led to a number of consequences.[3] The first important consequence was that the contract overlapped with family bonds, acting like a natural extension of kinship. The *paterfamilias* would teach his offspring his profession with the aim of turning them into business associates. Consequently, should the widow and their children take over the business after his death, his absence would not provoke the insolvency or liquidation of the company. This same practice applied to the husbands of one's daughters. Those were often young trade colleagues or even home employees—almost like sons who had been raised there and who culminated their careers by becoming junior partners of the boss.[4]

Secondly, those bases meant that the daily activity of any commercial company was similar to family life. Every company had its own name—a trading name—with which it was identified in the business world and which bound its partners before third parties. More often than not, the name was a reflection of the network of personal relations that underlay the contract ("X and Sons," "X and Z Bros," "Widow of X and Sons," and other such combinations). Furthermore, the *affectio societatis* enclosed a level of intimacy that was far more intense than the generic love and friendship that existed between colleagues of the same profession. In this regard, Savary would rightfully warn that

3 On the family origins of the commercial company, see Max Weber, *Historia económica general* (1923), Manuel Sánchez Sarto (trans.) (Madrid: Fondo de Cultura Económica, 2011), 264 *seq.* For a didactic and pertinent description, see also Umberto Santarelli, *Mercanti e società tra mercanti* (Turin: Giappichelli, 1989), 127 *seq.* (from "*Guadagnare e mangiare il medesimo pane*").

4 The following sociohistorical study on Cadiz clearly reflects those aspects: Manuel Bustos Rodríguez, *Los comerciantes de la Carrera de Indias en el Cádiz del siglo XVIII* (Cádiz: Universidad de Cádiz, 1995), 134 *seq.* (family and sons), 149 *seq.* (assistants and servants), and 177 *seq.* (commercial companies).

la première chose que doivent avoir deux associés est l'amitié et la déférence l'un pour l'autre, car c'est d'où dépend tout le bonheur ou le malheur de leurs affaires communes ("the first thing that two associates are owed towards each other is mutual friendship and respect, because on this the happiness or misery of their common affairs depends").[5] Another example of the manner in which business resembled family was the possibility that the partners had of designating each other as executors of wills or even as testamentary agents. However, the most frequent agreements implied a shared home and living costs, for those partners who were not united by blood led a family life. As we already know, the word *compañía* (company) means to eat the same bread.[6]

When the company was established between father and sons, the former usually assumed the living costs of the house. Paternal authority (*persona mayor de la compañía, padre y cabeza de la casa y compañía*, "the main partner", "father and head of the household and company") generally justified the inequality with which profit and loss quotas were defined as well as the inequality in the administration of common business. As one would expect, the deterioration of the father's health naturally led his sons to manage the company. Only then were they able to benefit from the prerogatives that belonged to the *caput*, including running the private business without requiring the consent of the partners.[7]

Thirdly, the closeness between the family and the company explains the characteristics of the contract. Its very personal nature (*intuitu personarum*) was based on reciprocal trust, thus justifying its dissolution when one of the partners passed away, unless an agreement was reached to continue doing business with the heirs. Those were certainly already known to the surviving partners and were held in esteem by them. In such cases, joint liability—a derivation of family debt liability—applied vis-à-vis common creditors.[8] This

5 Jacques Savary, *Le parfait négociant* (Paris: les frères Étienne, 1763), vol. 1, 386. See 388, in which it is asserted that among the "*ressources pour trouver de l'argent*" ("means to obtain funds") that are available to the partner who manages the finances "*la plus grande* (...) *est celle des amis particuliers qui sont puissans en argent, qui n'en refusent pas quand ils y trouvent leur sûreté*" ("the main resource to raise funds are rich friends, who are willing to lend money if they esteem their investment a surety"). It can thus be concluded that one cannot be a trader without friends.

6 According to the knowledgeable Joan Corominas, the etymology of the word "company" can be traced back to Merovingian Latin, where *con/cum-panis* was derived from the Gothic word *gahlaiba* (from *hlaifs*, which means "bread," and the prefix *ga*).

7 I documented those matters in *La compañía mercantil bajo el régimen de las Ordenanzas del Consulado de Bilbao, 1737–1829* (Seville: Universidad de Sevilla, 1980).

8 Let us also recall that despite the principle of the personal nature of penalties, in the most

rule was the exact opposite of what was foreseen within the framework of civil obligations.[9]

3 Partnerships and Mercantile Ordinances

Despite the fact that *ius commune* jurists produced a number of well-structured monographs that enjoyed wide circulation, including Pietro degli Ubaldis' *De duobus fratribus* (1472) or Ettore and Angelo Felicio's *Tractatus de societate* (1610), it was daily practice that defined the legal structure of the company. In this matter, as in many other matters that we associate with private law, regulatory norms were barely dictated by superior jurisdictions. At best, the task was assumed by lower ranking jurisdictions; in this case, it was the commercial guilds ("consulates"). Between the fifteenth and the eighteenth centuries, guild bylaws (the *ordenanzas* of the consulates of Burgos, Bilbao, Seville, Mexico, and Lima) were nevertheless scarce, and merely dealt with guild activities (government and consultation positions, honours, employees, elections, patron saints, and alms), the royal recognition of privileged jurisdictions, including procedural rules in trade matters, and a couple of contracts regarding maritime traffic (insurance, sea risks, and charter).

This situation changed in 1737. Following the example of France (*Ordonnances pour le commerce*, 1673; *Ordonnances pour la Marine*, 1681), the traders'

---

serious cases, the entire family group suffered (*unus potest puniri pro alio*) the consequences of the crime: Mario Sbriccoli, *Crimen laesae maiestatis. Il problema del reato politico alla soglie della scienza penalistica moderna* (Milan: Giuffrè, 1974), 239 *seq*.

9 Cf. *Nueva Recopilación* (1567) 5,16,1 (Enrique IV en Madrid, 1458) (= *Novísima Recopilación* (1805) 10,1,10): "*Establecemos, que si dos personas se obligaren simplemente por contrato o en otra manera alguna para hacer y cumplir alguna cosa, que por ese mismo hecho se entienda ser obligado cada uno por la mitad: salvo si en el contrato se dijere, que cada uno sea obligado in solidum, o entre sí en otra manera fuere convenido e igualado, y esto no embargante cualesquier leyes del Derecho común que contra esto hablan; y esto sea guardado en los contratos pasados como en los por venir*" ("We establish that if two people simply agree by contract or otherwise to do and accomplish something, that by that very fact it is understood that they are held each for the half; unless if the same contract provides that each party is obliged jointly and severally, or if the same were agreed in another way, and this irrespective of any contradicting laws of the *ius commune*; and this should be respected in past contracts and in contracts to come"). Doctrinal opinion, which was in favour of (exceptional) joint liability, understood that partners were bound by a relation of reciprocal mandate: Petit, *La compañía mercantil*, 204–205.

guild of the city of Bilbao, which constituted the main port of the northern peninsula, drafted a number of comprehensive ordinances that were soon after approved by the crown. Those were admirably written and innovative in nature. Unlike the French text, they dealt both with the institutions of terrestrial commerce and with maritime law, thus forming a sort of *avant la lettre* commercial code that would, by universal consensus and despite its local validity, be copied and applied myriad times in Spain and the Indies.[10]

The text was divided into 29 chapters that contained 723 laws, or "ordinances." Chapter 10, which was titled *De las compañías de comercio y de las calidades y circunstancias con que deberán hacerse* ("On trading companies and its qualities and circumstances"), had 17 articles. To a contemporary observer, the regulation of the institution may appear quite limited. Just like the 1673 *Ordonnance*, which was one of the code's main sources,[11] the guild rules of Bilbao primarily sought to guarantee trade security. This explains the numerous formal requirements they contained.[12] Substantial legal matters were relegated to a secondary position,[13] whereas the different types of company—of utmost importance today—were not even mentioned (only the *compañía general* is alluded to in section X,2). The quasi-family nature of the contract was reflected in the official stated intention of avoiding disputes (section X,16: submission to

10 Cf. *Ordenanzas de la Ilustre Universidad y Casa de contratación de la M.R. y M.L. Villa de Bilbao* (Madrid: Fernandez, 1775). The first eight chapters (jurisdiction of the consulate, appointment of positions and remunerations, elections, board meetings, damage management, and the responsibilities of the administrator) define commercial procedure and the corporation's regime. The following chapters, up to Chapter 18, cover the institutions of land commerce (accounting, companies, trading requirements and conditions, exchange instruments, representatives, bankruptcies). Chapters 18–24 cover maritime commerce (charters, shipwrecks, general average, insurances, bottomry loans, captains, and other staff of the ship). The last five chapters form a group of norms on the port and ships of Bilbao (master navigator and harbourmaster's office, the conservation of the estuary, shipwrights, bargemen, and boatmen).

11 José Martínez Gijón, "El capítulo X de las Ordenanzas del Consulado de Bilbao de 1737 (De las compañías de comercio y de las calidades y circunstancias con que deberán hacerse) y el título IV de la "Ordonnance sur le Commerce" de 1673 (Des sociétés)," *Revista de derecho mercantil* 175–176 (1985), 171–188.

12 The contract was turned into a public writ (sections X,4, X,8 and X,9); concerning its registration in the corporate archives, see section X,5. Rules regarding company accounting books and public announcements of dissolution are mentioned in sections X,6 and X,17 respectively.

13 With regard to the contract definition, see section X,1. Capital and contributions are dealt with in sections X,4, X,10, X,11, and X,14. Partners' liability is addressed in section X,13.

arbitrator judges), in partnership succession (section x,9), and in the prediction of possible family expenses that were to be considered common costs (section x,7).

In fact, the Bilbao ordinances allowed for a wide range of pacts; the parties were to determine *las (...) circunstancias, capítulos, y condiciones licitas, que se quisieren imponer, y pactar* ("freely the clauses, circumstances, and licit conditions") (section x,3). All that was required was for the public to be well informed of the establishment of the company and of its main clauses through announcements and the deposition of the contract at the consulate, *para manifestarle siempre que convenga* ("in order to display the agreement to anyone concerned") (section x,5).

The unclear Law No. 13 on the external liability of partners illustrates this issue well:

> Anyone interested in a company will be obliged to pay, and bring due execution, at loss, or gain, for any business agreed and executed by the partners with other persons and traders outside the company; each partner is responsible for losses that may occur according to his share in the capital and profits; but it is understood that the partner or partners under whose signature the company operates should respond, besides their share and profits that belong to them, with all their assets, present and future, even when they or any of them joined the partnership without any funds.[14]

It is likely that those who drafted that law had in mind the two precepts that were contained in the *Ordonnance pour le commerce* (IV,7–8), which they combined into a single and confusing text. In any case, the resulting text was a reflection of the company types that were known in Bilbao, and generally in Spain, during the eighteenth century. The law provided two kinds of partners with varying degrees of liability before third parties with regard to the activities that were carried out *nomine societatis*. On the one hand, *aquel, ó aquellos, bajo de cuya firma corriere la Compañía*, ("under whose signature the company oper-

14 "*Todos los interesados en una Compañía serán obligados á abonar, y llevar á debida execucion, á pérdida, ó ganancia, qualesquiera negocios que cada compañero haga, y execute en nombre de todos con otras personas, y negociantes fuera de ella; saneando cada uno las pérdidas que puedan suceder, hasta en la cantidad del capital, y ganancias en que fue interesado, y resultaren del total de la Compañía; entendiéndose, que aquel, ó aquellos, bajo de cuya firma corriere la Compañía, estarán obligados, demás del fondo, y ganancias que en ella les pertenezcan, con todo el resto de sus bienes, habidos, y por haber, al saneamiento de todas las pérdidas, aunque ellos tales, ó alguno de ellos entrase sin poner caudal en dicha Compañía*".

ates", that is the managers) who would respond *con todo[s] sus bienes, habidos y por haber* ("with all their assets, present and future"); on the other hand, the remaining partners (that is, the non-managers), who had the obligation of *sanea[r] cada uno las pérdidas que pueden suceder, hasta en la cantidad del capital, y ganancias en que fue interesado* ("to respond for the losses according to their share in the capital and profits"). Putting the ambiguous expression *correr bajo la firma* aside,[15] one could be led to assert that the company form that was contemplated in the ordinances (that, as mentioned before, only alluded to *las Compañías mas frequentes en el Comercio aquellas generales que usan, y practican muchos de sus individuos*, "the most common companies in commerce, the so-called general partnerships, which are widely used among merchants") was that of a limited partnership—a peculiar formula that was a reflection of the need to finance the merchant's activity[16] and which constituted a first and decisive step toward the disassociation between the commercial contract and its traditional family pattern.

Nevertheless, local practice contradicts that impression. The Bilbao contracts demonstrate that almost always, partners answered fully and jointly with regard to common debts, regardless of whether they had the power to conduct business in the name of the company or not. A judgment on the bankruptcy of Aréchaga e Hijo y Galíndez (1805–1806) describes the situation well:

> Although it is said that a partner is not held but in proportion to his share in the company, this applies to the relations among the partners, but not vis-à-vis the creditors of the company, in whose favour any and all of the partners are jointly liable to pay debts not only with the common fund but also with their separate property, as each and every debt is understood to be assumed by all partners as a result of a reciprocal mandate established among them.[17]

---

15 It should be interpreted as contract-making on behalf of the company, regardless of whether the name of the managers appears or not in the company name. In other words, the clause referred to the partners who were authorized to deal with third parties. This is suggested in the version of section X,13 of the Bilbao ordinance that is contained in an unpublished ordinance project (1794) for the Consulate of Seville (section VIII,12: "*pero el compañero, o compañeros, que hiciesen los tales negocios serán responsables a las pérdidas*": "because the partner authorized to trade is liable for losses"). See Petit, *La compañía mercantil*, 200–201.

16 See Santarelli, *Mercanti*, 148 *seq.*, 172 *seq.*, and 19 *seq.*

17 "*Aunque se dice que un socio no se obliga sino a prorrata de aquella porción o capitalidad que pone en compañía, esto rige y se entiende tan solamente para con los mismos socios*

In those cases in which it was agreed that the liability of one of the partners would be limited, with the exception of the previously mentioned limited partnership (that existed but was residual),[18] the liability-limiting clause responded to the mere will of the parties. There were companies with partners who were in charge of common business and who were authorized to sign in the name of the company, who nevertheless only responded with the capital they had contributed, in addition to profits, when they existed, or with a predetermined sum. The consulate accepted this, on the condition that at least one of the partners had the obligation to respond with all his goods, present and future. Given that such agreements were public, third parties had to trust in the solvency of the company, or in its main liable partner.[19]

4 Merchant Partnerships and Royal Companies

When the ordinances were approved, another form of association emerged in Spain. It was adopted by chartered companies whose capital was divided in shares and which served to explore colonial commerce or promote large-scale industrial production. The ordinances are completely silent with regard to those companies; nevertheless, upon the initiative of the consulate, Bilbao did experience a contemporary project of that sort (1736).[20] The fact that it failed does not justify, at least in principle, the surprising lack of corporate regulation.

---

entre sí, mas no para con los acreedores de la compañía, para con los cuales todos y cualesquiera de los compañeros son responsables con insolidación al pago no sólo con los caudales comunes sino también con los demás bienes separados y particulares, como que todas y cada una de las deudas se entienden contraídas por todos ellos por el concepto de mandatario recíproco que tienen entre sí los unos de los otros". See Petit, *La compañía mercantil*, 347 *seq*.

18 Only a little over 8% of the companies that were established in Bilbao between 1737 and 1829 adopted the scheme of limited partnership: Petit, *La compañía mercantil*, 49 *seq*. There were even fewer contracts that employed the term *comandita* or "limited": "*voz extranjera introducida en nuestras plazas de comercio*" ("a foreign word introduced lately in our merchant towns") according to Eugenio de Tapia, *Tratado de jurisprudencia mercantil* (Valencia: Mompié, 1828), 9.

19 Petit, *La compañía mercantil*, 206 *seq*.

20 On the desired "*Compañía de Real Fábrica y Comercio para la ciudad y las tres provincias de Buenos Aires, Tucumán y Paraguay*," see José María Mariluz Urquijo, *Bilbao y Buenos Aires. Proyectos dieciochescos de compañías de comercio* (Buenos Aires: Universidad de Buenos Aires, 1981).

In fact, there existed other reasons. To begin with, these royal companies bore no resemblance to genuine partnerships.[21] While the latter can be described as contractual, the former were, strictly speaking, institutional. Those who contributed to the establishment of royal companies by purchasing capital shares could not alter the legal regime that the company was subjected to within the framework of the decree that created it. This will be further explored below.

It should be added that these institutions were the result of an original concept of power.[22] During the seventeenth and eighteenth centuries, the monarch of the *ancien régime*, who had traditionally been in charge of "civil and political government", that is, *tutto quello, che riguarda gli affari publici di Stato per la conseruatione, aumento, decoro, e felicità del Principato* ("everything that relates to public affairs of state for the conservation, increase, decorum, and happiness of the principality"),[23] would additionally assume the responsibilities of a *paterfamilias*, the "economic" or "domestic government" that was necessary to keep a household: [*a*]*dministración y dispensación recta y prudente de las rentas y bienes temporales: lo que comunmente se dice Régimen y gobierno en las casas y famílias* ("prudent management and disposition of income and temporal goods: what is commonly said to be the regime and government of households and families").[24] Without going into the details of that cultural transformation which ultimately led to the emergence of the administrative state, it is enough to mention here that the fatherly monarch, who possessed broad economic power both in the public and private spheres, exercized the trade profession in his own way and devoted significant resources to promote the trade of the kingdom.

---

21 It was therefore inevitable that commercial literature would remain silent on privileged companies. See Henri Lévy-Bruhl, *Histoire juridique des sociétés de commerce en France aux XVIIe et XVIIIe siècles* (Paris: Domat-Montechrestien, 1938), 42 *seq.*, and Charles E. Freedeman, *Joint-Stock Entreprise in France, 1807–1867. From Privileged Company to Modern Corporation* (Chapel Hill: University of North Carolina Press, 1979), 4 *seq.*

22 Daniela Frigo, *Il padre di familia. Governo della casa e governo civile nella tradizione dell'economica tra Cinque e Seicento* (Rome: Bulzoni, 1985). Spanish sources include Ignacio Atienza Hernández, "Pater familias, señor y patrón: oeconómica, clientelismo y patronato en el antiguo régimen," in Reyna Pastor de Tognery (ed.), *Relaciones de poder, de producción y parentesco en la edad media y moderna. Aproximación a su estudio* (Madrid: CSIC, 1990), 411–458.

23 Giovan Battista De Luca, *Il Principe cristiano pratico* (Rome: Camera Apostolica, 1680), 66. See Frigo, *Il padre di famiglia*, 208 *seq.*

24 "Economía," in *Diccionario de Autoridades*, vol. 3 (Madrid: del Hierro, 1732), http://web.frl.es/DA.html (consulted on 17 January 2017).

It may seem paradoxical that the exercise of paternal power would allow the prince to establish companies that differed from the family model that company law had upheld to that point. In fact, the studies that have been carried out on the shareholders of those companies demonstrate that the "family" of the trader-monarch was a constellation of corporations, of more or less privileged estates, and of subjects of any condition, including foreigners.[25] The royal company was in turn an institution that was established by virtue of a sovereign decision of the king in the absence of a pre-existing contract; it drew a non-trading public that purchased the shares of a legally determined (*ope legis*) capital, and it was run by a small number of elected administrators whose mandates varied in duration.

The variety of investors formed an actual nation that supported the monarch in his *oeconomic* adventures and constitutes the third factor that allows us to differentiate between commercial companies and the privileged companies that attracted different people. In addition to the king himself, it drew noblemen who did not lose their condition, the under-aged and the legally incapable, religious and territorial institutions, and even literary and scientific academies. The commercial nature of the company was thus reduced to its object, which helps explain that the shares were transferable, for the personal condition of the partner was no longer relevant.

To highlight the differences between the two forms of association, the terminology was refined, and the term *sociedad* (*societas*, *société*, "partnership") was reserved for those associations where *il suffit de la volonté des associés* ("the free will of the parties is sufficient to conclude the contract"). The business initiatives of the monarchy—*établies* (…) *par la concession du prince* ("established by princely authority")—were in turn referred to as *compañías* (*collegium*, *compagnie*, "corporation").[26] This distinction became well rooted in France.[27]

---

25 For example, Teresa Tortella Casares, *Índice de los primitivos accionistas del Banco Nacional de San Carlos* (Madrid: Archivo Histórico del Banco de España, 1986).

26 See Levy-Bruhl, *Histoire juridique*, 43–44.

27 *Encyplopédie Méthodique, ou par ordre de matières. Commerce*, vol. 1 (Paris: Pancoucke, 1783), s.v. *compagnie*, 552: "*société se disant de deux ou trois négocians, ou de peu davantage* (…) *et compagnie s'entendant pour l'ordinaire d'un plus grand nombre d'associés, qui n'est fixé que suivant les secours, dont ceux qui s'associent, croyent avoir besoin pour les entreprises ou les établissements qu'ils veulent faire* (…). *Une autre différence* (…) *c'est que* (…) *les compagnies ne peuvent être établies que par la concession du prince* (…) *et que pour les autres, il suffit de la volonté des associés* (…) *le mot compagnie* (…) *ne se dise plus guères préssentement, que de ces grandes associations qui se sont fait* (…) *pour les commerces étrangers*" ("one speaks of *société* when there are two, or three partners, or

In Spain, Miguel de Zavala y Auñón distinguished in his *Representación* (…) *dirigida al más seguro aumento del Real Erario* between *la sociedad de pocos individuos que juntan sus caudales; y encargandose uno, ù dos de dirigir las negociaciones, hacen el trafico en aquellas cosas limitadas à que ſe estiende su fondo, y su crédito* ("the society of few individuals who pool their funds; with one or two of the partners taking charge of the business, and they trade in those limited things that their capital and their credit allow"), and genuine *companies*, which are a *cuerpo de muchos individuos, que contribuyen con sus caudales y su consejo, y con su inteligencia al logro de unas crecidas ganancias; se goviernan con methodo, y reglas fixas, y seguras para el acierto; y caminan, baxo la Real proteccion, con establecimientos, y con honores*[28] ("a body of many individuals, who contribute with their wealth and their advice, and with their intelligence to achieve high profits; they are methodically governed, according to fixed and safe rules, apt for success; and they march under the Royal protection, with establishments, and with honours"). Nevertheless, the Spanish language would not easily assimilate the commercial sense of the term *sociedad*.

Legally speaking, the royal companies were entities (*body politick, corporation, compañía* or *cuerpo*) that were established according to the law, or those *reglas fixas, y seguras* ("fixed and secure rules") that Miguel de Zavala would refer to. According to scholarly language—not many jurists (such as Johannes Marquardt) tackled those entities[29]—they constituted a *collegium* or *sodali-*

a few more, whereas *compagnie* is applied when there is a high number of parties, as high as the founders consider necessary to finance their common enterprise (…) There is another difference: *compagnies* only exist by royal decree, whereas other partnerships depend on the partners' free will (…). Also the word *compagnie* is rarely used nowadays, except for businesses trading abroad"). It was an *ad pedem litterae* reproduction of Jacques Savary des Bruslons, *Dictionnaire universel de commerce … 1/2: Contenant les articles du commerce et des compagnies*, Philemon-Louis Savary (ed.) (Geneva: Cramer & Philibert, 1742), s.v. *compagnie*, cols. 1039 *seq.*, in which he traced the distinction, while at the same time acknowledging "*quoi que compagnie et société soit* (…) *dans le fond la même chose*" ("*compagnie* and *société* are really the very same thing").

28 *Representació … dirigida al más seguro aumento del Real Erario, y la felicidad, mayor alivio, riqueza, y abundancia de su Monarquía* (s.l.: s.n., 1732 [1738]). The work contained an early proposal for trade through companies and was repeatedly published as a main part of the *Miscelánea económico-política* (1749, 1787).

29 Johannes Marquardt, *Tractatus politico-juridicus de jure mercatorum et commerciorum singulari libri IV* (Frankfurt am Main: Götzius, 1662), cf. book 3, chapter 1, "*De Judiciis & Curiis Mercatorum singularibus. Ubi primo de eorum Collegiis & Sodalitiis, vulgo Kompagnien*". See also Ralf Mehr, *Societas und universitas: Römischrechtliche Institute im Unternehmensgesellschaftsrecht vor 1800* (Cologne: Böhlau, 2008). Also, Johann Friedrich Bachoff von Echt,

tas. This was a form of *universitas*, according to Marquardt [*a*]*d horum Collegiorum exemplum commerciorumque promotionem faciliorem, institutae sunt hodiè societates seu Compagniae mercatorum, versus certas oras negotia tractantium* ("an example of these *collegia* for the better use of trade are those companies of merchants nowadays that were established for trade upon certain coasts"). They were thus subject to the approval of the sovereign, like any other *universitas* (for *collegia a superior sunt confirmanda*, "collegia are to be confirmed by the sovereign"). Their independent existence further rested on the existence of a business address (*collegiati quoque in certo loco conveniunt*, "the associates assemble in some location"), a common treasure (*collegiati communem possident arcam*, "associates hold a common treasury"), and a seal and insignia (*collegiati utuntur communi sigillo in obsignandis litteris & obligationibus liberationibusque ad collegia spectantibus*, "associates are to make use of a common seal in signing letters and obligations that concern the *collegium*"), in addition to the activity of their managing directors *quos omnis est directio et auctoritas*, ("every one has the administration and authority"), agents, and employees who executed the collective will (*collegiati suos habent officiales et minimos*). Furthermore, these companies were not subject to commercial jurisdiction and had the power to ensure the execution/implementation of their own regulations/rules (*quod si vero quis secus facere attentaverit, ille arbitrarie etiam exclusione punitur*, "he who will attempt to do otherwise, will be punished extrajudicially with exclusion").[30] Endowed with sovereign faculties and exclusive trading areas,[31] royal companies did not trade in an ordinary way ([*c*]*ommercia non ut simplices mercatores propagarunt*, "they will engage in trade not in the way of ordinary merchants"). But the main difference lay in the respective legal bases of the organizations. Whereas *las Compañías mas*

De eo quod iustum est circa commercia inter gentes (Jena: Litteris Hornianis, 1730), which is an academic essay that briefly mentions (at 34 *seq.*) shareholding companies, "*qvae octroyirte compagnien adpellari solent*".

30 Cf. Royal Decree of 25 September 1728, *Compañía de Caracas*, s. 7; Royal Decree of 18 December 1740, *Compañía de La Habana*, s. 23; Royal Decree of 4 May 1755, *Compañía de Barcelona*, s. 24, and the ordinances of April 11 1756, s. 84–92. See Raquel Rico Linage (ed.), *Las Reales Compañías de Comercio con América. Los órganos de gobierno* (Seville: Excma, 1983), documents at 26 *seq.*

31 "*Quibus rationibus*," wrote Marquardt on the Swedish East India Company, "*rex motus modò dictam Societatem eôdem anno 1626 egregio dotavit privilegio*." ("For these reasons, in the year 1626 the king endowed this partnership with a privilege"). We already know of some of those that were granted to the *Compañía de Barcelona*. However, the law that established them was referred to in its totality as a "grace" (cf. s. 19).

frequentes en el Comercio (...) que usan, y practican muchos de sus individuos (1737 Bilbao ordinance X,3), were regulated, as seen above, by means of a contract (*las circunstancias, capítulos, y condiciones licitas, que se quisieren imponer, y pactar* (1737 Bilbao ordinance X,4)), in the *collegia*-companies, the shareholders *secundum statute stricte vivunt* ("strictly obey the statutes"). And those mandatory statutes naturally bound the partners, starting with the *octroi* or creation privilege,[32] which was an imperative law that personified the company and established the framework of its activity according to the superior judgment of the monarch and his bureaucrats.[33] That is why their foundation laws often included more matters than was strictly necessary. For example, the Bank of San Carlos included the first general regulation of bills and notes that was known in Spain.[34] In addition, although the shareholders, or the corporate body that was established for that purpose, developed the internal regulations of the company, their confirmation pertained to the crown.[35]

5 The Kingdom as Corporation

Contract vs. *status*, one could thus conclude *à la* Maine. *Status* is a term that suggests predetermined rights and obligations, a pre-existing complex that is imposed upon the subjects who adhere to it. In this regard, it certainly helps in understanding the genesis of privileged companies and the secondary

32 The privilege was so inherent to this type of company that it helped name it: "[*a*] *Germanis vero*"—warned Bachoff von Echt in *De eo quod iustum est circa commercia inter gentes*, 41—"*privilegierte Compagnien vel, vti vulgo loquuntur, octroyrte Compagnien a voce ista belgica octroy, quae idem denotat ac permissio, nuncupari solent*." ("By Germans they should be called *privilegierte Compagnien* or, as they are commonly called, *octroyrte Compagnien*, after the Dutch word *octroy*, which means "permission"").

33 In addition, the privilege could only be interpreted by the prince who granted it: Bachoff von Echt, *De eo quod iustum est circa commercia*, 43.

34 Carlos Petit, "Signos financieros y cosas mercantiles, o los descubiertos de la Ilustración cambiaria," in Vito Piergiovanni (ed.), *The Growth of the Bank as Institution and the Development of Money-Business Law* (Berlin: Duncker & Humblot, 1993), 224–310, here 301 *seq.* The Royal Decree of the *Compañía de Filipinas* (12 July 1803) included, among other things, the concession of port liberty to Manila and the concession of free passages to professors and craftsmen (s. 44–45): Rico, *Las Reales Compañías*, 36 *seq.*

35 Cf. Royal Decree of the *Compañía de Barcelona*, s. 20. The *iuris communis* rule was applicable to the *potestas condere statuta* of corporations with minor degrees of jurisdiction: "Statuti delle arti nella dottrina del diritto commune" (1964), in Antonio Padoa Schioppa, *Saggi di storia del diritto commerciale* (Milan: LED, 1992), 11–62.

position that the partners held within that framework. The merely derived commercial nature of those associations of distinct political content inspired certain metaphors that philosophers used to explain the new social thinking:

> A kingdom is comparable to a corporation. Because the latter is subject to the narrow rules of trade, there is no reason to claim from each partner less than what has been earned, or more than what was lost, in proportion to the shares in the common mass; directors have no authority to undertake excessive spending, or to diminish what is necessary for the good of the company, but instead they have to maintain its existence and increase its prosperity.[36]

The comparison is admirable. The corporate metaphor served in the first place to attribute to the ruler the responsibility for collective interests. He was thus depicted as an attentive server of the company-nation and of the partner-citizens. Whether a sign of the times or a simple coincidence, the fact is that the Spanish king referred to himself at the time as the "supreme state administrator" (s. 8, royal letter-patent of 14 January 1783). The image further served to attribute positions and responsibilities within the company in accordance with the stock portion of the shareholder. This reflected a new rationality that was based on the equalitarian *actio pro socio*, and it imposed itself on the old estates.

However, it also revealed the consequences of commutative justice, which excluded from the *res publica* those who did not possess any shares. This was the painful result of the metaphor, as expressed in one of the *Patriotischen Phantasien* of German scholar Justus Möser, "*Der Bauernhof als eine Aktie betra-*

36 "*Un reino es comparable a una compañía de accionistas, sujetas a las estrechas reglas del comercio, que no hay razón para repetir a cada uno menos de lo que se gana, ni más de lo que se pierde, a proporción de sus acciones que tenga en la masa común; ni en los directores hay autoridad para hacer gastos superfluos, ni menos para escasear los necesarios al bien de la compañía, tanto para mantener su existencia como para aumentar su prosperidad*": León de Arroyal (1755–1813), *Cartas económico-políticas al Conde de Lerena* ..., José Caso (ed.) (Oviedo: Universidad de Oviedo, 1971), *ad litteram* v, 128–129. On this thinker, who can be classified as protoliberal, see Pablo Fernández Albaladejo, "León de Arroyal: Del Sistema de Rentas a la Buena Constitución," in Emiliano Fernández de Pinedo (ed.), *Haciendas forales y Hacienda Real. Homenaje a D. Miguel Artola y D. Felipe Ruiz Martín* (Bilbao: Universidad del País Vasco, 1990), 95–111.

chtet" ("The farm considered as share").[37] Without going into the full details of the text,[38] it is enough to note that privileged companies offered the author a model that helped explain the origin of the state and the political position that was reserved for the citizen. Thus, those problems that had not been addressed yet, or that had been incoherently addressed by the majority, could be better understood thanks to company law. For instance, slaves would be presented as men without shares (or rights) in the common body and thus legitimately excluded from representative mechanisms. This was only a step away from the ambiguous experience of primitive liberalism, where the constant demand for equality would call for the image of the shareholder as a justification of the unequal enjoyment of civic rights.[39]

Comparative constitutional history offers a number of instances of colonial companies that transformed into political entities. However, the analysis of the cases of Rhode Island, the Bermudas, or Connecticut would take us too far. Instead, we will turn our attention to a pending matter that is the limited liability of shareholding companies.

---

37 "Der Bauernhof als eine Aktie betrachtet," (1774) in Justus Möser, *Sämtliche Werke. II: Patriotische Phantasien und Zugehöriges*, L. Shirmeier and W. Kohlschmidt (eds.), vol. 3/6 (Oldemburg: Stalling, 1958), 255–270 (no. 63).

38 Thus the relation between agrarian property and the primitive social pact, according to the Möserian reconstruction of the hypothetical Germanic past, distinguishes the author from other scholars. Cf. Frederick C. Beiser, *The German Historicist Tradition* (Oxford: OUP, 2011), 9 *seq*. Also, Jerry Z. Muller, *The Mind and the Market. Capitalism in Western Thought* (New York: Anchor Books, 2003), especially chapter 4: "The Market as Destroyer of Culture."

39 Emmanuel J. Sieyès, *Proemio a la Constitución* (1789), in Ramón Máiz Suárez (ed.), *Escritos y discursos de la Revolución* (Madrid: Centro de Estudios Constitucionales, 1990), 101: "[*t*]*odos pueden disfrutar de las ventajas de la sociedad, pero solamente aquellos que contribuyan al mantenimiento de los poderes públicos son como los verdaderos accionistas de la gran empresa social*" ("all can enjoy the advantages of society, but only those who contribute to the maintenance of public authorities are considered as true shareholders of the great social enterprise"). Also, Edmund Burke, *Reflections on the Revolution in France* (London, Johnson, 1790; consulted edition Buffalo (NY): Prometheus, 1987), 100–101: "[s]ociety (...) it is a partnership in all science; a partnership in all art; a partnership in every virtue, and in all perfection (...) between those who are living, those who are dead, and those who are to be born," which brings to mind the "perpetual succession" of corporations in *common law*. From a different ideological stance: Thomas Paine, *Dissertations on First Principles of Government* (1795), in M. Foot and I. Kramer (eds.), *Thomas Paine Reader* (London: Penguin, 1987), 462.

6 The "Limited" Liability Question

Too many (often hasty) conclusions have been drawn with regard to the legal consequences that privileged companies had. Distinct assets, their corporate personality, and the ease with which shares could be sold limited the obligations of the shareholders to their original contribution. It has thus been asserted that the essential characteristic of the modern joint-stock partnership can also be traced back to the legal model of its direct predecessor.[40] Notwithstanding this, no proof beyond dogmatic reasoning has been successfully presented to support such allegations.[41]

The absence of provisions in this regard in the foundation laws indicate, in our view, that the Enlightenment culture dismissed such an essential aspect as partner responsibility within the framework of those privileged entities.[42] It has been asserted that the establishment of a mandatory regime that ran contrary to common regulations was intended to compensate for the risks inherent

---

40 Francesco Galgano, *Historia del derecho mercantil* (Barcelona: Laia, 1981), 7 *seq*. In "¿Crisis de la sociedad anónima?," *Revista de Estudios Politicos* 49 (1950), 51–106, Federico de Castro provides an intelligent analysis that is contrary to the establishment of a sort of continuity between privileged companies and the modern joint-stock partnership, in particular 77 *seq*.

41 María Jesús Matilla Quizá, "Las compañías privilegiadas en la España del Antiguo Régimen," in Miguel Artola (ed.), *La Hacienda del Antiguo Régimen*, vol. 4 (Madrid: Alianza, 1982), 323–401, at 340 *seq*. However, the clause of the *Real Compañía Marítima* (1789) that is invoked there contains a yardstick for the distribution of results. The clause concerning the *Compañía de Seguros Marítimos* (1800) is more ambiguous; the description of the capital ("[e]*l fondo capital de esta compañía será de pesos setecientos cincuenta mil de 128 cuartos cada uno*", "the capital will be of 750,000 pesos divided in 128 shares") was accompanied by a warning ("*sin más responsabilidad en los accionistas que la del número de acciones en que se halla interesado*", "without any liability beyond the number of their shares") that perhaps only implied the prohibition of contributions (see *infra*). In any case, given that it involved the insurance business, where the proclamation of unlimited liability was usual (cf. Jerònia Pons, "Compañías de seguro marítimo en España (1650–1800)," *Hispania: Revista española de historia* 67/225 (2007), 271–294), it would make sense to establish the opposite principle clearly.

42 A reference in the matter thus rightfully noted: "*So wichtig er uns heute für die Abgrenzung der Aktiengesellschaft von anderen Handelsgesellschaften erscheint*" that limited liability "*war nicht die treibende Kraft*" ("Even though it seems for us today so important as criterion to distinguish the corporation from other commercial companies, limited liability was not a driving force"). Cf. Karl Lehmann, *Die geschichtliche Entwicklung des Aktienrechts bis zum Code de commerce* (Berlin: Heymann, 1895), 23.

in the colonial adventure that the "commercial class" assumed.[43] Now, besides the fact that the presence of traders in those institutions was often limited (not only in Spain), my understanding is that the privileged condition was fundamentally due to the very existence of the corporation. There certainly existed other concessions and monopolies (especially in matters of navigation and fiscal taxation), but it seems to me that the main characteristic of those companies lay in the subjectivity that was granted by the *lex privata* promulgated by the sovereign. It was "the particular constitution" of the company (as expressed by Francisco Cabarrús in reference to the Real Banco de San Carlos, 1782) that conferred upon those companies their most outstanding characteristic.[44] It corresponded to that *privata lex* to establish the obligations of the partner and of the administrators (and for which the type of business would doubtless be relevant),[45] or to remain silent on the matter, as would be the case with regard to the Hispanic companies. Warnings such as [*a*]*ucun Actionnaire*

43 Francesco Galgano, *Historia del derecho mercantil*, 77. However, according to Montanari, *Impresa e responsabilità. Sviluppo storico e disciplina positive* (Milan: Giuffrè, 1990), 162: "[*l*]*'indagine storica sembra* (…) *smentire l'opinione che vede nella responsabilità limitata un 'privilegio' concesso dal sovrano alla sempre più potente classe mercantile*" ("historical inquiry (…) seems to deny the opinion that sees in limited liability a "privilege" granted by the sovereign to the merchant class that became increasingly powerful").

44 The edict of the "*Imperiale privilegiata Compagnia orientale*" (29 December 1719), which was approved by Carlos VI, is very eloquent: "*statuto composto di vari articoli* (…) *che debe costantemente servire come legge fondamentale e norma di detta Compagnia*," "*contratto e statuto fondamentale della Compagnia*," "*sua ordinaria legge fondamentale e regola obbligatoria* (…) [*che*] *verrà poi per parte Nostra dovunque efficacemente coadiuvata e sorretta*," etc. "bylaws are composed of various articles (…) that should constantly serve as a fundamental law of the company (…) the contract and fundamental statute of the Company (…) its ordinary fundamental law and mandatory rule (…) [which] will be then for Ourselves wherever effectively assisted and supported". Cf. Paolo Ungari (ed.), *Statuti di compagnie e società azionarie italiane (1638–1808): Per la storia delle società per azioni in Italia* (Milan: Giuffrè, 1993), 40–50.

45 For example, according to state provisions in New York and New Jersey, the liability of the shareholder was unlimited for banking companies. See Carlos Petit Calvo, "Ignorancias y otras historias, o sea, responsabilidades limitadas," *Anuario de historia del derecho español* 60 (1990), 497–508, here 501. During the eighteenth and nineteenth centuries in Scotland (prior to the 1879 legal reform) there existed three banks with limitation according to the letter granted by Parliament (the Bank of Scotland, the Royal Bank of Scotland, and the British Linen Company), whereas most existed without it (the so-called "free banks"); only the latter could issue bills. See Jack Carr, Sherry Glied and Frank Mathewson, "Unlimited Liability and Free Banking in Scotland: A Note," *The Journal of Economic History* 49/4 (1989), 974–978.

ne sera responsable au delà de sa mise ("shareholders are only liable for their investments"), which was inserted with no further explanation in the letter-patent of the *Société Imperiale pour le commerce Asiatique de Trieste et d'Anvers* (1781), were exceptions.[46]

In fact, it is not easy to establish on the basis of the foundational laws whether the shareholders were beyond the reach of creditors, and less so whether they were exonerated from having to increase their participation with approved contributions to settle their debts. A provision of the *Compagnie des Indes Orientales* (1674) nevertheless demonstrates that that was by no means extraordinary:

> Neither the directors nor individuals shareholders shall be held—by any cause or pretext whatsoever—to provide any money beyond that for which they will be obliged at the first establishment of the Company, either by way of supplement or otherwise.[47]

My understanding, contrary to Galgano's, is that the norm forbade recapitalization imposed *par manière de supplément ou autrement*.[48] The exact opposite occurred in the *Dr. Salomon* vs. *The Hamborough Company* (1671) case. Faced with the insufficiency of the corporate capital to handle a credit, the lords decided that the shareholders would contribute with new sums that were proportional to their shares. A few years later (cf. *Harvey* vs. *East India Company*, 1700), that ruling, which now constituted a precedent, allowed the conclusion that "the members in their private persons were made liable, the Company having no goods".[49] Thus, even when third parties lacked the means to pursue the shareholder, they could at least demand that the directors agree to request contributions and deal with the debts. The practice of recording the shares as registered securities in books provided for that purpose certainly allowed for

---

46 Ungari, *Statuti di compagnie e società azionarie*, 189.

47 "[*l*]*es directeurs ni les particuliers intéressés ne pourront être tenus—par quelque cause ou prétexte que ce soit—de fournir aucune somme au delà de celle pour laquelle ils seront obligés dans le premier établissement de la Compagnie, soit par manière de supplément ou autrement*".

48 It is thus asserted by Lévy-Bruhl, *Histoire juridique*, 244, in particular the cases examined at 23 *seq*. The author therefore concludes that "*les actionnaires de la Compagnie des Indes Orientales sont responsables in infinitum*" ("the shareholders in the Compagnie des Indes Orientales are responsible jointly and severally"), at 245.

49 Stefania Gialdroni, *East India Company. Una storia giuridica (1600–1708)* (Bologna: Il Mulino, 2011), 233 *seq*.

the identification of those affected. The triumph of limited liability in English corporate law would only arrive in the second half of the nineteenth century.[50]

Were there similar cases in Spain? Here, as in the rest of Europe, the silence of the *octroi* with regard to liability is remarkable, especially if one bears in mind that the foundational laws contained provisions aimed at protecting corporate assets against the particular creditors of the shareholders. Nevertheless, as far as we know, the failure of privileged companies was never addressed with compensation through contributions. For example, the crisis of the *Compañía guipuzcoana de Caracas* following the adoption of the Free Trade regulation (1788) and the war with Great Britain (1780–1783) led to the establishment of the *Real Compañía de Filipinas* (1785), where the assets of the Guipuzcoan company converged.[51] Something similar occurred with the *Banco de San Carlos* (1782), which was re-established in 1829 as the Banco de San Fernando, which received cash injections and good bills of exchange.[52] Although there is no proof that when those companies were liquidated, their shareholders responded directly before third parties (not even before those who made up for the initial capital insufficiency by means of a loan or census), the solution provided was in any case factual and does not allow us to identify the existence of a precise legal norm. When the High Court of the Dauphiné faced litigation that affected the *Compagnies du Corail*, the judges ruled *qu'un associé peut obliger les autres associez, comme la Cour avait déja prejugé (…) les participes solvables fuerent condamnez à payer la part même de leurs associez insolvables*[53] ("a partner may

50 H.A. Shannon, "The Coming of General Limited Liability," (1931) in E.M. Carus-Wilson (ed.), *Essays in Economic History*, vol. 1 (London: Arnold, repr. 1966), 358–379; Peter Stein, "Nineteenth Century English Company Law and Theories of Legal Personality," *Quaderni Fiorentini per la storia del pensiero giuridico moderno* 12 (1983), 503–519.

51 In 1796, the Caracas partners were paid a little over 377 *reales* per share over a total value of 500 pesos, that is, 7500 *reales*. Cf. María Lourdes Díaz-Trechuelo, *La Real Compañía de Filipinas* (Seville: 1965), 5 *seq*. At the same time, the liquidation of the new company was prolonged until 1840, but Díaz-Trechuelo, *La Real Compañía de Filipinas*, 149 *seq*., does not offer additional information.

52 Matthias Frey, *Die spanische Aktiengesellschaft im 18. Jahrhundert und unter dem Código de Comercio von 1829* (Frankfurt am Main: Lang, 1999), 24 *seq*., and 303 *seq*., on the royal decree of establishment; Pedro Tedde de Lorca, *El Banco de San Carlos (1782–1829)* (Madrid: Alianza, 1988), 358 *seq*. The *Compañía de La Habana* also perished because of its recalcitrant debtors: Monserrat Gárate Ojanguren, *Comercio ultramarino e Ilustración. La Real Compañía de La Habana* (Donostia: Amigos del País, 1993), 29 *seq*.

53 Mehr, *Societas und universitas*, 330. See at 344 *seq*. on the obligations for shareholders to assume capital increases in the case of "*quelque accident extraordinaire et imprévu*" ("for any extraordinary or unforeseen accident"), and 34 *seq*., on the liability of the partner in

obligate other associates, as the Court had already decided (…) creditworthy participants were condemned to pay for other associates").

In any case, it would be quite a few years before we would come across such declarations as those that were included in the statutes of the above-mentioned bank of San Fernando: [c]*onforme á las disposiciones del Código de Comercio sobre las Sociedades anónimas, la responsabilidad de los accionistas en operaciones del Banco se reducirá al importe de las acciones que tengan en él* ("according to the sections of the Commercial Code in matter of corporations, shareholders' liability in Bank operations is limited to the sum of their shares") (R.C., 9 July 1829, s. 7).

7 Partnerships by Shares

At the time, the Code was still in *vacatio*, but the matter is actually irrelevant. Indeed, the shareholding company would prove to be the ideal formula for the mobilization of resources and the pursuit of ambitious commercial objectives.[54] Setting the royal companies of the eighteenth century aside, the formula led to the existence of associations in which the possibility of investing capital by subscribing low quotas would allow anyone—*las personas de qualquier estado, sexo y calidad* ("persons of any class, sex and condition"), as it is stated in the founding documents of a Compañía Valenciana (1745)—to be interested in doing business. It can be said that those companies, far more than the limited partnership, helped finance commercial activities with non-business money.[55] Given that the general and corporate laws, in the same way as the Bilbao ordinances, remained silent with regard to this arrangement, the contracts constitute our main source of information. At this stage, it is interesting to consider the available data on commercial practice in a number of Spanish localities, amongst which the seafaring city of Cadiz stands out because of its objective importance. The shareholding companies found there from 1763 onward, all belonging to the insurance industry, responded, according to García-Baquero,[56] to the characteristics that were listed by Lévy-Bruhl:

---

the external relations of the company and the presence of what Lévy-Bruhl referred to as "*fausses commandites*" ("deceitful *commandites*").

54 José Martínez Gijón, "Las sociedades por acciones en el derecho español del siglo XVIII," in *Historia del derecho mercantil* (Seville: Universidad de Sevilla, 1999), 575–596.

55 Ricardo Franch, *Crecimiento comercial y enriquecimiento Burgués en la Valencia del siglo XVIII* (Valencia: Alfons el Magnánim, 1986), 281.

56 Antonio García-Baquero, *Cádiz y el Atlántico, 1717–1778. El comercio colonial español bajo*

a high amount of capital (the figure of half a million pesos was frequent); a precise description of that capital in the contract (fifty shares of ten thousand pesos, in the same case); and the company name (often a religious one). The existence of assemblies and boards and of directors and employees who ran the business is also worth mentioning.[57] The negotiability of the shares—a "capitalist" trait—was nevertheless non-existent, thus leading to the conclusion that those companies were

> A sort of hybrid form, a transitional type with some typically capitalist notes (...) but without that final stroke that serves to distinguish these companies from personalistic partnerships, namely: freely negotiation of their shares.[58]

Notwithstanding this, it is not possible to draw general conclusions when the transfer of shares, obviously hampered by the absence of sheets representing the capital, was entirely dependent on the corporate agreements. That which was absent in Cadiz, perhaps to offer an image of solvency, given that it was about maritime insurance, was sometimes possible in Valencia, as in the example of a company whose shareholders *en qualquier tiempo [podrían] transportar, vender o enajenar sus acciones con tal de que avisen a los Directores con seis días de antelación para hacer los asientos correspondientes al nuevo interesado* (*Compañía Valenciana*, 1745);[59] ("At any time the partner [could] carry, sell or dispose of its shares, reminding the Directors six days prior to the entry of the new partner"). From this perspective, "joint stock companies in the eighteenth century constitute a generic type of mercantile company, with the laws of each company (...) determining the specific nature of it, be personalistic or capitalistic."[60]

---

el monopolio gaditano, vol. 1 (Cadiz: Fundación Municipal de Cultura del Ayuntamiento 1988), 412 *seq*.

57 In addition to the previous, *see* Franch, *Crecimiento comercial*, 283 *seq*.

58 "(...) *una especie de híbridos, como unas sociedades de transición en las que se dan ya algunas notas típicamente capitalistas* (...) *pero en las que falta el trazo definitivo que sirve para distinguir a estas sociedades de las personalistas, a saber: la libre disposición por parte de los asociados de sus acciones con vistas a su posible negociación o venta*": García-Baquero, *Cádiz y el Atlántico*, 420.

59 In terms of the 11th clause of a "*Compañía Valenciana*" (1745), see Franch, *Crecimiento comercial*, 282, where other examples are mentioned.

60 "(...) *las sociedades por acciones del siglo* XVIII *constituyen un tipo genérico de sociedad mercantil, siendo los estatutos de cada sociedad* (...) *los que determinan la naturaleza*

The clauses that dealt with the liability of shareholders were more uniform in character. However, the genetic relation between those shareholding companies and the modern limited liability company should nevertheless still be refuted. Except in a very few contracts, such as the case of the *María Santísima Nuestra Señora de las Mercedes* (1777) company in Cadiz,[61] the statutes insisted that the shareholders were obliged to satisfy common debts beyond their contributions, as can be deduced from the clause on capital outlay and the obligation of distributing proportionally amongst the shareholders the sums required to settle the existing debts of the company.[62] I believe a careful con-

---

específica, personalista o capitalista de la misma": José Martínez Gijón, "Las sociedades por acciones," 588.

61 "[*E*]*ntendiéndose esta responsabilidad y obligación mancomunada, hasta en la concurrente cantidad del fondo en que deba cada cual contribuir para dichos quebrantos con los diez mil o veinte mil pesos importe de la una o dos acciones en que se han interesado, y no más: de forma que si sucediese que las pérdidas y quebrantos de los seguros y quiebras de los compañeros excediesen el valor del fondo, no quedarán en semejante caso obligados los otorgantes, sino solamente a cubrir y pagar las tales pérdidas y quebrantos hasta en la cantidad de la acción o acciones de su cargo*" ("This responsibility and joint liability should extend over the respective amount of the fund to which each partner should contribute, for the mentioned losses, with ten thousand or twenty thousand pesos, for one or two of their shares, and no more: so that if it happened that losses due to insurance underwriting or bankruptcy of the partners were for more than the value of the fund, partners are held to cover and pay for such losses only up to the amount of their shares"): García-Baquero, *Cádiz y el Atlántico*, 424.

62 "*En caso de omissión y morosidad de alguno de los Compañeros en contribuir su contingente*"—it was agreed in the company "María Santísima Nuestra Señora en el misterio de su Purísima Concepción y el patriarca señor San Joseph" (1763)—"*dexando, como dexan el derecho a salvo para repetir contra él y sus bienes la satisfacción de su importe, quedan y se constituyen los otorgantes junto de mancomún a voz de uno, y cada uno de por sí, y por el todo insolidum* (...) *y se obligan a la responsabilidad y efectiva paga y entrega de todas y cada una de las cantidades, que en virtud de esta Escriptura, y a nombre y por cuenta de esta Compañía se aseguren a fin de que sin embargo de la omissión, que se experimente en alguno de los socios, no padezca detrimento ni decadencia el crédito de ella*" ("in case of omitted or delayed contribution, aside from the right to file claims against the partner or his assets for satisfaction of the investment, partners are jointly liable (...) and they engage themselves to the liability and effective payment and delivery of all or any quantity which according to this text is required, and they are held and mutually ensured for the capital and account of the company, so that notwithstanding the omission by one of the partners there is no prejudice or decline of the company's credit"), which, according to García-Baquero, *Cádiz y el Atlántico*, 421, followed a repeated form. In contrast, the Valencian contracts were silent on any form of liability: Franch, *Crecimiento comercial*, 286.

sultation of the legal documents would allow for the discovery of those links between the shareholder and the external creditors.

8 From Partnerships to Corporations in the Commercial Code (1829) and the Company Law (1848)

The ordinances of 1737 and the last royal companies survived until the beginning of the liberal regime. During the last period of the rule of Fernando VII, a Code of Commerce (1829) was finally adopted in Spain. Although its provisions concerning companies owed much to the *Code de commerce*, they nevertheless contained two important novelties.

The first concerned the classification of commercial companies in a way that was unknown to the old Hispanic *ius mercatorum*. Despite a number of errors and hesitations, three categories of commercial companies were nevertheless identified (in addition to joint accounts), including the *compañía anónima* (i.e., joint-stock company). Notwithstanding the manner in which that designation had previously been used, the exceptional concession of privileges allowed by the code (s. 294) evokes a continuity with the royal companies. However, the liability of the shareholder was now clearly established, even if the limited liability still did not constitute, not even in the *Code de commerce*, a decisive element of the legal definition.[63]

The second innovation was a novelty both with regard to the tradition of privileged companies and to more recent regulations that had exerted their influence on the first Spanish Code of Commerce. This can be seen in section 293, which announced the obligation of presenting the founding statutes to the local tribunal of commerce, where they would be subjected to a brief control of legality that was a mandatory, prior, step for the company's registration at the *registro público del comercio*, as a *condición particular de las compañías anónimas*. This condition underlined the contractual nature of the new limited

63 "*Puede contraerse la compañía,*" stated s. 265, "3°. *Creándose un fondo por acciones determinadas para girarlo sobre uno ó muchos objetos que den nombre á la empresa social; cuyo manejo se encargue á mandatarios ó administradores amovibles á voluntad de los socios.*" In turn, s. 278 noted that "[*l*]*os socios no responden* (…) *de las obligaciones de la compañía anónima, sino hasta la cantidad del interés que tengan en ella*" ("the company can be agreed (…) by creating a fund of shares for investing in one or many objects that give name to the enterprise; the management of which is entrusted to agents who can be removed at the will of the shareholders". S. 278 states: "shareholders do not respond (…) for the obligations except up to the amount of the interest they have in corporation").

company in contrast to the institutional past of the old privileged company. However, it also side-lined the solution contained in the Napoleonic code, the approval by governmental decree of the establishment of the limited company (s. 37 of the *Code de commerce*). In fact, although the 1830s were marked by the protests against the Spanish code, which were accompanied by numerous texts (1837, 1838, 1839) and by the vain hope of the imminent adoption of the Civil Code (the 1836 project), the unique regime established in section 293 would pave the way for an almost constant special legislation.

In this regard, the 1848 Companies Law, which introduced the system of governmental control of corporations, is worth mentioning. The measure came as a response to a speculation fever that had led to the severe 1846–1847 crisis. The adverse financial situation, which was generalized in Europe during the second revolutionary cycle (1848), was further aggravated in Spain because of the ease with which shareholding companies could be created in the absence of capital that was adjusted to their business objectives.

> When this hobby grew [i.e. the foundation of corporations] to a fever pitch from 1845 to 48, when hundreds of companies were founded with a fabulous capital and different objects for all kinds of industry, including mining, agriculture, irrigation, roads, construction, factories, water supplies, grains, fish, gas and even pastry and sweets ... The most fantastic programs, the most poetic emblems or mythological and allegorical titles were, it can be said, exhausted in those sublime associations; and the most ambitious projects offered to the astonished country led it to think of itself as being on the eve of a magical transformation into an earthly paradise. But unfortunately the case came which gave effect to those ridiculous perspectives, and they were scattered as images of make belief, or they went up in smoke, the Iris and the Auroras, the Phoenix, the Ceres, the Foresighted, the Fertilizer, the Advertizing, the Promotion, the Persevering, the Illustration, the Ermine, the Fire, the Mercury, the Probability, the Commerce, the Villa de Madrid, the Hispano-Filipino, the Great Antilla, the Regenerating, the Fortuna, the Hope, the Happiness and other theological virtues, gifts of the Holy Spirit and Olympian deities.[64]

64 "*Cuando creció esta manía hasta un punto febril fue desde 1845 al 48*"—as is recorded by a contemporal witness—"*en términos que no bajaron de ciento las sociedades improvisadas con un capital fabuloso y con objetos diferentes aplicados a todo género de industria, de minería, de agricultura, de riego, de caminos, de construcción, de fábricas, de consumos, de abastecimientos de aguas, de granos, de pescados, de gas y hasta de hojaldre y caramelos* (...). *Los programas más fantásticos, los emblemas más poéticos, los títulos mitológicos*

Satire aside, the statistics were as follows. Between 1844, when "moderate" liberals reached government, and 1847, around fifty shareholding companies were established in Madrid, from which the following stood out: 7 insurance companies; 11 banks and lending companies: 9 wholesale companies; and 8 transportation companies, with a nominal capital of around 3,649,000,000 *reales*, of which 927,247,250 were disbursed, that is, around a fourth part. There were also many fabulous projects that promised to mobilize many more hundreds of millions.[65]

The solutions contained in the Code had already been generally evoked:

> It is a particular condition of corporations that the deeds of their founding and all regulations upon administration and management, have to be examined by the Commercial Court of the jurisdiction where it is founded; and without the Court's approval the agreement is not implemented.[66]

This implied, in practical terms, a liberty of constitution, which was unknown to Europe.[67] The author of the Code of Commerce would claim that this option responded to the desire to implement the intrinsically capitalist formula in

---

y alegóricos quedaron, puede decirse, agotados en aquellas sublimes asociaciones; y los proyectos más gigantescos ofrecidos bajo su consigna al pais atónito hicieron que éste se creyera en vísperas de verse transformado mágicamente en un paraíso terrenal. Pero desgraciadamente llegó el caso de hacer efectivas aquellas risueñas perspectivas, y se disiparon como cuadros disolventes, o resolvieron en humo los Iris y Auroras, los Fénix, las Ceres, Previsora, Fertilizadora, Publicidad, Fomento, Perseverante, Ilustración, Armiño, Fuego, Mercurio, Probabilidad, Comercio, Villa de Madrid, Hispano-filipino, Grande Antilla, Confianza, Regeneradora, Fortuna, Proveedora, Esperanza, Felicidad y demás virtudes teologales, dones del Espíritu Santo y Deidades olímpicas": Ramón Mesonero Romanos, *Nuevo manual histórico-topográfico-estadístico y descripcion de Madrid* (Madrid: Yenes, 1854), 555–556, cited by Angel Bahamonde Magro and Julián Toro Mérida, *Burguesía, especulación y cuestión social en el Madrid del siglo XIX* (Madrid: Siglo Veintiuno de España, 1978), 200–201. On the protagonists of those establishments, see Alfonso Otazu, *Los Rothschild y sus socios en España, 1820–1850* (Madrid: O. Hs., 1987).

65 Data collected by Bahamonde and Toro, *Burguesía, especulación y cuestión social en el Madrid*, 198, on the basis of Madoz' *Diccionario geográfico*.

66 S. 293: "[*e*]*s condición particular de las compañías anónimas que las escrituras de su establecimiento y todos los reglamentos que han de regir para su administración y manejo directivo y económico, se han de sujetar al examen del Tribunal de Comercio del territorio en donde se establezca; y sin su aprobación no podrán llevarse a efecto*".

67 Bernhard Grossfeld, "Die rechtspolitische Beurteilung der Aktiengesellschaft im 19. Jahrhundert," in Helmut Coing and Walter Wilhelm (eds.), *Wissenschaft und Kodifikation des*

Spain. His claim, for which he offered no basis, nevertheless seems to have been driven by interest, or rather, by the desire to excuse himself.

Amidst the failure to adopt another code, the law on joint-stock companies was adopted on 28 January, 1848. Beforehand, during the worst period of the crisis, a royal order that was issued on 9 February 1847, ordained that the tribunals of commerce were to abstain from authorizing the establishment of new companies while the work was still being done on the reform of the system in force. This temporary decision was reinforced by another royal decree adopted on 15 April, which granted the government the authority to approve the constitution of limited companies, while the project it had submitted shortly before to the Cortes (27 February 1847) was being processed.[68] Before long, an extensive decree was adopted (Royal Decree of 17 February 1848).

The parliamentary material pertaining to the 1848 law, which it took the Cortes almost a year to approve, has been analyzed by María Jesús Matilla. But the two studies that have been published by Francisco de Cárdenas concerning the decree that was adopted in April 1847, and the ministerial project, respectively, are less well-known.[69] In general terms, both Cárdenas' proposals and

Privatrechts im 19. Jahrhundert, IV: Eigentum und industrielle Entwicklung, Wettbewerbsordnung und Wettbewerbsrecht (Frankfurt am Main: Klostermann, 1979), 236–254; Anne Lefebvre-Teillard, *La société anonyme au XIX siècle. Du Code de Commerce à la loi de 1867: Histoire d'un instrument juridique du développement capitaliste* (Paris: PUF, 1985); Antonio Padoa Schioppa, "Le società commerciali nei progetti di codificazione del Regno Italico (1806–1807)," (1977) in Antonio Padoa Schioppa, *Saggi di storia del diritto commerciale* (Milan: LED, 1992), 113–135; Claes Peterson, "Juristische Person und Begrenzte Haftung der Aktionäre. Ein Beitrag zur Geschichte des Aktienrechts in Schweden," *Quaderni fiorentini* 11–12 (1982–1983), 321–387; H.A. Shannon, "The Limited Companies of 1866–1883," in E.M. Carus-Wilson (ed.), *Essays in Economic History*, vol. 3 (London: Arnold, 1933; repr. 1966), 380–405; Paolo Ungari, *Profilo storico del diritto delle anonime in Italia. Lezioni* (Rome: Bulzoni, 1974), 29 *seq*.

68 In January 1846, Minister Armero presented a project on companies before the Senate. However, it was abandoned following a change of government members: cfr. María Jesús Matilla Quiza, "La regulación del sistema capitalista en España (1829–1923): la constitución de las sociedades por acciones," *Estudios de historia social* 38–39 (1986), 7–56, in particular 16–17.

69 Francisco de Cárdenas, "Examen del proyecto de ley sobre sociedades por acciones," in Francisco de Cárdenas, *El Derecho moderno. Revista de jurisprudencia y administración*, vol. 1 (Madrid: Rodriguez de Rivera, 1847), 126–145; Francisco de Cárdenas, "Legislación actual sobre sociedades por acciones," in Francisco de Cárdenas, *El Derecho moderno: Revista de jurisprudencia y administración*, vol. 1 (Madrid: Rodriguez de Rivera, 1847), 256–268.

the governmental project and April decree coincided with regard to the objective of the reform, which was to introduce the authorization system in Spain. The latter was approved by a majority of the parliament (s. 1: *No se podrá constituir ninguna compañía mercantil, cuyo capital se divida en todo o en parte en acciones, sino en virtud de una ley o de un Real decreto*, "It shall not be constituted any commercial company, whose capital is divided wholly or partly in shares, but under a law or a royal decree"), which based its arguments on a criticism of the codified regime, cast in years, as Cárdenas said, *en que el capital nacional crecía lenta y pesadamente, en que se necesitaba más bien promover el tráfico por todos los medios posibles que cuidarse del abuso que pudiera hacerse de ellos* ("when the national wealth grew slowly and heavenly, and when it was needed to promote the economic traffic by all possible means, rather than to consider the abuses that might be made of it"). However,

> thanks to the secularization of communitarian and ecclesiastical estates, the reforms made fifteen years ago and the strong impulse that gave the revolution to the ideas, to the customs and all the elements of our civilization, national wealth has increased rapidly.[70]

The situation would appear to be completely different by the middle of the century. Within that context, limited liability in companies would come to be understood for the first time as a sort of privilege that justified that its establishment was controlled. It was also about preserving the activities of minor traders, which explains the legal measures, in section 4, against the monopoly of basic products. Although this regulation was criticized by some, who suggested the adoption of the normative system (1849) instead, the idea of public intervention continued to dominate.

There were certain nuances in the manner in which the new solutions were articulated. The extent of public intervention in the authorization of companies was a subject of debate. Although the provisional governmental regulations, the project, and the parliamentary opinion consistently referred to joint-stock companies and limited partnerships, which explains section 1 of the law (*cuyo capital en todo o en parte se divida en acciones*, "the capital of which is divided, as a whole or in part, in shares"), some progressive voices (*Ordax Avecilla*) sought to exclude the latter from the strict legal requirements

70 "(…) [*m*]*erced a la desamortización civil y eclesiástica, a las reformas hechas de quince años a esta parte y al impulso violento que ha dado la revolución a las ideas, a las costumbres y a todos los elementos de nuestra civilización, el capital nacional ha recibido un aumento rápido*".

for their authorization. This position found support in comparative law—including the French example, where it constituted the basis for capitalism—but nonetheless it was not widely shared. Cárdenas' suggestion of adopting a capital limit beyond which the authorization of the limited companies became necessary (200,000 *duros*), was barely echoed, thus impeding the adoption of an intermediate solution that would have encouraged the development of this company form, which at the time had acquired great importance in other countries.

A second controversial issue was the legal form of the governmental approval. Although the text that was approved by the Cortes accepted the decree as a mechanism of ordinary authorization, it nevertheless requested that a statute be resorted to in specific instances (s. 2: issuing banks, railroads, road and canal construction). Furthermore, the archaic possibility of privilege granting was upheld (s. 294 of the Code), but it now pertained to the legislative body.

In addition to the approval by decree or statute, other requirements were foreseen. The legal obsession with defining the object of the company was reflected in the emphasis that was placed on the exceptional nature of shareholding companies in addition to their causal nature—it was public utility that justified, by means of an authorization, the subjection of the company to the regime of limited liability (s. 4 *Ley*; s. 13,2 *Reglamento*) and of authorization.[71] That obsession is but a reflection of the historical period in which shareholding companies were being articulated and which the Spanish reform process sought to address. The suggestions that were put forward in the Cortes (Gonzalo Morón, Armendáriz) to exclude specific commercial branches from the scope of shareholding companies did not succeed. However, the government did commit to rejecting those companies that might violate the prohibition of monopolies.

The rules imposed on the capital reflected the fear of fictitious companies or investments that were disproportional to the object. Thus, it was mandatory to subscribe to (at least) half the capital (s. 7 *Ley*; s. 9 *Reglamento*) with letters of intent as to the acquisition of shares. That it was mandatory was underlined

71 s. 5 (Ley): "*Toda compañía por acciones, se constituirá precisamente para objetos determinados*", "any company by shares should have a precise object". See also Reglamento, s. 13,2: "*Las escrituras de fundación de las compañías mercantiles por acciones han de contener necesariamente: 3. El objeto o ramo de industria o de comercio a que exclusivamente ha de dedicarse la compañía*" ("the notarial documents of commercial companies by shares must necessarily contain: 3. The object or branch of industry or commerce of the company").

in the decree (s. 10). The crisis had led to the contemplation of an automatic dissolution in cases in which more than 60 per cent of the capital was lost.[72] However, the law limited itself to company inspection (s. 17), which could eventually lead to the suspension or annulment of the authorization that had been granted (s. 30 *Reglamento*). To this end, and in general terms with regard to the authorization, the decree placed its trust in the provincial governors or *jefes políticos* (right of inspection, s. 37–38 *Reglamento*; prior reports on the establishment proposals, s. 13–14 *Reglamento*).

Naturally, the regulations contained in the Code of Commerce still constituted the general law that acted in a subsidiary manner with regard to the new statute. The decree contained a number of explicit references to the 1829 text (s. 8: null nature of secret pacts; section 1,14: annual balance; etc.). However, given that the legislation on companies was limited, it would develop by means of special laws. Thus, section 2 *Reglamento* established that:

> it is an essential and common condition in all mercantile companies with shares that the partners have equal rights and participation in the profits of the company, distributed proportionally according to the number of shares held by them.[73]

This expressed an equalitarian principle that was further reflected in a number of contemporary proposals that advocated for the acceptance of a special category of shares ("industrial shares") in case of investment in patents or in the work itself. Section 33 of the decree contained another substantial rule with regard to the conditions for transferring shares, which were always registered securities (s. 12 *Ley*; s. 15 forbade shares to bearer in the absence of legal authorization). In short, the 1848 legislation introduced the system of

---

72 de Cárdenas, "Examen," 145: "*Cuando la pérdida ascienda al 60 por 100 del capital, se disolverá de derecho la compañía, y los gerentes o administradores son responsables personalmente respecto a los terceros interesados de las obligaciones que contrajeren, después que tuvieron o debieron tener conocimiento de la pérdida*" ("when the loss amounts to 60 per 100 of the stock, the company should be dissolved by law, and directors or managers are personally liable vis-à-vis third parties that entered into obligations with them, after the managers had or should have had knowledge of the loss"). The author's suggestion was to publicize, including by means of advertisements in the Gaceta, the loss of half of the capital.

73 "[s]*erá condición esencial y común en todas las sociedades mercantiles por acciones, que los socios tendrán iguales derechos y participación en los beneficios de la empresa, distribuyéndose proporcionalmente al número de acciones que posea cada socio*".

authorization of shareholding companies in Spain in terms that were strict but which were nevertheless quite common in the European landscape.

A comprehensive study of authorization rules has not yet been undertaken. What is mainly lacking is an analysis of the decrees (and laws) on authorization as an instrument around which the law on shareholding companies, which was barely dealt with in the Code or in special laws, was articulated. In short, we still need to determine whether the authorization system generated a commercial doctrine on companies similar to the French jurisprudence produced by the *Conseil d'État*.[74]

This future research work is further encouraged by the fact that the 1829 legislator, Pedro Sainz de Andino, was appointed a member of the Spanish Council of State as president of Department of Trade, Instruction, and Public Works, that is, of the section that was responsible for issuing opinions on the provisions that affected industrial and commercial activities, such as the decree of authorization of shareholding companies. In other words, the same person who conceived of the lax (rather formal) control system for joint-stock companies that was implemented by the tribunal of commerce also became, as of 1848, the main person in charge of the company authorization system that was established by governmental decree. That Andino made use of his position to filter information to his politician friends should not concern us here. It is enough to recall only that this occurred, as can be seen in his correspondence with Mª Cristina of Naples, queen widow of Fernando VII, and her second husband, Antonio Muñoz. It would be much more relevant to consult the files that are conserved at the archive of the *Consejo de Estado*. Indeed, the Council was not just about issuing the report regarding the decree of authorization; it acted as a full company police force that, for instance, looked into the opportunity of selecting determined company types, the liquidation of a limited company, the claims of the shareholders upon their invitation to a general junta, the reduction of capital, and many other similar matters that it would be important to approach with much attention at a future stage.

---

74 Anne Lefebvre-Teillard, "L'intervention de l'État dans la constitution des sociétés anonymes," *Revue historique de droit français et étranger* 59 (1981), 383–418.

CHAPTER 8

Partnerships as Flexible and Open-Purpose Entities: Legal and Commercial Practice in Nineteenth-Century Antwerp (*c.* 1830–*c.* 1850)*

Dave De ruysscher

1 Introduction

It is a striking fact that during the Industrial Revolution and in the first decades of the nineteenth century, in many European countries and also in the United States, general and ordinary partnerships[1] were regularly chosen as vehicles for business ventures. They were often more popular than limited companies and corporations. This practice has elicited different explanations. An older view was that the start-up of corporations was closely watched over by governments and that control was strict, which resulted in entrepreneurs and traders choosing less efficient but more accessible company types. The corporation has indeed generally been considered to be most appropriate for attracting and securing capital. A corporation combines the limited liability of investors with

* This chapter has benefited from the support of the European Research Council (Starting Grant 714759), FWO-Flanders (projects 1229814N and G053214N), The Academy of Finland and VUB. I'd like to thank Johan Dambruyne (State Archives of Antwerp), Hilde Greefs (University of Antwerp) and participants at the workshop "The Small, Medium-Sized and Large Company in Law and Economic Practice (Middle Ages–*c.* 1900)" (Brussels, 21–22 May 2015). I also extend my thanks to Luisa Brunori (Lille-II) for sending copies of articles and chapters on French companies in the nineteenth century. The results in this chapter, to a modest extent, correct and above all supplement those contained in Dave De ruysscher, "Handelsvennootschappen in Antwerpen (1830–1850): tussen flexibiliteit en continuïteit," *Pro Memorie. Bijdragen tot de rechtsgeschiedenis der Nederlanden* 17/2 (2015), 176–193.

1 Hereafter, the notion of "general partnership" is used as a label for the academic *societas*, whereas "ordinary partnership" refers to the French *société en nom collectif* or comparable company types (e.g. the German *Offene Handelsgesellschaft*). General and ordinary partnerships are commonly considered as being the same. Indeed, they were largely comparable. However, when the French *Code de commerce* was imposed in 1808, the rules relating to general and ordinary partnerships were different, in respect of publicity requirements for example (see hereafter). "Limited partnership" hereafter refers to the French *société en commandite* or comparable company types.

 | DOI: 10.1163/9789004351868_010

autonomy and continuity, making the firm less vulnerable to internal and external threats (e.g. the death of partners, and claims of their personal creditors).

Over the past decade, these opinions have been given more detailed attention, and more scholars are currently emphasizing the fact that general and ordinary partnerships were not as alien to business as has long been thought. Admittedly, partnerships could be dissolved before their planned purposes had been reached, as well as quite unexpectedly (e.g. when a partner resigned).[2] Associates in mercantile partnerships were generally deemed to be jointly and severally liable for debts incurred by one of the partners, even including their own assets. Within such partnerships mutual agency applied: every associate could sign contracts on behalf of the other partners, thus binding even their own personal properties.[3]

Irrespective of these features, though, there were numerous advantages as well. General and ordinary partnerships allowed for lower transaction costs when it came to obtaining credit. Corporations were less transparent in this regard because shareholders had to authorize loans, which made lenders reluctant.[4] In addition, on account of delegated management practices, minority oppression and moral hazards were risks that were avoided when opting for partnerships. In limited partnerships and corporations, investors and administering agents were largely separated, which could invite directors to pursue their own interests more keenly than those of the investors (moral hazard). In terms of control over the management of the firm, within corporations, majority shareholders could ignore the interests of shareholders who held fewer equity stakes (minority oppression).[5] By contrast, partnerships allowed for the continuous and reciprocal monitoring of partners, whether

2 Timothy Guinnane, Ron Harris, Noami R. Lamoreaux and Jean-Laurent Rosenthal, "Putting the Corporation in its Place," *Enterprise & Society* 8 (2007), 687–729, here 693–694; Naomi R. Lamoreaux and Jean-Laurent Rosenthal, "Organizing Middle-Size Firms in the United States and France, 1830–2000," working paper 2006, 13, http://people.hss.caltech.edu/~jlr/Papers/NRLJLRSMES.pdf (consulted on 17 January 2017).

3 E.g. Robert Cull, Lance E. Davis, Naomi R. Lamoreaux and Jean-Laurent Rosenthal, "Historical Financing of Small- and Medium-Size Enterprises," *Journal of Banking and Finance* 30 (2006), 3017–3042, here 3021.

4 Ryan Bubb, "Choosing the Partnership. English Business Organization Law During the Industrial Revolution," *Seattle University Law Review* 38 (2015), 337–364, here 339, 356; Lamoreaux and Rosenthal, "Organizing Middle-Size Firms," 5.

5 Timothy W. Guinnane and Jean-Laurent Rosenthal, "Making Do With Imperfect Law. Small Firms in France and Germany, 1890–1935," *Entreprises et Histoire* 57 (2009), 79–95, here 81; Lamoreaux and Rosenthal, "Organizing Middle-Size Firms," 14.

they were investors, managers, or both.[6] Moreover, partnerships were very flexible as to their structure.[7] In line with these beneficial features, the formerly acclaimed attractiveness of corporations and limited companies has been differentiated to a large extent. As has been discovered, furthermore, some of the characteristics commonly associated with corporations were not always present in the first half of the nineteenth century but date, rather, from a later period.[8]

Law is considered an important variable in the choices concerning the organizing of business ventures. Since the 1990s scholars such as Naomi Lamoreaux have underlined that official law provided supporting structural schemes for commercial enterprises. This view came after a period in which it was assumed that "(official) law didn't matter", for it was thought that merchants circumvented legislation and adopted their own standards, which were eventually acknowledged in both case law and statutes alike. Economic development and the facilitating effects of official law have since been addressed in debates on the "New Institutional Economics", "legal origins" and "varieties of capitalism". As a result, legal context is now commonly deemed an *ex ante* factor influencing the economic actions of entrepreneurs. The efficiency of legal regimes is widely discussed. In these discussions, La Porta, Lopez-de-Silanez, Shleifer and Vishny have categorized France and other countries with codifications as being more resistant in their ability to change and to adapt to new economic developments, whereas the judge-made common law was more flexible according to these scholars. However, this perspective has provoked the argument that common law could be—and for company-related questions in fact was—slow in changing, and that it was thus more uncertain than codified law and laws containing organizational schemes for companies.[9] Company contracts that

6 Among others, Jean-Pierre Hirsch, "Naissance des sociétés, personnes et capitaux à Paris, Lille et Lyon en 1846 et 1866," in Michael Moss and Philippe Jobert (eds.), *Naissance et mort des entreprises en Europe XIXe–XXe siècles* (Dijon: Université de Dijon, 1994), 141–156, here 155.

7 Cull, Davis, Lamoreaux and Rosenthal, "Historical Financing," 3022; Naomi R. Lamoreaux and Jean-Laurent Rosenthal, "Legal Regime and Business's Organizational Choice. A Comparison of France and the United States During the Era of Industrialization," *American Law and Economics Review* 7 (2005), 28–61, here 37–41.

8 Naomi R. Lamoreaux, "Partnerships, Corporations, and the Limits on Contractual Freedom in U.S. History: An Essay in Economics, Law, and Culture," in Kenneth Lipartito and David B. Sicilia (eds.), *Constructing Corporate America. History, Politics, Culture* (Oxford: OUP, 2004), 29–65, here 32–35.

9 Lamoreaux and Rosenthal, "Legal Regime and Business's Organizational Choice," 55–56.

cannot be linked to detailed provisions in laws or to fixed precedents in case law are often considered to be weak vehicles for business ventures.[10]

In addition to the legal framework, institutional arguments must refer to the economic context as well. The aforementioned views have been combined, for instance, with assessments of the impact of variables of scale and type of industry on the organizational choices of entrepreneurs.[11] This approach came after earlier attention to regional differences in nineteenth-century France regarding to company form, branches of business and economic factors.[12] In considering the variables mentioned, this chapter therefore combines an economic-historical approach with a legal-historical perspective. In this latter regard, taking legislation as the prime mover and as the only source of law in the period of industrialization is too narrow; even though codifications were paramount in the first half of the nineteenth century, judges and lawyers interpreted legislation and addressed problems that arose in practice and that had not been solved in a straightforward way in the black-letter law.

This chapter analyzes 145 company statutes that were drafted in Antwerp, in the period 1830–1850. The focus is on the essential elements of business ventures, above all, as reflected in these contracts. They include capital, agency and liability. This investigation thus examines how these elements corresponded to the sections of the French codifications of the early 1800s, which were also in force in the subsequent Belgian period; to what extent judges dealt with deficiencies and lacunae in the codes; and how contracts responded to these approaches.

Antwerp was a typical port city in this period; it excelled in services and transit rather than in industrial enterprise. Commercial activities were concerned with, foremost, wholesaling and commission sales, brokerage and insurance.[13] However, manufacturing shops were not entirely absent. True, the tex-

10 Guinnane, Harris, Lamoreaux and Rosenthal, "Putting the Corporation," 7; Henry Hansmann, Reinier Kraakman and Richard Squire, "Law and the Rise of the Firm," *Harvard Law Review* 119 (2006), 1333–1403, here 1339.

11 Pierre Cayez, "Structures juridiques et structures économiques, Lyon 1808–1863," in Alain Plessis (ed.), *Naissance des libertés économiques. Liberté de travail et liberté d'entreprendre, le décret d'Allarde et la loi Le Chapelier, leurs conséquences, 1791–fin XIXe siècle* (Paris: Institut d'histoire de l'industrie, 1993), 236–241; Lamoreaux and Rosenthal, "Organizing Middle-Size Firms," 32–41.

12 See the papers and books by Pierre Cayez, Jean-Pierre Hirsch, Philippe Jobert, Michel Lescure and André Straus, among others.

13 Hilde Greefs, "Foreign Entrepreneurs in Early Nineteenth-Century Antwerp," in Clé Lesger and Leo Noordegraaf (eds.), *Entrepreneurs and Entrepreneurship in Early Modern Times.*

tiles industry, which had been important in the eighteenth century, was already waning in the early nineteenth century.[14] Yet in the first half of the nineteenth century, manufacturing shops still processed goods that had been imported through the port of Antwerp, including rice, sugar and tobacco.[15] In the first half of the 1800s their activities remained largely preindustrial, as steam engines for example were not yet widely used.[16] Economic conditions were not that favourable between 1830 and 1850, and the developing Belgian state was itself endangered until 1839. As a result, the economic policy of the new government was unsettled. Tariffs could be increased from one year to the next. Trade and entrepreneurial initiatives not only suffered from threats of war, but also from international upsets in the prices of raw materials.[17] However, in spite of all this uncertainty, merchants and entrepreneurs did establish firms and shops.

2 Antwerp Company Contracts (1830–1850): Some Remarks on the Sources and Their Representative Qualities

2.1 *Pools of Sources and Circuits of Registration and Publication*

The results presented here were gathered from two series of archival sources, which are connected in some respects, and separate in others. These are the record books of the Antwerp registration offices, as well as notarial deeds. In the record books of the registration offices of Antwerp,[18] several company statutes (called "*actes de société*") can be found. Nearly all of these contracts

---

Merchants and Industrialists Within the Orbit of the Dutch Staple Market (The Hague: Stichting Hollandse Historische Reeks, 1995), 101–117, here 106.

14 Hilde Greefs, *Zakenlieden in Antwerpen tijdens de eerste helft van de negentiende eeuw* (PhD thesis, University of Antwerp, 2004), 77–79; Catharina Lis, *Social Change and the Labouring Poor. Antwerp, 1770–1860* (New Haven: Yale University Press, 1986), 17–38.

15 Greefs, "Foreign Entrepreneurs," 106. The Antwerp sugar industry in the first half of the nineteenth century has been analyzed in Greefs, *Zakenlieden*, 79–83; Helma Houtman-De Smedt, "Korte historische schets van de suikerraffinaderij "Cels, Aerts en Co" (1760–1806) en van haar latere evolutie (1806–1951)," *Bijdragen tot de Geschiedenis* 63 (1980), 293–311; Alfons K.L. Thijs, "De geschiedenis van de suikernijverheid te Antwerpen (16de–19de eeuw): een terreinverkenning," *Bijdragen tot de geschiedenis, bijzonderlijk van het hertogdom Brabant* 62 (1979), 23–50.

16 Greefs, *Zakenlieden*, 76–77; Thijs, "De geschiedenis van de suikernijverheid," 42–47.

17 Greefs, *Zakenlieden*, 43–85; Karel Veraghtert, "De Antwerpse bankwereld en de expansie van de haven," *Revue de la Banque* 9 (1980), 191–203.

18 There were two registration offices (South and North) until 1835. After 1835, both were merged together.

were copied verbatim from the original,[19] which was either a notarial deed or a privately written agreement. Registration at the offices mentioned was compulsory for some company statutes (see below), yet optional for others. Even when registration was not required by law, it could be advisable in order to prevent that disputes would arise, for example, over the contents or date of the contract. The ledgers mentioned also contain "*actes de dissolution*", which demonstrate fundamental modifications in the structure of firms, such as a change of partner or the demise of the company (a partial or full liquidation).[20]

In addition, company contracts can be found in notarial ledgers. If parties wanted to start up a firm they could ask a notary to draw up statutes, or they could have their privately written agreement recognized in a notarial deed. When the notary himself drafted the deed that structured a business venture, the law required that he registered the deed at a registration office.[21] Furthermore, privately written contracts that were copied into or rephrased in a notarial deed could be presented at the registration offices, but this was not required by the law.[22] At the registration offices, notarial deeds concerning companies that had been drafted in their entirety by a notary were enacted in the ledgers of series 5 (*actes publics*). Privately written contracts that had acquired the form of a notarial deed were often inserted in the registration volumes of series 5, and less often in the record books of series 6 (*actes sous seing privé*).[23] This latter series was mainly used for private contracts that had not been brought before a notary.

When notaries submitted deeds at the registration offices, they advanced the fees and forwarded them to their clients. Fees were not high: in the 1840s, for

19 This convention is fortunate and relies on an established practice in registration offices, one which also concerned marriage contracts, for example. Other contracts given at the registration offices (writs of sale, for example) were not copied in full. See Théodore Vuarnier, *Traité de la manutention des employés de l'enregistrement et des domaines*, vol. 1 (Paris: Pissin, 1848) 244 (no. 800). Vuarnier mentions it with regard to "*actes publics*" (series 5), but in practice these copies were also made—at least at the Antwerp registration offices—in series 6.

20 *Actes de dissolution* were usually also copied in full.

21 The notary had to have the deed concerning company statutes or dissolution registered within ten days at the office of the company's location, if this office was in his constituency.

22 Vuarnier, *Traité de la manutention*, 1, 234 (no. 763).

23 This ran counter to what was required according to doctrine, see Vuarnier, *Traité de la manutention*, 1, 234 (no. 763).

actes de société the registration and clerk fees combined usually amounted to 6 (Belgian) francs 62 cents. Later, around 1850, this cost corresponded in today's prices to some 45 euros.[24] Fees were fixed. Company contracts and also *actes de dissolution* benefited from a fiscal exemption, which meant that the object of the contract (its capital) was not assessed, as long as no immovable properties were or had been invested in the firm.[25] Since privately written company statutes were provided for registration, too, notaries did not have a monopoly in assisting parties with drafting their company contracts. Advocates, translators, or "writers" could have a part in this practice as well. Such intermediaries sometimes presented the written contract at a registration office, for enactment in series 6.[26]

There was also a third method for enacting agreements on business ventures (besides the registration offices and notaries' ledgers). Since 1799, Antwerp had a commercial court, which, starting in 1808, was called the *tribunal de commerce*. Its judges were businessmen from the elite, who were not obliged to have any legal training.[27] The 1807 Napoleonic *Code de commerce*, which had come into effect in 1808, provided that summary excerpts of company con-

---

24 This calculation is based on the historical development of the consumption index and a weighed consumption index coefficient for the year 1850. See Peter Scholliers, "A Century of Real Industrial Wages in Belgium, 1840–1939," in Peter Scholliers and Vera Zamagni (eds.), *Labour's Reward. Real Wages and Economic Change in 19th and 20th Century Europe* (Aldershot: Ashgate, 1995), 106–137, and 203–205.

25 s. 68 § 3, 4° *loi sur l'enregistrement* 12 December 1798. See also Raymond-Théodore Troplong, *Commentaire du contrat de société en matière civile et commercial* (Brussels: Meline, Cans & Cie, 1843), 414 (no. 1067). This same section of the law referred to was considered to apply to *actes de dissolution*. See Charles François Philippe Masson de Longpré, *Code annoté de l'enregistrement. Répértoire complet des lois sur l'enregistrement, le timbre, les droits de greffe, d'hypothèque …*, vol. 1 (Paris: Pissin, 1848), 446–448 (nos. 2696–2710). In practice, even when immovable property was invested (for example, the premises of the office location of a shop), the fixed fee was deemed sufficient. See, for example, Antwerp, State Archives (henceforth referred to as SAA), Registration offices of Antwerp, BA Noord (inventory F350) (henceforth referred to as ROA, BA), 107, fols. 182^{r-v} (registered on 22 July 1829). However, it seems that investment in kind of immovable property was rare, and that if a house or storage facility of one of the partners was used for company purposes, it was expressed in terms of letting and renting. In that case there was no doubt that the fixed fee applied. See, for example, SAA, Registration offices of Antwerp (general inventory F349) (henceforth referred to as ROA), 565, fols. 55^{v}–56^{r} (reg. 2 Dec. 1837), 599, fols. 91^{r-v} (reg. 31 Jan. 1851).

26 SAA, ROA, 610, fol. 142^{r-v} (reg. 18 Dec. 1856, "*avocat Augez*"), 611, fol. 93^{v}–94^{v} (reg. 9 June 1857, "*presenté par Mr Hickendorff, traducteur juré à Anvers*"). Both volumes belong to series 6.

27 Greta Devos, "De rechtbank van koophandel te Antwerpen. 200 jaar ten dienste van

tracts mentioned in the Code had to be handed in at the commercial court in the location of the company's office, within a period of two weeks after it had been created.[28] The excerpts had to mention the names, profession and domicile of partners, the name of the firm (*raison sociale*), the investments, and the projected duration of the venture.[29] These rules applied for all company agreements with commercial purposes that were mentioned in the Code, including those that were privately written and that had not been drafted or recognized by a notary or had not been enacted at a registration office. The clerks of the commercial courts were required to register these excerpts, and these summaries were put on display in the form of posters that were shown in the courtrooms for a period of three months.[30]

The goal of the aforementioned rules was publicity. In this regard, the law regarding information which was exchanged through the commercial courts was different to the legal duties of registration offices and notaries. Contracts filed with the commercial court were—at least as far as the contents mentioned in the excerpts were concerned—made known to the mercantile and industrial community within the judicature of the court. Creditors could go to the court clerk's office to check how a company was structured.[31] By contrast, contracts that had been inserted into the record books of registration offices, or which had been enacted before a notary, were not public. For statutes that had been copied at the registration offices, an official request for consultation had to be filed with the First Instance Court. Access could be granted only to those with a "direct interest", which meant that the applicant had to be mentioned in the registered contract.[32] The same requirement was imposed when requests were made for disclosure of notarial deeds.[33] All these conditions meant that creditors could not check the notarial and registered company contracts of their debtors.

---

handel en industrie," in Greta Devos, Paul Buysse and Herman Hellenbosch (eds.), *200 jaar Rechtbank van Koophandel Antwerpen, 1798–1998* (Antwerp: s.n., 1998), 59–74.

28 s. 42 *Code de commerce*.

29 s. 43 *Code de commerce*.

30 s. 42 *Code de commerce*.

31 As suggested in Troplong, *Commentaire*, 274 (no. 693).

32 Vuarnier, *Traité de la manutention*, 1, 327 (nos. 1143–1144). A direct interest related to the fact that the applicant was either party to or beneficiary of the registered contract. Not even notaries were given access, unless they substantiated a mandate and direct interest on behalf of their client(s). See Vuarnier, *Traité de la manutention*, 1, 329 (no. 1149).

33 Jean-Baptiste Massart, *Commentaire générale de la loi organique du notariat du 25 ventôse an XI* ... (Lessines: s.n., 1863), 278–279 (nos. 1209–1218).

Of the three circuits of enactment mentioned, for the period under study, notarial deeds and the ledgers of the Antwerp registration offices are complete.[34] However, this is not the case for the excerpts submitted to the commercial court of Antwerp. Due to a fire at the Exchange in 1858—where the commercial court was located—few court records dating from before this calamity have been preserved. Lost documents include the volumes containing the summaries of company contracts. Moreover, unlike in France, the newspaper publication of excerpts of company statutes registered at commercial courts was not in use in Antwerp during the first half of the nineteenth century.[35]

Nonetheless, an analysis of those company contracts brought before the Antwerp registration office and Antwerp notaries does still provide a view into the practice of starting up and continuing business ventures in Antwerp during the years 1830–1850. For this paper, the notarial deeds of the four most important Antwerp notaries of this period were analyzed, thus yielding 27 contracts.[36] Scrutiny of the record books for series 6 of the Antwerp registration offices yielded another 118 contracts.[37]

2.2 *Representativeness of the Sample*

With regard to these materials, two issues must be addressed initially. First, there is the question as to whether the absence of data concerning documents handed in at the Antwerp commercial court affects the representativeness of the abovementioned contracts collected. A second question relates to the

34 As for the notarial ledgers, address inventories of the period of 1830–1850 were consulted (*Almanach royal officiel de Belgique* (Namur: De Mortier, 1841), and *Almanach royal officiel* (Brussels: Tarlier, 1859)). They include all notaries having offices in Antwerp. The names of notaries in these lists were compared with the preserved records of Antwerp notaries in the Antwerp State Archives. This yielded the result that all notaries' record books have been preserved. Moreover, there are no lacunae in the record series.

35 For French practice, see Jean Hilaire, "L'évolution des formes. Les publicités légales," in Jean Hilaire (ed.), *Le Droit, les Affaires et l'Histoire* (Paris: Économica, 1995), 285–291. Samples were taken from the main Antwerp newspapers: *Le Précurseur*, *Het Handelsblad*, and *Journal du Commerce d'Anvers*. They contain data on commerce, such as price lists, news on ships and stock, yet no mentions of contracts or company statutes deposited at the commercial court.

36 These are Pierre Joseph Antonissen (active between 1826 and 1870), Jean François Gellynck (active in the period 1825–1850), Xavier Antoine Ghyssens (active 1830–1867), and Josse Hanegraeff (for the period 1820–1849).

37 See SAA, ROA, 559–599, 609–612; SAA, ROA, BA2 0000 (inventory F351, henceforth referred to as BA2), 95–99, and SAA, ROA, BA, 103–111.

proportion of contracts that remained entirely private, and which accordingly do not show up in the pools of archival sources mentioned.

As to the first question, it was perfectly lawful for mercantile company contracts—with the exception of corporations (*sociétés anonymes*)—to be registered only at the commercial court's office and not with a registration office or notary. In other words, submission to the commercial court was always required. If the contract was drafted by a notary, then it also had to be sent over to a registration office. In order to assess to what extent all this was done, one must consider the numbers of contracts that were handed in at the registration offices and at the commercial court, as well as those that were written by notaries.

As was previously mentioned, for the period up to 1858, no records of the Antwerp commercial court can be used. However, starting with 1856, the legal journal *Jurisprudence du port d'Anvers* lists the excerpts of contracts that had been turned in at the law clerk's office for this court (the journal was in fact published by the law clerk's office itself). A comparison of these published summaries—including those for the period from July 1856 until December 1857,[38] along with all company contracts that were registered in the registration office of Antwerp and/or with Antwerp notaries in this same period[39]—shows that company contracts enacted before notaries and/or at the registration office constituted 43.75 per cent (28/64) of all the company contracts that were brought before the commercial court. For these contracts, either registration had been solicited at the registration office, or they had the form of a notarial deed, or both. In addition, some 11 per cent (8/72) of all company contracts found in all three series of sources combined were registered by a notary and/or at a registration office, yet they did not end up at the commercial court. All this demonstrates that it was an established practice to draw up company contracts privately, and then have them published via the commercial court, without intervention from notaries and without going through a registration office. Moreover, not all company contracts that were drafted were brought before the commercial court, either. If the abovementioned proportions are applied to the aforementioned materials found in registration and notarial records for

38 *Jurisprudence du port d'Anvers et des autres villes commerciales et industrielles de la Belgique* (henceforth *Jur. Port d'Anvers*), 1 (1856), and 2 (1857). The official editor was Joseph Conard, chief law clerk of the Antwerp *tribunal de commerce.*

39 See SAA, ROA, 281–289 (years 1856–1857), 610–612 (years 1856–1857). The first volumes concern series 5, the second series 6. Moreover, the inventories of ledgers of notaries working in Antwerp in 1856 and 1857 were analyzed.

TABLE 8.1 *Number of registered and/or published company contracts July 1856–Dec. 1857*

	N
COMM, REG, NOT	9
COMM, REG, no NOT	19
COMM, NOT, no REG	0
COMM, no REG, no NOT	36
no COMM, REG, no NOT	5
no COMM, NOT, no REG	0
no COMM, REG, NOT	3
total	72

REG: registered at the registration office; NOT: registered in a notarial deed (recognizing a private contract or containing statutes that were drafted by the notary); COMM: deposited at the Antwerp commercial court.

the period 1830–1850, then, the estimated number of company contracts that were drawn up in writing in Antwerp in 1830–1850 amounts to 311.[40]

As for the second question, according to the prevailing law, agreements that were not registered or published in one way or another were considered legally sufficient for partnerships with a civil purpose. They were not always required to have a written form.[41] These rules did not apply to commercial companies, though. For firms mentioned in the commercial code, a written agreement was obligated by law, irrespective of the value of the contract (s. 39 *Code de*

40 145 contracts were registered before notaries or at the registration offices. If this number is reduced by 16 (i.e. 11%, or the number of contracts that were enacted before notaries or the registration offices but not submitted to the commercial court), the number can be estimated at 129. If this is considered 43.75% of the total of contracts deposited at the commercial court, another 166 statutes were submitted there but had not been enacted before notaries or at the registration offices. The total (129 + 16 + 166) amounts to 311.

41 For purposes of evidence, an agreement of a civil partnership had to be drawn up in writing if the object of the contract was above 150 (first French, then Belgian) francs (s. 1341 and s. 1834 *Code civil*). If the value was less, then an oral agreement was deemed lawful, and evidence by testimony was allowed. The mentioned sections provided that any written partnership contract (also for below 150 *francs*) could not be challenged or supplemented by means of witnesses.

commerce), and publicity through the commercial court was required as well (see above).

There are strong indications, however, that many contracts concerning cooperation between merchants or entrepreneurs, or for purposes of trade or manufacturing, were not presented to the commercial court, or before a notary, or for registration. Furthermore, it is very likely that a good deal of company agreements did not have the form of a written contract but were oral and informal only. Given the nature of such arrangements and their absence from official records, it is very difficult to provide hard data as to their numbers and contents. Even so, some cautious estimates can be made by extrapolating from the contents of registered *actes de dissolution*. For the abovementioned period of 1830–1850, some 18 of 40 *actes* (45 per cent) that concerned *dissolutions*, and which were registered at the Antwerp registration offices, do not mention a written company statute, a reference that was nonetheless compulsory.[42] Another nine refer to a written agreement that had not been registered and had not been deposited at the commercial court. The 18 contracts mentioned do not contain references to advertizing before the commercial court, either. A *dissolution* could encompass anything from a liquidation through public sale or otherwise, a partial split-off of assets, and also a change of partner. It seems that *dissolutions* were more usually registered at registration offices than company contracts; furthermore, there are some examples of contracts being registered some time, indeed in some cases long after they had been written,[43] and shortly before the company underwent some major change, which then provoked an "*acte de dissolution*".[44] In short, 27 out of 40 *dissolutions* reg-

42 Clerks at the registration offices were obligated to ask someone presenting a contract whether it had an impact on earlier (registered and unregistered) agreements, and these were mentioned. If the earlier contract had been registered, a reference to the volume and page of the registration ledger in which it had been enacted was added. See Vuarnier, *Traité de la manutention*, 1, 206 (no. 645). Notarial deeds and submissions to the commercial court were also mentioned.

43 An extreme example is a contract of January 1815 that was registered in July 1846. See SAA, ROA, 587, fols. 29^{r-v} (reg. 3 July 1846). A delay of some months was not uncommon. Sometimes the period between the signing and registration was long, and the registration was accompanied with supplements to the contract, mentioning new partners, for example. See, for example SAA, ROA, 579, fols. 52^{r-v} (reg. 3 Aug. 1843, original contract of 21 Sept. 1840).

44 E.g. SAA, ROA, 572, fols. 60^{v}–61^{v} (reg. 2 Apr. 1841), 574, fols. 24^{r-v} (reg. 26 Sept. 1841). The first contract was an "*acte de société*" providing the introduction of a new partner, the second one an "*acte de dissolution*" referring to one partner leaving the company (which nonetheless continued to operate).

istered at the Antwerp registration offices during the years 1830–1850 refer to oral agreements and privately written non-registered contracts.

Even though "*actes de dissolution*" were commonly drafted, informal contracts can still be expected to have ended up in informal liquidations and changes of partner as well. Moreover, when contracts of commercial business ventures were not written down, registered or made public, the official penalty was that the contract was null and void, though in practice—as will be detailed in the further paragraphs of this chapter—the company agreement was often honoured or maintained. The lack of differentiation in judicial practice did not provide an incentive to formalize and make arrangements public. Therefore, another method of estimating the unwritten and the written yet unregistered and unpublished contracts can be based on the proportions of contract types mentioned in the abovementioned 40 *actes de dissolution*. In these 40 registered dissolutions, 45 per cent concerned companies with unwritten non-published agreements (18/40), 22.5 per cent related to privately written, unregistered and unpublished agreements (9/40) and 32.5 per cent dealt with registered and/or published contracts (13/40). Accordingly, these proportions can be copied onto the known numbers of registered contracts. The estimated number of contracts enacted in one way or another is 311. When projecting the aforementioned proportions onto this number, then, the total number of company agreements would be 797.[45]

Given due exercise of caution, this number of 797 company agreements in Antwerp, which corresponds to a yearly average of around 40, can be compared with other cities. For Lille, for instance, it turns out that in the early 1830s, some 32 to 33 company contracts were deposited at the commercial court each year.[46] In the 1840s and 1850s, in Marseille—which was a deindustrialized port as was Antwerp, though with a larger population (*c.* 150,000 in 1836, whereas

45 If the proportion of written/unwritten company statutes is (maximum) 55% vs. (minimum) 45% (based on the mentioned *actes de dissolution*), if the number of contracts registered at registration offices as compared to the population of written and enacted (registered and/or published) company statutes was around 50 percent (see table 1), and considering the proportion of written vs. registered statutes at 3/2 (based on the *actes de dissolution*), then the share of statutes brought before the registration offices can be estimated a maximum of 16.06% of the total number of company contracts (both written and unwritten). From 128, one can thus infer the number of 797, of which some 438 were written and around 358 were not. The number of 797 does not include those agreements that were not put into writing, and which were ended informally as well. Please note that in De ruysscher, "Handelsvennootschappen," 182, footnote 25, there are factual errors: for number 448 read "438", and for 349 read "358".

46 Pierre Deyon and Jean-Pierre Hirsch, "Entreprise et association dans l'arrondissement de

the Antwerp population at that time was around 80,000)—between 15 and 45 company contracts were brought before the local *tribunal de commerce* annually.[47] Admittedly, these numbers only concern those *actes de société* that were submitted to the local commercial court and not those that were unwritten or unpublished. For Antwerp, during the period mentioned, the number of contracts deposited at the court can be estimated to be about 15 on average each year,[48] which in view of the figures for Marseille is not unlikely.

3 Company Types: Legal and Commercial Approaches

3.1 *The Legal Regime*

According to the official law, as made explicit in legal doctrine, a company entailed a cooperative venture with a purpose and a contribution from partners.[49] A typology of commercial companies was more or less clearly defined in the *Code de commerce*. A *société en nom collectif* (henceforth SNC) gathered unlimitedly liable partners, all of which were held responsible for debts that had been made when the name of the firm (*raison sociale*) had been used. A *société en commandite* (henceforth SC) had one or more *gérants*, i.e. directors or working partners, who were held liable for the debts of the company, as well as *commanditaires*, who were liable for no more than their investments. The *commanditaires* were non-working associates: they were prohibited from

Lille 1830–1862," in *Entreprises et entrepreneurs XIXe–XXe siècles* (Paris: Université de Paris-Sorbonne, 1983), 5–21, here 15.

47 Michel Lescure, "Companies and Manufacturers of the First Period of Industrialization in Marseilles 1810–1860," in Philippe Jobert and Michael Moss (eds.), *The Birth and Death of Companies. An Historical Perspective* (Carnforth: Parthenon, 1990), 105–120, here 107.

48 A comparison of contracts brought before the commercial court and contracts registered with notaries and at registration offices has—to my knowledge—not been pursued, for France or for Belgium. In publications regarding French companies, however, many authors advise caution on the data extracted from deposited contracts. See Cayez, "Structures juridiques," 240 (on the alternative way around construing a commercial firm as *société civile*, which was not required to publish its statutes); Michel Lescure and André Straus, "Rythmes et espaces dans la première industrialization. Une approche par les actes de société," in Alain Plessis (ed.), *Naissance des libertés économiques. Liberté de travail et liberté d'entreprendre, le décret d'Allarde et la loi Le Chapelier, leurs conséquences, 1791–fin XIXe siècle* (Paris: Institut d'histoire de l'industrie, 1993), 193–211, here 202 (on the difficulty of assessing which commercial court was competent for the submittal of contracts, since many firms had a broad geographical scope).

49 Jean-Marie Pardessus, *Cours de droit commercial*, vol. 3 (Paris: Garnery, 1815), 4–8 (nos. 969–972).

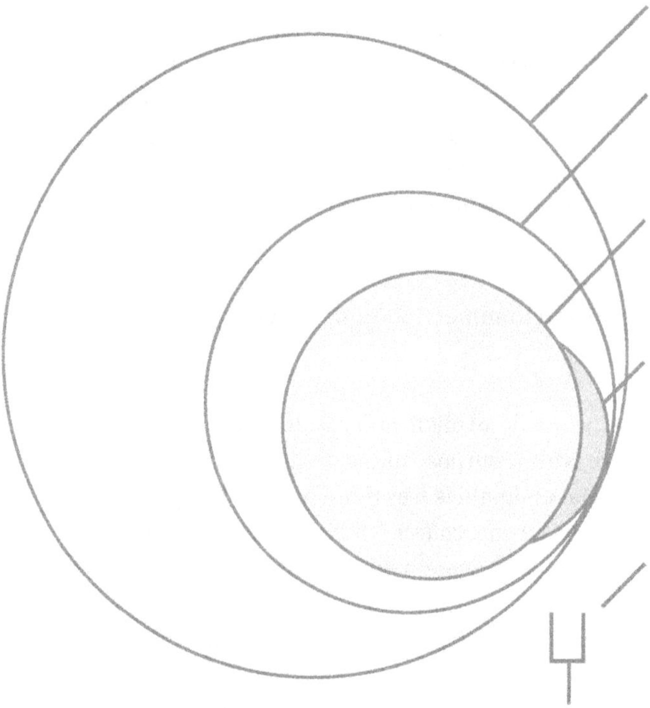

FIGURE 8.1 *Estimated numbers of company statutes, written and unwritten (yet formally dissolved) (Antwerp 1830–1850). The circles in colour indicate written and enacted (deposited and/or registered) contracts.*

participating in the trade for which the SC was set up. SCs could have equity that was divided in shares, which the law did not provide for the SNC. In addition to the SC and SNC, there was the *société anonyme* (henceforth SA); the SA had a structure similar to that of the SC in that directors managed the firm and paid the debts, but the firm's liability was limited to the company's capital and the directors were not personally liable. Participants (*actionnaires*) were held responsible for no more than that which they had invested. The capital was divided in shares, which were transferable and could be "to bearer". Moreover, a fundamental difference between the SA, on the one hand, and the SC and SNC, on the other, was that for the SA a governmental approval had to be obtained after enactment before a notary. A fourth type was the "*association commerciale en participation*", which was an association that could remain informal, and which concerned one or a few commercial operations only.[50]

50 s. 19–50 *Code de commerce.*

The characteristics of limited liability of investors were thus only acknowledged by law for the *actionnaires* in a SA, as well as for the *commanditaires* in a SC. For the SNC, limited liability of (some) partners went against the core elements of the contract type,[51] whereas for the *association commerciale en participation* this obligation was not regulated in detail.

Legal personhood did not yet exist in 1807 in the same form as does today. Corporations nowadays combine autonomy with limited liability of investors; they are creditors and debtors themselves. In the first half of the nineteenth century, the company was only granted the capacity of debtor in some respects. Summonses on debts of commercial companies had to be brought "*en leurs maison sociale*" (s. 69, 6° *Code de procédure civile* of 1806), for example. This definition hints at the assimilation of a firm with its business office. However, in practice, the liabilities of *gérants* and (working) partners were still paramount, as had been the case in the Old Regime,[52] and a firm was largely identified with those who represented it in public (see further paragraphs below).

With the exception of the SA, continuity was hampered by the possible withdrawal or death of partners. If one of the associates passed away, the company could continue if an arrangement had been made in the statutes, such as stating that an heir would replace the deceased partner, or that the remaining partners would continue the business venture (s. 1868 *Code civil* of 1804). The resignation of associates was not allowed if the duration of the venture had been detailed in the contract, except for when the duration was unlimited. In that latter case, resignation was only lawful if due notice was given to all partners, if it was timely (e.g. not if profits were expected) and without bad intent (for example, when an associate left in order to receive as much profits as possible) (s. 1869–1870 *Code civil*).

Another corporate characteristic known as entity shielding—i.e. company assets and capital are fenced off from actions of personal creditors of partners—was not detailed in the law, but it was generally accepted for commercial companies. This feature was read in section 529 of the *Code civil* (1804), which provided that for "*actions ou intérêts dans les compagnies de finance, de com-*

51 Pardessus, *Cours de droit commercial*, 3, 79–80 (no. 1013), and 92–93 (no. 1022).

52 Dave De ruysscher, "A Business Trust for Partnerships? Early Conceptions of Company-Related Assets in Legal Literature, and Antwerp Forensic and Commercial Practice (Later Sixteenth-Early Seventeenth Century)," in Bram Van Hofstraeten and Wim Decock (eds.), *Companies and Company Law in Late-Medieval and Early Modern Europe* (Leuven: Peeters, 2016), 9–27.

merce ou d'industrie" seizure was not possible by partners or their personal creditors for as long as the company lasted.[53] Rules relating thereto, which were not made explicit in legislation but which were widely acknowledged in case law and doctrine, included that creditors of commercial companies had priority over personal creditors of partners,[54] and that set-off of personal debts of partners with claims of the company, or vice versa, was impossible.[55] Sometimes it was said that summonses for company-related debts could not be brought against partners before the "*fonds social*"—i.e. the company's equity and assets—had been addressed and/or exhausted,[56] but this was an exceptional view. Most of these characteristics had been accepted for all partnerships before 1804/7, including the civil ones. However, due to the civil/commercial divide that was enforced through the Napoleonic codifications, and following on from a growing restrictive attitude towards civil initiatives over the course of the 1840s and 1850s (in Belgium as well as in France), from the 1860s and 1870s onwards the abovementioned features were excluded for civil partnerships.[57] In the 1830s and 1840s, prior to these developments, there were fierce scholarly

53 Until the later 1820s, it was sometimes said that this rule applied only to "large" or "substantial" companies. See, for example, Charles-Bonaventure-Marie Toullier, *Le droit civil français …*, vol. 12 (Paris: Warée, 1823), 143–144 (no. 97), and 148 (no. 101). By the 1840s, this had unanimously been decided in favour of all companies, even for civil ones. See Alexandre Duranton, *Cours de droit civil suivant le code français*, vol. 2 (Brussels: Société belge de Librairie, 1841), 284 (no. 930); Karl Salomo Zachariae, *Cours de droit civil français*, vol. 1 (Brussels: Société belge de Librairie, 1842), 144, footnote 6.

54 In 1821, Vincens was the first to state this position without hesitation. It became a common point of view in the years thereafter. See "Société," in *Dalloz Répertoire* (Paris: Dalloz, 1859), 497 (no. 628); A[ntoine] Frémery, *Études de droit commercial: du droit fondé par la coutume universelle des commerçants* (Paris: Gobelet, 1833), 32; Émile Vincens, *Des sociétés par actions* (Paris: Huzard, 1837), 6; Émile Vincens, *Exposition raisonnée de la législation commerciale et examen critique du Code de commerce*, vol. 1 (Paris: Barrois, 1821), 20. There was debate as to whether this approach also applied to civil partnerships. See Edouard Richard, ""Mon nom est personne". La construction de la personnalité morale ou les vertus de la patience," *Entreprises et Histoire* 57 (2009), 14–44, here 35.

55 Pardessus, *Cours de droit commercial*, 3, 17 (no. 975); Toullier, *Le droit français suivant l'ordre du Code*, vol. 7 (Paris: Renouard, 1829), 378. Also, concerning set-off between partners, see Troplong, *Commentaire*, 35 (no. 73), and 195 (no. 526).

56 Pardessus, *Cours de droit commercial*, 3, 19 (no. 976); Troplong, *Commentaire*, 324 (no. 821).

57 Dave De ruysscher, "Een rechtshistorische kijk op schaalgrootte in het Belgische en Franse handels- en economisch recht (vroege negentiende eeuw tot ca. 1960)," in Koen Reniers and Melissa Vanmeenen (eds.), *Regelgeving op maat van KMO's* (Antwerp: Intersentia, 2013), 213–234, here 226–228.

discussions over the distinctive characteristics of civil and commercial companies. Debates, too, took place regarding the legal status of companies that did not meet the publicity requirements of the *Code de commerce* (see hereafter).[58]

3.2 *Company Types in Contracts*

The 145 company contracts that were found in Antwerp records for the period 1830–1850, and also some other materials predating that period, allow for a nuanced view both on the acceptance of the Napoleonic legislation and on the legal rules regarding company types that were applied in practice. From the 145 statutes, it is evident that labels referring to the four types of business venture mentioned in the *Code de commerce* were very rare.

The notion of "company type" presupposes that certain features are clustered together in company statutes or that combinations of clauses are recognized as default schemes. When reading early nineteenth-century company statutes, however, it immediately becomes clear that concepts used to describe companies varied to a large extent. For Antwerp, and for the Low Countries in general, the linguistic context had some part in this divergence. Consistent Dutch ("Flemish") legal terminology was absent. For a large part of the nineteenth century, there was no official Dutch vocabulary in Belgium for either legal or company-related matters. Only in 1898 did legislation in Belgium come to be issued in two official versions, in French and Dutch, with both having the same legal force. Dutch legal language—in fact, even the Dutch language in general—had not been standardized in Belgium before that time. This lack did not mean that only French was used in legal environments. Dutch, of course, was also the language of the region where Antwerp is located. Moreover, political changes could provoke the renewed importance of Dutch. In 1815, the Southern Netherlands were reunited with the Kingdom of the Netherlands in the North—after some 330 years of separation—into the newly established United Kingdom of the Netherlands. Hence, Dutch became a language of public administration again. Yet this revival came only after a French occupation

58 French doctrine on these issues has been studied in De ruysscher, "Een rechtshistorische kijk," and Richard, "Mon nom est personne". Other papers provide succinct passages in this regard. See, for example, Carlo Angelici, "Discorsi di diritto societario," in Carlo Angelici et al. (eds.), *Negozianti e imprenditori. 200 anni dal Code de commerce* (Milan: Mondadori, 2008), 141–182, here 142–147; Laura Moscati, "Dopo e al di là del *Code de commerce*: l'apporto di Jean-Marie Pardessus," in Carlo Angelici et al. (eds.), *Negozianti e imprenditori. 200 anni dal Code de commerce* (Milan: Mondadori, 2008), 47–80, here 61–64.

that began in 1794/5 and lasted for twenty years, thereby pushing Dutch aside as the language for government.[59]

In terms of languages known and applied, all these transitions did not pose too many problems among merchants and entrepreneurs in the South. In Antwerp, the mercantile community had always made use of several languages. In eighteenth-century Antwerp, French and Dutch had been the most common, and the municipal government had used both, too, even though the official language was Dutch (French was a language of diplomacy and for correspondence with the central government only).[60] Since 1814, contracts could again be registered and be recognized as notarial deed in French, Dutch or any other language.[61] After the Belgian Revolt of 1830 and the creation of the Kingdom of Belgium, French was again dominant in government affairs, but Dutch was still used in contracts, even when they were officially enacted. Nevertheless, despite the common usage of Dutch as a vernacular, merchants in Antwerp were, as ever, international. Their language use also reflected their attachment to elitist milieus, in which French was the standard.[62] Moreover, to a large extent, French was a *lingua franca* in business environments, particularly in Belgium.[63]

---

59 A general overview of the language situation during the French period and under the United Kingdom is provided in Roland Willemyns, *Dutch. Biography of a Language* (Oxford: OUP, 2013), 104–113.

60 See throughout Edward Poffé, *Antwerpen in de XVIIIe eeuw voor den inval der Franschen* (Ghent: Siffer, 1895).

61 On the 1814 regulation, see Fred Stevens, *Revolutie en notariaat. Antwerpen 1794–1814* (Leuven: Van Gorcum, 1994), 174–175. The rule that written agreements could be enacted before a notary or at a registration office in all languages was limited to those languages which the clerks or notary mastered. A regulation of 5 June 1830 confirmed this rule. See Massart, *Commentaire générale*, 609–612.

62 On the gentrification processes among Antwerp merchants in the eighteenth century, see Karel Degryse, *De Antwerpse fortuinen. Kapitaalsaccumulatie, -investering en -rendement te Antwerpen in de 18de eeuw* (Antwerp: Genootschap voor Antwerpse Geschiedenis, 2005), 180–194.

63 German immigrant entrepreneurs and bankers, who were numerous in early nineteenth-century Antwerp, used their native language within their community of compatriots. See Geert Pelckmans and Jan Van Doorslaer, *De Duitse kolonie 1796–1914* (Kapellen: Pelckmans, 2000), 23–26 (referring to a *Kaufmännische Verein*, for example). However, their notarial deeds of company contracts and privately written *actes de société* were never in German, but always in French or Dutch. In business correspondence, German immigrant traders also usually resorted to French.

Taking these contextual elements into consideration thus makes possible the appropriate evaluation of the language and terminology of the 145 company statutes. Of the 145 company contracts examined, only 31 are in Dutch, and all others in French. The distinction notarial/privately written is a proxy in this regard: notarial deeds were relatively more frequently drawn up in Dutch (29.6 per cent) than private contracts registered at the registration offices in series 6 (19.49 per cent). A likely explanation is that at registration offices the prevailing language of government, French, was preferred. However, the language of the contract seems not to have been a variable in relation to the types and contents of company statutes.

A detailed analysis of the contents of the Dutch statutes yields further arguments supporting the abovementioned weakness of Dutch as a legal language in the period under study. In the first half of the nineteenth century there were some (foreign) legal texts and a number of (mostly private) translations and dictionaries that listed "Dutch" transpositions of French legal terms. Still, their variety was enormous. Under the United Kingdom of the Netherlands, preparations had been made to issue a commercial code in Dutch, but this project had not yet been completed when Belgium proclaimed its independence in September 1830.[64] The Dutch commercial code, which was imposed in the North in 1838, used the term "*vennootschap*" for commercial companies. However, an earlier Dutch translation of the French 1807 commercial code, made in 1808 by Johannes Van der Linden, and the 1809 draft of a commercial code for the Kingdom of Holland, had applied the notions "*compagnieschap*" and "*societeit*".[65] When around 1808 P.J. Lorio from Ghent made a Flemish translation of the French commercial code of 1807, he chose "*societeyt*" as label for companies,[66] and this term was also used in the contemporary official *Bulletin flamand*, which contained unofficial "Flemish" versions of French legislation.[67] Dictionaries and Dutch translations of the early nineteenth century mentioned other expressions such as "*genootschap*", "*maatschappij*" or "*zamen-*

64 Ernst Holthöfer, "Belgien," in Helmut Coing (ed.), *Handbuch der Quellen und Literatur der neueren europäischen Privatrechtsgeschichte* vol. 3/3 (Munich: Beck, 1986), 3287–3289.

65 Arnoldus van Gennep, Mozes S. Asser, and Joannes Van der Linden, *Wetboek van den Koophandel voor het Koningrijk Holland* (s.l.: s.n., 1809), 6 (ch. 3); Joannes Van der Linden, *Wetboek van den Koophandel voor het Fransche Rijk* (Amsterdam: Allart, 1808), 161–170.

66 P.J. Lorio, *Commercialen wetboek* (Ghent: Bogaert-De Clercq, *c.* 1808), 9–16.

67 See Dirk Heirbaut, "Inleiding," in Dirk Heirbaut and Gustaaf Baeteman (eds.), *Cumulatieve editie van het Burgerlijk Wetboek. Édition cumulative du Code civil*, vol. 1 (Ghent, 2004), li, and vol. 2 (Ghent: Wolters Kluwer, 2004), 1797–1814.

leving".[68] In his 1841 Flemish-Dutch translation of the *Code civil*, the Flemish judge Carel Ledeganck used "*maetschap*",[69] following the example of the Dutch Civil code of 1838. In this code, "*maetschap*" was a civil partnership, with "*vennootschap*" being reserved for commercial companies. However, "*compagnieschap*", "*vennootschap*" and "*maetschap*" were terms that were not very well known in the South before the union with the North, and they did not survive after Belgian independence.[70] By contrast, "*societeyt*" had been and remained a common translation of "*societas*", which in the Old Regime was the academic label for a general partnership. In the eighteenth century, "*associatie*" and "*compagnie*" had been widespread terms in the Southern Low Countries as well.[71] "*Societeyt*" remained very popular under the Belgian regime, but many other terms were also used ("*associatie*", "*maetschappij*", "*genootschap*"), which was the case for the entire period from 1830–1850.[72] In this regard, there is no difference between notarial contracts and the ones that were drawn up privately. Formulary books for notaries were equally diverse in terminology.[73]

Quite surprisingly, many labels were used in French, too, and they did not often rephrase the French commercial code, even though the appropriate legal terminology was used in French-language company contracts as well. Many statutes mentioned "*l'établissement d'une maison de commerce*"[74] or a "*mai-*

68 E.g. Abraham Blussé, *Dictionnaire portatif françois et hollandois, et hollandois et françois* (Dordrecht: Blussé, 1828), 872.

69 Carel Ledeganck, *Het burgerlyk wetboek uit het Fransch vertaeld* (Ghent: Hoste, 1849), 434.

70 In Antwerp, the term "*compagnieschap*" gained some popularity in the 1820s, but it faded away after 1830. See SAA, ROA, BA2, 95, fols. 42^{v}–44^{r} (reg. 18 Jan. 1830); SAA, ROA, BA, 103, fol. 195^{r} (reg. 1 Aug. 1823), 107, fols. 58^{v}–60^{r} (reg. 23 Aug. 1828). The last mention dates from 1844. See SAA, ROA, 582, fol. 38^{r} (reg. 2 Oct. 1844).

71 See for example Houtman-De Smedt, "Korte historische schets," 293–294.

72 SAA, Notaries, 7476, deed no. 4740 (16 Nov. 1848: "*genootschap*"); SAA, ROA, 585, fols. 85^{v}–86^{r} (reg. 23 Dec. 1845, "*maetschappij*"), 588, fols. 5^{v}–6^{r} (reg. 13 Nov. 1846, "*genootschap*"), 590, fol. 15^{v} (reg. 19 July 1847, "*associatie*"). "*Zamenleving*", "*maetschap*", "*vennootschap*" and "*compagnie*" were not used, however. The terms "*gemeenschap*", "*deelgemeenschap*" or "*gemeenschappelykheit*" were only mentioned one time in the period 1830–1850, but they had been more common in 1815–1830. See SAA, ROA, 584, fol. 6^{v} (reg. 17 May 1845, "*gemeenschappelykheyd*"); SAA, ROA, BA, 103, fols. 38^{v}–39^{r} (reg. 17 June 1822, "*gemeenschap*"), and 106, fols. 56^{r-v} (reg. 7 Apr. 1827, "*deelgemeenschap*").

73 E.g. *Formulier der notariële akten voor het Koninkrijk der Nederlanden. Formulaire des actes notariés pour le Royaume des Pays-Bas* ... (Brussels: Wahlen & Cie, 1823), 535–536 ("*societeit*", "*maetschappij*").

74 E.g. SAA, ROA, 571, fols. 43^{r-v} (reg. 10 Nov. 1840), fols. 74^{r}–75^{v} (reg. 17 Dec. 1840), 588, fol. 78^{v} (reg. 3 Febr. 1847).

son de commission".[75] These terms have no equivalent in the *Code de commerce*. Many contracts only stipulated that the partners "*s'associent*", "are associated", and nothing more, with no hints as to type of company mentioned in the commercial code.[76] Others detailed a "*société de commerce à pertes et gains*".[77] Such generic descriptions of "*sociétés*" or "*associations*" were the most common. No less than 104 out of 160 Antwerp company statutes for the period 1830–1850 (i.e. those 145 of the sample and 15 SA statutes) defined the business venture in generalizing terms that had no basis in the commercial code (see Table 8.2). If legal wording was chosen, then the SNC was opted for the most. By contrast, company contracts defining partners as limitedly liable did so mostly by means of legal terminology: the ventures were then described as *sociétés en commandite* or the silent partners as *commanditaires*. However, SCs were not very popular: only 12 out of 160 contracts referred to this company type. The abovementioned proportions among company descriptions did not change much over time, even though near the end of the 1840s generic partnerships seem to have gained popularity over other company types (see table 8.2 and figure 8.2). In other regards, too, references to sections of the commercial code were largely absent: only 11 of 118 registered company statutes and 3 out of 27 notarial contracts refer to a provision of the *Code de commerce*. In most cases, this citation concerned the article regarding publication at the commercial court. Sometimes, it was said that books would be kept according to the code's requirements.[78] In regard to references to the commercial code, there was not much difference between privately written and notarial contracts.

3.3 *Judicial Approaches and Views in Doctrine*

The lack of distinction in commercial practice between "types" was equally prevalent in legal doctrine and in decisions of courts. It was very common, even in the 1850s, to label mercantile and manufacturing partnerships as "*société de commerce*", and not to categorize these firms as one of the types in the commercial code.[79] This custom followed on from some gaps in legislation and from uncertainties relating to the official law.

---

75 SAA, Notaries, 4523, deed no. 267 (3 Sept. 1836); *Jur. Port d'Anvers* 2 (1857), *renseignements commerciaux*, 13 (Oct. 1857).

76 E.g. SAA, ROA, 569, fols. 38^v–39^v (reg. 13 Jan. 1840).

77 E.g. SAA, ROA, 569, fols. 55^v–56 (reg. 7 Jan. 1841).

78 E.g. SAA, Notaries, 9754, deed no. 84 (9 Aug. 1838).

79 E.g. Brussels 6 July 1854, *La Belgique Judiciaire* (henceforth referred to as *BJ*) 1857, 333.

TABLE 8.2 *Numbers of types, as described in company statutes (Antwerp 1830–1850)*

	SOC	SNC	SC	PART	SA (date recognition)	Total
1830–1834	19	1	2	0	2	24
1835–1839	18	10	2	1	11	42
1840–1844	27	8	4	0	0	39
1845–1849	28	5	4	0	2	39
1850	12	2	0	2	0	16
total	104	26	12	3	15	160

SOC refers to the generic "*société*" or "*association*", SC to "*société en commandite*", SNC to "*société en nom collectif*", PART to "*association en participation*" (meaning a temporary or silent partnership) and SA to "*société anonyme*". For the latter, data was gathered from Demeur, Greefs, Trioen and Veraghtert.[80] Remarkably, statutes of SAs were not found in the ledgers of the registration offices for the period 1830–1850, or even in the notarial deeds consulted (see also the comment under table 8.9 below). The date of all statutes referred to is the date when the contract was written (not the date of registration or the starting date). For SAs, the date of governmental approval was chosen.

In the early nineteenth century, the divide between commercial and civil law, which had been instituted by the Napoleonic codes, was very much debated and derived from a lack of clarity concerning many issues. Yet it was also more fundamental in that the legislature had poorly defined the relation between the civil and commercial code. The *Code de commerce* provided that laws as well as the 1804 Civil code could supplement its contents (s. 18). One would expect on the basis of this section that the commercial code stood largely apart from the Civil code. However, the *Code civil* contained sections on partnerships with a commercial purpose, and it was not always evident whether they had been abolished by the commercial code. Moreover, the Civil code

80 Adolphe Demeur, *Les Sociétés anonymes en Belgique en 1857. Collection complète des statuts collationés sur les textes officiels avec une introduction et des notes* (Brussels: L'éditeur, 1859); Greefs, *Zakenlieden*; Julienne Laureyssens, *De naamloze vennootschappen en de ontwikkeling van het kapitalisme in België (1819–1850)* (PhD thesis, Ghent University, 1970), 4 vols.; Louis François Bernard Trioen, *Collection des statuts de toutes les societés anonymes et en commandite par actions de la Belgique. Recueilles et mis en ordre d'après les renseignements fournis par les societés elles-mêmes; suivies de tableaux synoptiques et d'une notice sur les emprunts et les fonds publiques cotés dans toutes les bourses de l'Europe* (Brussels: Trioen, 1839), 2 vols.; Veraghtert, "De Antwerpse bankwereld," 191–203.

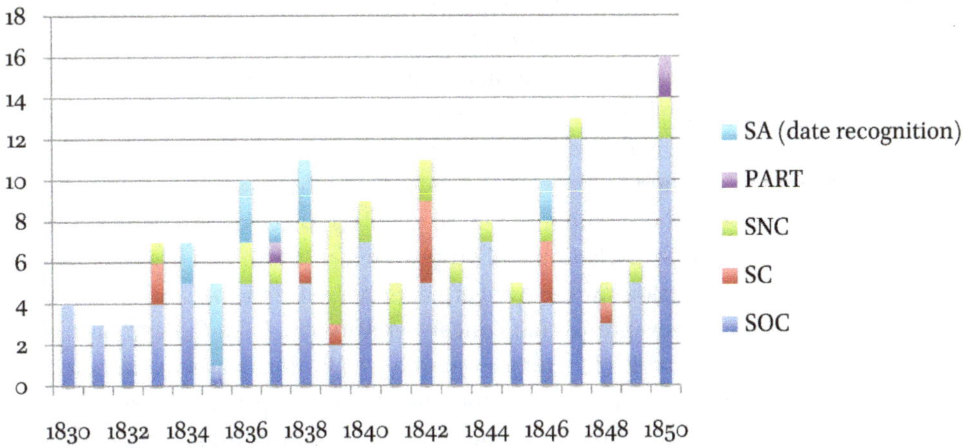

FIGURE 8.2 *Types of companies, according to year (Antwerp 1830–1850)*

provided that its contents applied only insofar as there were no specific laws or trade usages (s. 1873). The commercial code could be considered to be a specific law in some respects, but in others it remained unclear which of the codes prevailed.

As a result of all this inconsistency, legal scholars had to assemble sections of the two codes into a coherent legal doctrine. This had a direct impact on legal views regarding companies. In this period, French academic writings were widely read in Belgium, where they influenced court decisions and the arguments of Belgian legal scholars.[81] Some French academics (Pardessus, Vincens) maintained that only mercantile firms had a "*personne morale*", which meant that the capital and assets acquired during their lifespan were distinguished from personal properties of partners.[82] Yet others (Troplong, Delangle) acknowledged this feature, which was linked to section 529 of the Civil code, for both civil and commercial companies.[83] Another debate concerned the publicity requirements imposed by the commercial code. Some scholars maintained that disrespect for the sections of the code brought about the absolute and retroactive nullity of the company contract, whereas others (Delangle, Vincens) stated that the firm could be upheld to some extent, at least among the

81 Dirk Heirbaut, "The Belgian Legal Tradition. Does it Exist?," in Hubert Bocken and Walter De Bondt (eds.), *Introduction to Belgian Law* (Brussels: Bruylant, 2000), 10–13.

82 Pardessus, *Cours de droit commercial*, 3, 17 (no. 975); Vincens, *Des sociétés par actions*, 6.

83 Claude-Alphonse Delangle, *Commentaire sur les sociétés commerciales* (Brussels: Wahlen, 1843), 439 (nos. 14–15), and 441 (no. 20); Troplong, *Commentaire*, 29 (no. 58), and 33–34 (no. 69).

partners, or that it was possible that among them communal assets existed, being more or less independent from their personal estate.[84] Depending on the position, it was possible to argue that partnerships that were for commercial purposes, but which had not been made public, and which did not correspond to types mentioned in the *Code de commerce*, were nonetheless lawful *sociétés*, in one way or another.

The questions that confounded legal scholars affected case law as well. The policy of the Brussels Court of Appeal, which heard appeals that were lodged against decisions of the Antwerp commercial court, was important in matters of business ventures that concerned Antwerp. First, the approach of the Brussels Court, which in practice was followed by the Antwerp commercial court, was highly relevant for companies that did not keep with the regulations (hereafter "irregular companies"). Such firms had statutes that had duly been published, but they had structural features that were contrary to the contents of the *Code de commerce*. Notwithstanding their irregularities, and irrespective of the strict wording of the code, in several decisions taken between 1815 and 1860, the Brussels Court maintained that agreements that set up companies had to be considered as a whole, based on the contents of the contract but also on facts, and that decisions for the application of sections of laws depended on those.[85]

As a result, the French codes were not followed to the letter and irregular companies could still be considered to be lawful. Admittedly, in principle, the Brussels Court imposed strict criteria. Only firms with specific characteristics were defined as SNCs. The first criterion, which until the early 1860s was the only one, concerned the firm's name ("*raison sociale*"). If no company signature specifying "*& Cie*" or containing the names of at least two partners had been used, then the partnership did not qualify as a SNC.[86] Another criterion,

84 Delangle, *Commentaire*, 584 (no. 512), 599–600 (no. 539) ("*communauté d'intérêts*" for the past, not for the future); Vincens, *Exposition raisonnée*, 1, 310–313 (nos. 10–13) ("*union de fait*").

85 Brussels 31 January 1855, *Pasicrisie* (henceforth referred to as *Pas.*) 1857, vol. 2, 82–84. This argument was also generally accepted by other Courts of Appeal. See Ghent 2 May 1853, *BJ* 1854, 691; Liège 3 June 1871, *Pas.* 1871, vol. 2, 435. This approach seems at odds with the policy of the Brussels Court to systematically repeat that non-published commercial companies were "null and void" in an absolute sense. This view did not rule out the possibility that unpublished company statutes were factually honoured at least to some extent. See, for example, Brussels 16 February 1839, *Pas.* 1839, vol. 2, 27; Brussels 26 April 1855, *BJ* 1856, 1390.

86 Brussels 29 May 1830, *Pas.* 1830, 142; Brussels 30 November 1831, *Pas.* 1831, 320; Brussels

which was imposed from around 1860, was the company's office: if it had been provided in the statutes that the firm would have a fixed "*domicile*", then this did—together with the use of a "*raison sociale*"—entail the labelling of the firm as SNC.[87] However, notwithstanding these categorizations, the Brussels Court of Appeal also maintained that if the two mentioned conditions were not fulfilled, the company (which then was no SNC) was considered to be an "*association en participation*". A requirement for this default categorization of irregular companies was that the venture had been limited in duration. This condition was sufficient even when no specific project had been agreed upon between the partners, or when the cooperation encompassed several undetermined operations, sales or projects.[88] The Brussels Court of Appeal stretched the sections of the code on these *associations*, which considered them to be temporary but for one or two operations only (s. 48).

Secondly, any company statute that could be categorized as SNC, SC or SA on the basis of its contents was nonetheless considered to be an "*association en participation*" if the publicity requirements were not met.[89] The Brussels Court made use of a loophole in the official law in this respect. According to the *Code de commerce*, publicity was not required for the "*association en participation*" (henceforth AP).

The recourse to considering irregular and unpublished companies as APs allowed for maintaining some of the previously mentioned features of the "*personne morale*" for them. Even though in principle the Brussels Court did not allow the "*personne morale*" for these APs,[90] it was nonetheless accepted that they entailed "common interests",[91] or a "community of interests".[92] It seems that this referred to a modest priority of claims by creditors of the firm over those of personal creditors of partners. In general terms, according

---

30 April 1842, *Pas.* 1842, vol. 2, 166; Brussels 21 July 1846, *Pas.* 1851, vol. 2, 186; Brussels 22 June 1860, *Pas.* 1860, vol. 2, 387.

87 Brussels 16 January 1860, *Pas.* 1860, vol. 2, 377–378.

88 Brussels 15 February 1861, *Pas.* 1861, vol. 2, 106–109; Brussels 10 May 1869, *Pas.* 1870, vol. 2, 195–196. Please note that the Brussels Court of Appeal used the term "*association en participation*" in a different sense to the usage in the commercial code. The term "*association en participation*" (abbreviated PART) in table 8.2 and figure 8.2 above refers to the legislative variety, not to the one crafted by the Brussels Court.

89 Brussels 21 July 1846, *Pas* 1851, vol. 2, 186–188.

90 Brussels 11 July 1861, *BJ* 1861, 1419.

91 Brussels 21 July 1846, *Pas.* 1851, vol. 2, 188 ("*attendu que, malgré la dissolution de l'association, des intérêts subsistent en commun jusqu'à la liquidation complète entre parties*").

92 Brussels 12 January 1860, *Pas.* 1860, vol. 2, 273–277. This point was raised in the first instance, and not addressed in the phase of appeal, however.

to the Brussels Court, for APs there was no separation between personal and company-related properties. However, within the personal properties of each partner the Court acknowledged a share of the so-called "*fonds commun*" of the business venture, which referred to the nominal capital of the firm. It was assumed that the capital had not been paid up, and that the investments of each associate were still part of their personal estates. The abovementioned modest priority for company-related debts meant that they were compensated first with the "*fonds commun*" share in the personal properties of the associate that had been summoned. If this share did not suffice (or when no capital had been provided in the company statutes), personal assets were addressed. Both the "*fonds commun*" share and the liability with personal assets were limited proportionally, taking the number of partners into account.[93]

Two exceptions to the "*fonds commun*" rule were acknowledged. First, in cases where the company statute appointed one partner as *gérant* (i.e. as working associate who was in charge of the firm's funds, assets and books), then according to the Brussels Court he was considered to be the sole owner of the company's estate.[94] As a result, a *gérant* could be held liable to pay creditors the full "*fonds*" of the company. The remainder of the debt that was not compensated could thereafter be claimed *pro rata* from the *gérant* as well as from the other associates. A second exception related to joint actions. If associates had signed together for debts, they were considered to be jointly and severally liable.[95]

It is quite remarkable that for partners this understanding of irregular and unpublished *sociétés de commerce* as APs actually provided advantages vis-à-vis creditors compared to lawful and published SNCs. The latter had "*personne morale*", but its associates were jointly and severally liable for the entire debt, and creditors were not obliged to expropriate the funds of the SNC first, before they addressed individual partners.[96] For APs as categorized by the Brussels

93 Brussels 10 May 1869, *Pas.* 1870, vol. 2, 196 ("… *qu'en effet, dans toute espèce de société, il y a une chose commune, dont on se propose de tirer profit; qu'il est à remarquer toutefois que, dans l'association en participation, le fonds commun reste dans le patrimoine particulier des associés, tandis que, dans les sociétés en nom collectif, il est distinct et séparé de l'avoir particulier des associés et appartient à un être moral*").

94 Brussels 15 February 1861, *Pas.* 1861, vol. 2, 106. See also "Société," in *Dalloz Répertoire* (Paris: Dalloz, 1859), 759 (no. 1674).

95 *Jur. Port d'Anvers*, vol. 2 (1857), 122–123 (commercial court Antwerp 29 April 1857).

96 Brussels 14 August 1841, *Pas.* 1841, vol. 2, 379. This is remarkable, when considering the law predating the *Code de commerce*, and in view of the opinions of prominent legal scholars (Pardessus and Troplong). The ruling of the Brussels Court of Appeal was linked

Court there was a "*fonds commun*", albeit within each partner's estate only. All this meant that the creditors of an AP had to bring suit against all partners of the AP and not against one associate, as was the case with the SNC. If the creditor wanted to circumvent this procedural difficulty, he could have the summoned associate of the AP qualify as *gérant*, but then he had to provide evidence of his appointment by the other partners. However, for APs that supported undisclosed firms, with statutes not being published, this procedure was factually very difficult. As for an SNC, one active associate could be sued for the full amount of the debt, even if there were others that were publicly known; in regard of an AP, it was best to summon all partners to court, and the fact that they were not known publicly was not considered to be a legitimate reason to claim the total debt from one of them. As for an SNC, the entirety of the company-related debt was compensated with the estate of the partner that was sued, even when it exceeded his share in the partnership. By contrast, for APs, claims of creditors against individual partners were limited to the extent of the "*fonds commun*" and the proportionate share of the partner in the debts of the firm that exceeded the "*fonds commun*".

If, for example, two (trading) associates had set up a SNC in full accordance with the official law, providing capital of 500 francs, and the SNC had 1,000 francs of debt with one creditor, then one of the partners could be held liable to pay up 1,000 francs to the latter. If, however, the same venture were considered to be an AP, the creditor who brought suit against only one of the associates could recover no more than 500 francs (i.e. 250 as referring to the *fonds commun* and 250 as rateable share in the firm's debts) if the associate that was addressed could not be considered *gérant*. The Court of Appeal of Brussels confirmed several times that this rule applied: APs did not entail joint and several liability.[97] In fact, this view went against the spirit of the *Code civil*, which provided that partnerships with a commercial object by law had jointly and severally liable partners (s. 1862).[98] The Brussels Court thus clearly envisaged

to the explicit provision in the code confirming the unlimited, joint and several liability of partners in a SNC. Presumably, the Court changed its position later on. See Brussels 20 June 1860, *Pas.* 1860, vol. 2, 301 (creditors of a SNC can pursue their debts against partners only after having obtained condemnation of the *société*).

97 Brussels 18 November 1815, *Pas.* 1815, 527; Brussels 31 May 1816, *Pas.* 1816, 140; Brussels 28 July 1820, *Pas.* 1820, 203; Brussels 12 January 1822, *Pas.* 1822, 24; Brussels 16 July 1834, *Pas.* 1834, vol. 2, 189; Brussels 13 April 1848, *Pas.* 1848, vol. 2, 253.

98 On this issue, and in regard of the AP, there was debate among legal scholars. See, for example, Eugène Persil, *Des sociétés commerciales ou commentaire sur les sociétés en général, les diverses espèces de sociétés de commerce, la manière de constater l'arbitrage*

commercial law as being entirely separate from civil law, that is, as standing beside the *Code civil*. The Court preferred to construe new solutions within the framework of the *Code de commerce*, instead of applying relevant sections of the Civil Code.

The *pro rata* policy of the Brussels Court of Appeal entailed a favourable attitude towards business partners who were given the opportunity to protect their personal properties from company creditors, at least to a certain extent. However, the approach of the Brussels Court did not affect all associates in the same way. Under the *pro rata* system, directors and working partners—even when they had invested sums themselves—were better off than non-active partners who had contributed in kind (by providing expertise or labour). If the latter were known, they were held to pay *pro rata* for the firm's debts. In fact, when calculating the "*fonds commun*" only the nominal capital that was mentioned in the company statutes was taken into consideration.[99] A non-working partner who had invested in kind could thus face claims based on a portion of capital stock to which he had not contributed. All this proved advantageous for trading associate-directors in companies in which non-financial partners were involved, because the former saw their liabilities reduced at the expense of the latter.

Indeed, even when the company statutes stressed joint and several liability, the Brussels Court imposed *pro rata* liability for irregular and undisclosed companies. The Brussels Court of Appeal distinguished between essential and non-essential provisions in irregular and unpublished company contracts. The non-essential ones (e.g. non-competition clauses) could not be invoked,[100] whereas the essential ones (in particular, the liability for debts) were considered to be enforceable.[101] Among the non-essential provisions were those concerning joint liability and mutual agency of associates.

---

forcé, la dissolution de sociétés, etc (Paris: Nève, 1833), 229–230; Troplong, *Commentaire,* 629–631 (nos. 603–604).

99 It was debated among legal scholars whether an investor in kind co-owned the company assets and stock, and if so, to what extent. See "Société," in *Dalloz Répertoire* (Paris: Dalloz, 1859), 448 (no. 374).

100 Brussels 28 April 1852, *BJ* 1853, 522; Commercial court Antwerp 17 December 1875, *Jur. Port d'Anvers* 1876, vol. 1, 51. Perhaps the Brussels Court changed its position later on. See Brussels 8 June 1870, *BJ* 1870, 1143 (the liquidation of the community of interests "*doît être opérée conformément à l'intention commune des parties*", i.e. has to be done according to the shared intentions of those involved).

101 Brussels 3 May 1823, *Pas.* 1823, 402; Brussels 13 February 1830, *Pas.* 1830, 42. See also Commercial court Antwerp 26 November 1869, *Jur. Port d'Anvers* 1870, vol. 1, 21.

Furthermore, one can summarize the policy of the Brussels Court of Appeal in terms of varieties of legal personhood. The Court distinguished between legal personhood "light" (entailing priority of company-related debts over personal debts and exclusion of set-off, which was applied to lawful and published SNCs) and legal personhood "ultra light" (separation of company funds but only within the personal funds of partners, for irregular and undisclosed SNCs, SCs[102] and SAs[103]). Joint liability of partners and mutual agency was acknowledged for the first, but not for the latter. The liability of the *gérant* in an "*association en participation*" was higher than for other associates, but for what exceeded the "*fonds commun*" was limited to a share of personal properties.

4 Organizational Structures and the Purpose of the Firm

The policy that was set out by the Brussels and Antwerp judges is important when analyzing the functionality of Antwerp company statutes. First, many of the contracts in the sample of 145 firms using indistinct labels such as *société* or *association* were to be considered "*associations en participation*" in the sense given by the Brussels Court of Appeal because they did not have a proper "*raison sociale*" (firm name). In at least 13.79 per cent of the statutes in the sample of 145 (i.e. 20/145), only some of the partners were mentioned in the signature of the company—moreover, without the addition "*& Cie*". Secondly, many contracts for partnerships were not published via the commercial court (some 45 per cent of company agreements remained unwritten, see above). As a result of all these divergent designations, the judicial tactics of the Brussels and Antwerp courts were highly relevant. In cases where a lawsuit was brought against a business venture, the features and form of the company determined the extent of the associates' liabilities. This section will analyze the purposes for which partnerships, which were often unpublished or irregular, were used (under 4.1). Moreover, it will examine to what extent the approaches of judges and entrepreneurs connected with each other (under 4.2).

4.1 *To What Extent were Partnerships Used for Corporate Finance?*

For Belgium, arguments as to the inherent advantages of partnerships, also in legal terms, have not been raised thus far, for a number of reasons. First among them is that scholarly interest in company structures and their relative impact

102 Brussels 22 February 1875, *Pas*. 1875, vol. 2, 100.

103 Brussels 16 February 1839, *Pas*. 1839, vol. 2, 27.

has faded over the past three decades, meaning that the debates over English, American and French counterparts have not been linked to the Belgian situation. The focus in earlier scholarly literature is much more orientated towards corporations and limited partnerships.[104] A second reason is that Belgium was an early leader in the Industrial Revolution, and that the share of corporations in this process was more significant than it was in France.[105] This level of industrialization means that the country aligns with the traditional assumption that industry needed capital, which could be pursued and secured by means of corporations. However, general and ordinary partnerships were very abundant in Belgium, as elsewhere. For the entire Kingdom of Belgium, numbers based on *actes de société* brought before commercial courts are available from 1845 onwards. They show that between August 1845 and January 1852 a vast majority of submitted *actes* concerned SNCs (511, designated as such) and that SCs (110) were also widely in use.[106] Even though in Belgium SAs in industry were more common than they were in France, the numbers were rather restricted; admittedly, the corporations were core players in their business sector, but even by 1850 most of them were not concerned with industrial activities.[107]

There are some indications that the traditional arguments regarding the limited access of the SA-acknowledgment by the government, upon request of authorization, as well as those concerning the characteristics of the SA vis-à-vis general and ordinary partnerships, do not entirely correspond with views of contemporaries. For example, in his *De l'état de l'industrie et du commerce en Belgique* (1861), Clerfeyt refers to SNCs. He states:

> This form of company (*société*) [meaning the SNC] provides third parties [i.e. creditors] with an energetic and efficient security (*garantie*), but it

104 Laureyssens, *De naamloze vennootschappen*; Julienne Laureyssens, "*L'Esprit d'Association* and the *Société Anonyme* in Early 19th-Century Belgium," *Revue belge de philologie et d'histoire* 2002, 517–530; Fred Stevens, "Vie et mort des sociétés commerciales en Belgique. Évolution du cadre légal, XIXe–XXe siècles," in Michael Moss and Philippe Jobert (eds.), *Naissance et mort des entreprises en Europe XIXe–XXe siècles* (Dijon: Université de Dijon, 1994), 3–16.

105 Laureyssens, "*L'Esprit d'Association*," 519–521.

106 François-Xavier-Théodore Heuschling, *Résumé de la statistique générale de la Belgique … pour la période décennale de 1841 à 1850* (Brussels: Hayez, 1852), 256.

107 Laureyssens, *De naamloze vennootschappen*, 1, 25–40, 60–62; Laureyssens, "*L'Esprit d'Association*," 519–521; Ginette Kurgan Van Hentenryk, "L'apport des actes de société à l'histoire des entreprises en Belgique," in *Entreprises et entrepreneurs, XIXe–XXe siècles* (Paris: Université de Paris-Sorbonne, 1983), 32–45, here 32–34.

> is not—one has to admit—fit for undertakings that are more significant (such as the construction of a railroad). It is feasible only for a restricted number of partners and does not provide for attracting modest investors. Moreover, it is very difficult to find people having so much confidence in one another that they are willing to risk their entire estate to rely on their individual behaviours. This company form is too rigid, and it oversteps its purpose. Moreover, it is incomplete and insufficient [for the purpose of significant ventures].[108]

On the SC, he noted the following:

> With these companies, the capital can be high, low or divided, and the number of silent partners can be significant; but, on the other hand, disadvantages are present as well. The unlimited and discretionary powers of the directors, the threat of unlimited liability for the silent partner when he participates in the business, the impossibility for the investor to halt damaging transactions of directors, and the common antagonism of those who should work together in their common interests, are the main disadvantages of these sorts of companies.[109]

SAs, too, were criticized. In his *De l'industrie en Belgique* from 1839, Natalis Briavoinne emphasized that many SAs, as well as SCs, had gone bankrupt in the preceding years, because "money cannot be a substitute for expertise and work". Briavoinne suggested that directors had held concurrent positions in many SAs and as a result had not monitored these businesses thoroughly. The same was said of SCs, which according to Briavoinne were for a large part to be considered as non-authorized SAs.[110] Briavoinne's remarks hint at corporate governance problems. Flawed selection processes seem to have been an issue. Directors were appointed not for their ability to administer the firm but for other reasons. One can presume that they were mostly bankers or that they belonged to the elitist networks of the corporation founders.

Furthermore, the abovementioned opinions are only partially corroborated by the 145 company statutes. The distinction capital-based (SC, SA) vs. non-capital-based companies (SNC) fits with the situation in Antwerp only to a

---

108 J. Clerfeyt, *De l'état de l'industrie et du commerce en Belgique et des institutions qui s'y rattachent* (Brussels: Lesigne, 1863), 244.

109 Ib.

110 Natalis Briavoinne, *De l'industrie en Belgique. Causes de décadence et de prospérité. Sa situation actuelle*, vol. 2 (Brussels: Wahlen, 1839), 237–241.

TABLE 8.3 *Nominal capital (in Belgian francs) mentioned in company contracts, divided over company type (Antwerp 1830–1850)*

	SOC	SNC	SC	SA
undetermined	54	10	1	1
<10,000	8	4	3	1
10,000-<50,000	26	5	0	0
50,000-<100,000	11	2	4	0
100,000-<1,000000	5	3	4	1
1,000000+	0	0	0	12
other	0	1	0	0
unknown	0	1	0	0
total	104	26	12	15

certain extent. It is true that a significant number of *sociétés* and SNCs were founded without any nominal capital, and that most of their founders purported to build up capital by ploughing back profits (see table 8.3).[111] Moreover, SAs had high nominal capital. However, the general partnership was also often used for locking in funds before the firm started its activities. The *société en commandite*, which was mostly devised as without shares (only 1 out of 12 was *par actions*), was used not only to draw in large amounts but also to attract smaller capital investments.

It is evident that many company contracts were used to confirm plans for cooperating rather than to make arrangements on capital. One can distinguish between company contracts that were collaborative structures and those that contained provisions on corporate finance, either with the specification of a nominal capital or with deliberately vague descriptions (e.g. "the capital will be raised when necessary,"[112] "the partners will pay up according to the needs of the firm"[113]). For both, a difference arises between contracts that served the

111 This was demonstrated for other contemporary cities, as well as for the SNC. See Cayez, "Structures juridiques," 229–230; Hirsch, "Naissance des sociétés," 143; André Straus and Pierre Verley, "Parisian Industries and National Capitalism in the First Half of the Nineteenth Century (1830–1850)," in Philippe Jobert and Michael Moss (eds.), *The Birth and Death of Companies. An Historical Perspective* (Carnforth: Parthenon, 1990), 89–103, here 99.

112 E.g. SAA, Notaries, 9749, deed no. 160 (6 Dec. 1833).

113 E.g. SAA, Notaries, 9754, deed no. 84 (9 Aug. 1838).

TABLE 8.4 *Purpose of companies (Antwerp 1830–1850)*

	SOC	SNC	SC	SA
NCF	31	10	0	0
NCF/BUS	5	3	0	0
NCF/BUSCON	0	0	0	0
NCF/BUSEX	13	0	0	0
CF	15	4	10	10
CF/BUS	7	2	1	0
CF/BUSCON	1	0	0	0
CF/BUSEX	23	6	1	5
BUSCON	2	0	0	0
BUSCON/BUSEX	1	0	0	0
other	1	0	0	0
unknown	5	1	0	0
total	104	26	12	15

NCF: no corporate finance, BUS: establishment of a business venture, BUSCON: consolidation of a functioning business venture, BUSEX: running of a business in combination with attracting expertise, CF: corporate finance purpose.

purpose of establishing or continuing a firm, and those that were aimed to attract expertise (in that case one partner was an expert, and his participation was typically in kind; other partners provided infrastructure or capital) (see table 8.4).

These numbers show that for *sociétés* 44.23 per cent (46/104) of contracts had the purpose of locking in capital investments. For other types, this share is higher (somewhat higher for SNCs: 46.15 per cent (12/26)). Indeed it is very pronounced for the SA and SC: both 100 per cent ((12/12) and (15/15)). However, Clerfeyt's opinion that the SNC (and *a fortiori* the general partnership) was not fit for "larger undertakings" does not entirely correspond with the data. The *société* was used for starting up business ventures for which capital was collected.

Some 30.77 per cent of *sociétés* (32/104, see table 8.5) were for manufacturing firms; for SNCs this percentage was 19.23 per cent (5/26); for SCs 8.5 per cent (1/12) and for SAs it was 13.33 per cent (2/15). As was mentioned above, in the period under examination the appetite for investments in manufacturing shops and industry in Antwerp was generally limited. Nonetheless, the mainly preindustrial processing shops that were set up in Antwerp during the first half of the nineteenth century required financing as well.[114] The raw materials of sugar refineries and tobacco shops were also expensive because of import tariffs,[115] and when new locations were used, the installation of mills and chimneys was often necessary.[116]

What was true for manufacturing ventures did not apply to trading houses. In practice, new ventures in insurance, brokerage and commission business sectors did generally require less starting capital than manufacturing firms.[117] The predominant use of SAs for insurance and banking must be analyzed with care in this regard. The nominal capital of these companies was devised as a public offering: it was a projection rather than a reflection of a presence of funds. Shareholders were invited to buy stock, and only when all shares were bought was the purported capital acquired. Even though for other company types such projections were possible as well, they were less common.[118] The general partnership was popular for general trading companies (30.77 per cent, 32/104, see table 8.5), but the SNC (57.69 per cent, 15/26) and SC (58.33 per cent, 7/12) were used relatively more often. SNC contracts for general wholesale and commission ventures often provided for ploughed-back profits and lacked provisions on nominal capital. By contrast, SCs and SAs always served the purpose of finance. Clerfeyt was correct in stating that the SC and SA were combined with higher capital than were other company types. Yet SCs and SAs were used more generally for commercial services and trading houses, though seldom in ventures of industry or manufacturing shops.

The abovementioned results correspond to data from other nineteenth-century cities, including Paris, Marseille, Lille, and Lyon. The fact that many general partnerships and SNCs were also used for manufacturing has been explained in terms of family relations and close monitoring (henceforth

114 Please note that in De ruysscher, "Handelsvennootschappen" the labels of "manufacturing" and "industry" were largely combined. However, a more subtle distinction between the nature of activity, size of the business and corporate finance purposes is fruitful for the present argument. Even though manufacturing shops were largely preindustrial (in terms of size and methods of processing and production), the purpose of drawing in capital, which has mainly been linked to industry, could be vital for them as well.

115 Greefs, *Zakenlieden*, 79; Thijs, "De geschiedenis van de suikernijverheid," 43–44.

116 Thijs, "De geschiedenis van de suikernijverheid," 42–43.

117 Hilde Greefs, "Enkele zwaartepunten in het onderzoek naar ondernemerschap en ondernemersstrategieën te Antwerpen gedurende de periode 1794–1870," *Revue belge de philologie et d'histoire* 76 (1998), 419–442, here 433–434.

118 If company statutes provided the nominal capital they usually also mentioned the date on which it had to be paid. See SAA, ROA, 571, fols. 59^{v}–61^{r} (SNC, reg. 26 Nov. 1840), 576, fols. 91^{v}–92^{v} (SNC, reg. 3 Oct. 1842), 579, fols. 84^{r}–85^{r} (SNC, reg. 2 Oct. 1843).

TABLE 8.5 *Type of industry, per company type (Antwerp 1830–1850); these numbers are based on the description of the purpose of the company in the contract.*

	SOC	SNC	SC	SA
general trade	32	15	7	0
manufacturing (sugar)	4	1	0	1
manufacturing (tobacco)	4	0	0	0
manufacturing (other)	24	4	1	1
store	10	0	0	0
invention	1	0	0	3
insurance	0	0	0	7
banking	0	0	0	3
unknown	16	5	2	0
other	13	1	2	0
total	104	26	12	15

"General trade" encompasses wholesale activities, commissioning and/or financial services, which were usually not strictly separated from each other. Manufacturing firms were defined as those enterprises that the parties at the company contract labelled "*fabrique*", or which involved production activities with specialized infrastructure (e.g. sugar refineries, leather shops).

referred to as the "monitoring" argument).[119] It has also been stated that they served as start-up instruments for enterprises, which when they became more successful were switched to the SC or SA-type (henceforth referred to as the "maturing" argument).[120] For Paris, for example, it has been found out that the SNC was used not only between relatives, however, but also to a large extent between non-relatives. SNCs of this type included companies established for the sale of manufactured products in a wider region around the city and for cooperative ventures between craftsmen.[121]

For Antwerp, previous research by Hilde Greefs has pointed out to what extent non-relatives were working in business together during the first half of the nineteenth century. In a population of 234 merchants and entrepreneurs,

---

119 Pierre Caron, "Commerçants et industriels de la Côte-d'Or au XIXe siècle vus à travers les actes de société," *Annales de Bourgogne* 1982, 89–121, here 105–106, 120; Cayez, "Structures juridiques," 235; Hirsch, "Naissance des sociétés," 154–155.

120 Cayez, "Structures juridiques," 240–241; Lescure, "Companies and Manufacturers," 111–112.

121 Straus and Verley, "Parisian Industries," 100–101.

TABLE 8.6 *Relations between partners, per company type (Antwerp 1830–1850)*

	SOC	SNC	SC	Total
2 or more family members	31	6	7	44
not relatives	73	18	5	96
unknown	0	2	0	2
total	104	26	12	142

only 45 worked with non-relatives; the family venture, consisting of at least two family members, was dominant (56 per cent of firms).[122] The majority of these family firms had not been established as such but had evolved into one, when children were made partners after some time, for example, or when heirs and/or the widow of deceased founders continued the business.[123] Most of this information was based on practice-related documents that show collaborative undertakings and contacts. The data from the sample of 145 firms yield a less significant number of family businesses. The criterion used to label companies in the sample of 145 as family firms is the presence of two or more associates who have the same family name or who are named as spouses. Using this benchmark, at least 67.61 per cent (96/142, see table 8.6) of the 145 company contracts concerned ventures that were not family firms. This lower share of family firms is most probably due to the fact that collaboration was not always structured in the form of a company contract. It can thus be presumed that many unwritten and unregistered agreements on business ventures involved family members, and that enactment of company statutes was more common when non-relatives were involved. Nonetheless, it is remarkable that the relationship between associates did not influence the choice of company type even when statutes were written, enacted and published. Distribution of company types over firms of relatives and non-relatives largely corresponds to the proportions in the general population of company statutes. SCs are excepted because they were used relatively more often for collaboration between relatives than other company types.[124]

122 Greefs, *Zakenlieden*, 294.

123 Greefs, *Zakenlieden*, 300.

124 These findings have also been obtained for Lyon. See Cayez, "Structures juridiques," 235; Lescure and Straus, "Rythmes et espaces," 204. Please note the error of "68.75%" for "68.57%" in De ruysscher, "Handelsvennootschappen," 189.

TABLE 8.7 *Company statutes for manufacturing firms, per company type (Antwerp 1830–1850); these numbers are based on the agency provisions in the statutes.*

	SOC	SNC	SC
EQINV, EQAG	8	0	0
EQINV, UNEQAG	3	1	1
UNEQINV, EQAG	5	2	0
UNEQINV, UNEQAG	12	1	1
unknown	4	1	0
total	32	5	1

EQINV: partners invested the same share of capital in money or the statutes do not provide capital. UNEQINV: partners invested a different share of capital or some contributed in kind whereas others invested financial sums—in cases where the statutes did not provide any nominal capital and when investment in kind was not made by all partners, the company was categorized under this label. EQAG: all partners had mutual agency. UNEQAG: the statutes may or may not provide restrictions on agency of partners, though they contain a firm name that does not include all partners' names (or the addition "*& Cie*"). SAs are not included because they always combined unequal investments with unequal agency.

Manufacturing firms could be structured as general and ordinary partnerships when they purported to delegate the management to an agent-director. However, in a substantial share of general partnerships for manufacturing firms, partners—who were typically investors of capital as well as craftsmen or experts investing in kind—were considered as equals (8/32, 25 per cent, see table 8.7). This was less the case when capital was invested from the start and was not devised as an accrual of ploughed-back profits. Typically, in such "management firms" one or more financial investors were the directors. Most *sociétés* for manufacturing firms entailed unequal investments in combination with agency restrictions (12/32, 37.5 per cent). For trading associations general partnership contracts were more conventionally egalitarian than for manufacturing firms (13/32, 40.63 per cent vs 25 per cent), because they more often lacked provisions on capital or had associates who all invested financial sums and not labour or expertise.

4.2 *Mercantile Strategies Responding to Legal Requirements and Judicial Approaches*

Did partners avoid publication in order to profit from the *pro rata* approach of the Brussels and Antwerp judges? It is possible that managing partners avoided

TABLE 8.8 *Company statutes for trading associations, per company type (Antwerp 1830–1850); these numbers are based on the description of the purpose of the firm in the contract.*

	SOC	SNC	SC
EQINV, EQAG	13	5	0
EQINV, UNEQAG	4	0	2
UNEQINV, EQAG	7	2	0
UNEQINV, UNEQAG	8	1	0
unknown	0	7	5
total	32	15	7

For abbreviations, see the notes below table 8.7. SAs were not included for the same reason as mentioned under table 8.7.

the proper publication of statutes in order to reduce their external liabilities vis-à-vis creditors. This option may have been linked to the fact that trading and administering partners, in particular, took the initiative of having a contract drafted and published. Another possible trend may have been that associates arranged factual limited liability when the statutes mentioned some partners that were not included in the company's signature and remained unpublished. As a result, they were "hidden" from the creditors of the firm. When partners were not publicly known, they could not be sued for company-related debts. Publishing the statutes of a firm meant that all names of partners were made known publicly.

The proportions of company types over the population of published, enacted and privately written contracts can be inferred to a large extent from the 1856–1857 sample. It yields the finding that some types of companies are more prominent among the statutes exclusively published via the commercial court than were others. For SNCs and general partnerships many statutes were brought before the commercial court only, and these had not already been registered (43.48 per cent, 20/46, see table 8.9). If contracts of SNCs and *sociétés* were registered before being submitted at the court, then in the majority of cases it was done at the registration office alone, and not with a notary (72.73 per cent (16/22) v. 27.27 per cent (6/22)). For SCs, too, there was a tradition of submitting private contracts directly to the court without any registration one way or another (50 per cent, 4/8). For SCs, however, registration before a notary was more popular than for the *société* and SNC (25 per cent (2/8) vs. 15.22 per cent (7/46)). When considering all this, it can be assumed that in 1830–1850

TABLE 8.9 *Proportions of company contracts in the sample of July 1856 – Dec. 1857 (see above), per type and method of registration and publicity*

	SOC/SNC	SC	SA	Other/un-known	Total
COMM, REG, NOT	6	1	2	0	9
COMM, REG, no NOT	16	2	1	0	19
COMM, NOT, no REG	0	0	0	0	0
COMM, no REG, no NOT	20	4	7	5	36
no COMM, REG, no NOT	3	0	0	2	5
no COMM, NOT, no REG	0	0	0	0	0
no COMM, REG, NOT	1	1	1	0	3
total	46	8	11	7	72

Note that the SNC and *société* (general partnership) cannot be distinguished on the basis of the mentions in *Jurisprudence du Port d'Anvers*. The numbers for SAs must be interpreted with care. In particular the number of statutes brought before the commercial court, though without a counterpart in the ledgers of the registration offices or in notarial deeds (in italics), can be biased because of the timing of administrative formalities. Presumably governmental approval and publicity were solicited before (full) notarial registration.[125]

there were many more contracts of *sociétés* and SNCs than those in the sample of 145. Within this same period, moreover, the number of *sociétés en commandite* must have been more significant than can be deduced from the 1830–1850 sample. When considering this data, it cannot be ruled out that higher numbers of generic *sociétés* in the population of unpublished statutes reflect a tendency to manage partners to circumvent joint and full liability, or of devising factual limited liability.

However, the aforementioned question also touches upon the contents of company statutes, and considering the problem from that perspective largely rules out the above explanations. Counter-indications for liability reduction in favour of directors are found in those company statutes that were duly published. They contain incomplete company signatures as well, even though they were not functional. The 1856–1857 sample shows that 16.67 per cent (9/54) of excerpts of published statutes contained unlawful company names.

125 In De ruysscher, "Handelsvennootschappen," 187 it is presumed that all SA statutes were notarial from the start. The data there corresponds to the 145-sample. The 1856–1857 sample invites for nuances at this point.

This proportion is largely comparable to the share of registered statutes with incomplete "*raisons sociales*" (13.79 per cent, 20/145). The deficient company names in these samples cannot have been devised so as to opt for the *pro rata* regime, because the statutes were made public and contained the names of all partners. In a published SNC, a director-associate was jointly and severally liable, as were all associates.[126] Moreover, those contracts with unlawful firm names that were registered at the registration offices—of which most were published in the commercial court—were signed by all associates, as well as by those who invested in kind.

Furthermore, the data of tables 8.7 and 8.8 do not demonstrate any systematic director-managed opting-in for the liability regime that was instituted by the Brussels Court of Appeal and the Antwerp commercial court. Since manufacturing firms had a shop and equipment, the personal liability of partners and directors for these ventures may have posed less of a problem than for trading associations, which worked with merchandise that was often not present or which had intangible assets. If assets were easily found, they could be seized. This was more likely the case for manufacturing firms than in respect of trading ventures. However, associations for trade that provided equal agency of partners in their statutes were more common than manufacturing shops that treated associates on the same footing. One would expect attempts at shielding administrators within the company statutes when personal liability was an issue, but this was not the case.

Another explanation for the high numbers of unpublished partnership contracts may be that lack of publication was *de facto* a limitation of liability. However, when considering the 1856–1857 sample, the share of non-published (written) statutes does not reflect a higher number of companies having incomplete firm names or unequal agency compared to the published ones. It is possible that unwritten contracts were mostly devised in such terms, but that cannot be proved. There are some indications that firm names could remain private; they were not always communicated to the outside world.[127] Another possible hint that unwritten statutes more often served to shield investors is the higher

126 s. 22 *Code de commerce*.

127 Some address books of merchants and shopkeepers list their names with mention of their firm's name. It seems that not all of them revealed that they were representing a company. See, for example, Léonard Van den Wijngaert, *Almanach. Indicateur commercial de la ville d'Anvers* (Antwerp: Van den Wijngaert, 1828), 149 (Fr. J. Ferd. Theunissen, general trader), and 169 (Pierre Michel Ergo, sugar refiner). Both were involved in a company for their listed profession at that time. See SAA, ROA, B2, 96, fo. 26^{v}–27^{r} (reg. 8 Febr. 1831) and SAA, ROA, BA, 108, fo. 101 r–103^{v}. (reg. 1 July 1830).

number of family firms mentioned in documents stemming from practice, as compared to (written and enacted) company statutes. But then again, if limited liability was an important problem, why was the safest option (a SC), even among the unpublished (yet written) statutes, so unpopular?

The abovementioned arrangements of incomplete company signatures in published statutes were more likely chosen to appoint some or one of the partners as administrators. These agents were not comparable to *gérants*, who were liable with their personal properties but to the extent of the "*fonds commun*" and a surplus share only. By contrast, administrators were fully liable with their personal properties. It would have been an advantage for associates delegating powers to an agent to publish the statutes (the agent was then unlimitedly liable), rather than keep the statutes unpublished (meaning that personal liability of the *gérant* was capped). But, as the abovementioned sample of 1856–1857 shows, the unpublished and published statutes do not differ much in regards of incomplete company signatures. The choice for agents was thus a matter of administration rather than liability. Associates who were not active in trade accepted their liabilities, but they appointed administrators who would answer first for the debts of the company.

In summary, therefore, there are few indications that the judicial approaches of the Brussels Court and Antwerp commercial court fundamentally determined contractual provisions on agency restrictions. It is more likely that there was a general path dependence in commercial practice, irrespective of the contents of the French codes and interpretation of judges, while building on the traditions of the Old Regime. Courts did not merely corroborate irregular and unpublished statutes but did go a long way in upholding them. The differences between judicial strategies and associates' views were limited overall. Path dependence is evident in the continuity of designations for companies between the eighteenth and nineteenth century. Moreover, path dependence among entrepreneurs explains why notaries also drafted company statutes without having support in the official law, or even in judicial policies. It was judges who adapted the legal framework on the basis of contractual practice, rather than the other way round.

5 Conclusion

The data analyzed above is rather counter-intuitive. Company structures typically associated with small business could be used for activities of manufacturing. *Sociétés* and SNCs were chosen often even when capital was locked in. *Sociétés en commandite*, typically considered as vehicles for large companies with outside investors, were mainly used to structure family firms, even though they always encompassed invested capital. Moreover, company contracts were not, to a large extent, used to finance commercial activities, even when they were written down and registered. The arguments mentioned as to monitoring and maturing thus invite further reflection when considering the Antwerp case. The maturing argument cannot explain why both new and consolidated businesses were typically structured as *sociétés* and SNCs. Similarly, the monitoring argument does not support the relatively frequent use of SCs among family members, although only if family ties are taken as supplementing the contents of the company contract. Indeed, SCs separated investment from control, as Clerfeyt rightly stated. Moreover, there were not more partnerships for collaboration with non-relatives, which one could infer from the monitoring argument. As a result, the functionalities and intended uses of partnerships were much broader than has often been thought.

The abovementioned legal approaches, by jurists and courts, lowered the bar for considering business ventures to be valid, even when they had not been formalized in a contract. A likely reason was the balancing of creditors' and associates' interests. In this regard, "absolute nullity" of unpublished and irregular companies, which was proposed by some legal scholars on the basis of sections in the *Code de commerce*, was a blunt concept. If a company agreement was pronounced as being null and void in this sense, the contracts that had been signed on its behalf were also affected. Retroactivity in categorizing irregular and undisclosed firms as non-existent technically deprived creditors of their guarantee, which lay in the joint and several liabilities of the associates mentioned in the firm's name. Moreover, in cases where a winding up occurred on account of retroactive nullity, associates lost what they had built up (reputation, capital). As a result, the Brussels Court of Appeal, and the Antwerp commercial court in its wake, accepted an intermediate form between joint and limited liability of associates in irregular and unpublished companies.

Another conclusion following on from the combined analysis of commercial and legal practices in this particular period of 1830–1850 is that limited liability was not yet a fundamental feature of companies. The approaches of the Antwerp and Brussels courts technically opened up the possibility of bringing "hidden" partners into general partnerships. In theory, such outsiders could be sued for the debts of the firm, but in practice—when the contract had not been deposited at the commercial court, and the firm's name did not mention them—who could know that they were involved? "Hidden" partners in undisclosed partnerships could be better off than silent partners in officialized *sociétés en commandite*. The latter could be sued for their share in the capital, if it had not been paid up,[128] whereas the former could remain under the creditors' radar. However, when considering the numbers of company statutes, it is not likely that deliberate tactics to avoid publication in order to protect associates from creditors were widespread, perhaps with the exception of unwritten company agreements. Furthermore, in terms of liability and agency in judicial and contractual practice, company types, as mentioned in the *Code de commerce*, were largely interchangeable, if not altogether ignored. It seems that parties to company agreements of any form could devise more or less full liability of some associates in combination with restricted liability of others.

It is likely that path dependence in commercial practice explains the lasting popularity of these general partnerships that were not in line with the commercial code. Judges in the Antwerp and Brussels courts bridged the gap between the official law and mercantile practices to a large extent. In any case, and considering that judicial approaches and mercantile practice did not entirely overlap, the former did not provide any significant incentive for the business community to adjust agreements of company. Considering all this, the activity of organizing and structuring enterprises must be reappraised. For example, in view of the above, the alleged "weak" structure of many large associations of dockers and transporters in the Antwerp port poses less of a problem.[129] Moreover, the legal-economic history of the era of industrialization can be reconsidered: networks and informal constraints were undoubtedly important, but collaboration was also based on support from legal actors, even though the incentives for change came from below, including from local courts, rather than from within the spheres of government.[130]

128 Brussels 31 Oct. 1871, *Pas.* 1872, vol. 2, 55.

129 The "maturing" argument and respect for tradition are commonly brought forward in debates concerning the "*naties*" (i.e. associations) in the Antwerp port. However, they often deliberately opted for the structure of *société* or SNC. See H. Bosmans, "De Antwerpse naties," in *Liber amicorum Tricot* (Antwerp: Kluwer, 1988), 95–105; Greta Devos, "Het juridisch statuut van de Antwerpse naties—19de–20ste eeuw," in *Publiek recht ruim bekeken. Opstellen aangeboden aan prof. J. Gijssels* (Deurne: Kluwer, 1994), 230–240; Hugo van Driel and Greta Devos, "Path Dependence in Ports. The Persistence of Cooperative Forms," *Business History Review* 81 (2007), 681–708, here 691, and 704–705.

130 Many authors have emphasized that commercial credit was in crisis in mid-nineteenth century Antwerp, especially from the end of the 1830s onwards. See Bernard S. Chlepner, *La Banque en Belgique. Étude historique et économique*, vol. 1 (Brussels: Lamertin, 1926), 80–85; Veraghtert, "De Antwerpse bankwereld," 196–203. However, this crisis mostly concerned bank loans and advances on deliveries. The authors mentioned have not considered the widespread use of letters of credit, order notes and private current accounts.

In view of a large factual comparability of company types, one possible method of further explaining differences in choices of entrepreneurs as to the structure of their business ventures would be to detail the social strata to which partners and directors belonged. Presumably the social profile of associates not only determined the type of business in which they engaged, but also the methods used to organize their undertakings. Would a banker who wanted to set up a family firm use the same tactics and methods as a shopkeeper who intended to introduce his son or daughter into his business? Maybe the former would go to a notary and set up a SC, whereas the latter would draw up a private contract of general partnership or SNC that was immediately brought before the commercial court. From these perspectives, further scrutiny of the sample of 145 contracts might provide answers to these questions in future.

Moreover, they have not taken the flexible legal approaches towards security and cooperation into account.

CHAPTER 9

Form, Size, "Governance": Remarks on Italian Late Nineteenth-Century Companies

Annamaria Monti

1 Introduction

The late nineteenth century Italian experience concerning the form, size and governance of companies and partnerships limited by shares represents a good case study in the contemporary European context, especially for the coexistence of small and large companies, each with a specific role and different needs. Small companies were established, above all, in the Northern part of the Peninsula, where preindustrial manufacturers were already operating in the late eighteenth century and throughout the nineteenth century, before the Industrial Revolution had reached the country. In the late nineteenth century these small firms, most of which became modern manufacturing industries, played an important economic role, a role they continued to have throughout the twentieth century and up to today.[1]

In fact, in Italy the industrial development was very much characterized by territory and the small dimension that always generally characterized the country's industrial structure. Besides these small businesses, there were a few big firms which led the industrialization in strategic sectors such as the electrical and chemical industries, iron metallurgy, and mechanics.[2]

Moreover, neither the few big businesses nor the many smaller companies chose the classical corporation form, namely a company limited by shares, which in Italy, as in France, was called *società anonima*. At least at the beginning of their business activities, they mainly preferred the juridical form of the so called *accomandita per azioni*, i.e. limited partnerships with shares, where in addition to one or more general partners who did not enjoy limited liability, there were one or more limited partners, i.e. partners with limited lia-

1 Franco Amatori, "Entrepreneurial Typologies in the History of Industrial Italy: Reconsiderations," *Business History Review* 85 (Spring 2011), 151–180.

2 For a general overview, see Franco Amatori and Andrea Colli, *Impresa e industria in Italia. Dall'Unità a oggi* (Venice: Marsilio, 2003), as well as Valerio Castronovo, *Storia economica d'Italia. Dall'Ottocento ai giorni nostri* (Turin: Einaudi, 2013).

 | DOI: 10.1163/9789004351868_011

bility. And this was for different reasons which I will discuss in the following study.

Certainly, from an economic and business history point of view, Italy was a "latecomer" among industrial countries, which meant that both the development of the firms and the legislation suffered in many ways due to this.[3] Shortly after the Unification in 1861, the country still had an agricultural and a craft based economy. Industrialization arrived in the late nineteenth century, when other northern European countries such as Germany had already entered the so called "second industrialization". Italy, however, was the first country in southern Europe to reach a stable stage of industrialization.

In fact, in the 1880s, things changed: in addition to modern manufacturing industries which operated in traditional Italian craft sectors such as food and textiles, others such as metallurgy and chemical and mechanical production became "visible". More precisely, historians say that, for Italy, we can really only talk of an industrial revolution when we reach the period that goes from 1896 up to 1914. And it is with World War I that industrialization appears to have passed the point of no return.[4] In synthesis, Italy, a latecomer, managed to catch up with the other industrialized countries at the time of the second Industrial Revolution: steel, heavy machinery, transportation equipment, electric and chemical industries were as present in Italy as in the world's leading nations.[5]

The companies which are today considered to be the most important Italian corporations were all founded around the turn of the twentieth century. And, as happened everywhere in the industrialized world, the first big businesses were the railway corporations. By 1905 the railways were nationalized and the indemnities to the companies were often used to finance the growing electric industry.[6] Generally speaking, Italian industrialization was made

---

3 Franco Amatori and Andrea Colli, "Models of Entrepreneurship in a Latecomer Country: Italy," in Youssef Cassis and Ioanna Pepelasis Minoglou (eds.), *Country Studies in Entrepreneurship. A Historical Perspective* (Basingstoke: Palgrave Macmillan, 2006), 129–148.

4 Franco Amatori, "Italy: The Tormented Rise of Organizational Capabilities Between Government and Families," in Alfred D. Chandler Jr., Franco Amatori and Takashi Hikino (eds.), *Big Business and the Wealth of Nations* (Cambridge: CUP, 1997), 246–276.

5 Franco Amatori and Andrea Colli, "European Corporations: Ownership, Governance, Strategies and Structures. A Review of Five Countries: United Kingdom, Germany, France, Italy and Spain," in Harm G. Schröter (ed.), *The European Enterprise. Historical Investigation into Future Species* (Berlin: Springer, 2008), 23–36.

6 Giuseppe Berta, *L'Italia delle fabbriche. La parabola dell'industrialismo nel Novecento* (Bologna: Il Mulino, 2014).

possible through State aid, mainly through fiscal benefits, protective tariffs, and direct financial aid. The government also supported big business through orders. Furthermore, financial support was given by banks, which were "mixed banks", following the so-called German model. In particular, Italian capitalism was open to foreign investments, especially from Germany. Italian business was also confined within a family framework. Appropriately, Italy's capitalism has been defined as one of "limited suffrage", which was controlled by the state and by prominent families.[7]

Therefore, the Italian model has also been defined as "precocious State capitalism". In fact, it would probably have been impossible for Italy to have acquired a modern industrial apparatus without strong government intervention.[8] Later on, during the twentieth century, bigger firms started building monopolistic corporate groups.[9] Indeed, such a process of industrialization—a mix of private businessmen, State aid and bank investments—together with the growth of smaller firms challenged lawyers and jurists at the turn of the twentieth century.

2 The Italian Debate on Company Law

In 1882 a new Commercial Code was promulgated: it was the result of the multi-decennial efforts of a well-known Italian jurist, Pasquale Stanislao Mancini, a lawyer and professor of International Law who was also a prominent politician and Minister for Justice.[10] Concerning company law specifically, the so called

---

7 Amatori, "Entrepreneurial Typologies," 154.

8 Franco Bonelli, "Il capitalismo italiano. Linee generali di interpretazione," in Ruggiero Romano and Corrado Vivanti (eds.), *Storia d'Italia. Annali I. Dal feudalesimo al capitalismo* (Turin: Einaudi, 1978), 1193–1255, in particular 1204, as quoted by Amatori, "Italy: The Tormented Rise," 255. See also Fabrizio Barca, *Il capitalismo italiano, storia di un compromesso senza riforme* (Rome: Donzelli, 1997).

9 Raffaele Teti, "Imprese, imprenditori e diritto," in Franco Amatori et al. (eds.), *Storia d'Italia. Annali XV. L'industria* (Turin: Einaudi, 1999), 1213–1303.

10 Reference to Claudia Storti, "Mancini, Pasquale Stanislao," in Italo Birocchi, Ennio Cortese, Antonello Mattone and Marco Nicola Miletti (eds.), *Dizionario Biografico dei Giuristi Italiani (XII–XX secolo)*, vol. 2 (Bologna: Il Mulino, 2013), 1244–1248, with extensive bibliographical references. Among other recent contributions see Gian Savino Pene Vidari, "La prolusione di Pasquale Stanislao Mancini sul principio di nazionalità (Turin 1851)," in Giovanni Cazzetta (ed.), *Retoriche dei giuristi e costruzione dell'identità nazionale* (Bologna: Il Mulino, 2013), 117–134; Bernardo Sordi, "Plaidoyer per l'unità della giurisdizione: Pasquale Stanislao Mancini e l'abolizione del contenzioso amministrativo," in Stefano Borsacchi

Mancini Code, even if it was mainly inspired by the French law of 1867,[11] made some original choices.[12] To incorporate a company, the Code of 1882 imposed the complete subscription of the capital (of the company), and it also required each shareholder to pay 30 per cent of the due contribution. However, the most important reform was the abolition of the governmental permission previously required for the formation of companies limited by shares: from that point on, the articles of incorporation had to be executed and filed, and the deed had to be checked and approved by a civil tribunal judge.[13]

This was a very important achievement for Italy and it seemed to be a very modern and efficient regulation. However, it very soon showed its limits, as it was enacted when the country was first caught up in the Industrial Revolution. So, when the first industrial plant was created around the 1880s and a mixed banking system started to operate, mainly thanks to foreign capital, Italian corporate legislation was far from being appropriate for the investors' needs. That is why businessmen as well as scholars were involved in the reform process.

The demand for a comprehensive reform of company law was deeply rooted in real needs. In particular, the small firms needed an adequate regulation: they did not benefit from State aid as did the bigger industrial businesses, and they called for legislative support. Indeed, starting in 1894–1895, official

---

and Gian Savino Pene Vidari (eds.), *Avvocati protagonisti e rinnovatori del primo diritto unitario* (Bologna: Il Mulino, 2014), 845–858.

11 Jean Hilaire, *Introduction historique au droit commercial* (Paris: PUF, 1986), 208–243; Anne Lefebvre-Teillard, *La société anonyme au 19ème siècle: du Code de Commerce à la loi de 1867. Histoire d'un instrument juridique du développement capitaliste* (Paris: PUF, 1985). See also Jean-Pierre Alline, "Le développement du droit commercial en dehors du Code et l'influence des droits étrangers 1807–1925," in Corinne Saint-Alary-Houin (ed.), *Qu'en est-il du Code de Commerce 200 ans après? État des lieux et projections* (Toulouse: Presses de l'Université des sciences sociales de Toulouse, 2009), 84–87; Edouard Richard (ed.), *Droits des affaires. Questions actuelles et perspectives historiques* (Rennes: Presses universitaires de Rennes, 2005), and the papers joined in Carlo Angelici et al., *Negozianti e imprenditori. 200 anni dal Code de commerce* (Milan: Mondadori, 2008). Recently, Johannes W. Flume, "Law and Commerce. The Evolution of Codified Business Law in Europe," *Comparative Legal History* 2 (2014), 45–83.

12 Antonio Padoa-Schioppa, *La genesi del codice di commercio del 1882*, now in Antonio Padoa-Schioppa, *Saggi di storia del diritto commerciale* (Milan: LED, 1992), 157–203.

13 Antonio Padoa-Schioppa, "Disciplina legislativa e progetti di riforma delle società per azioni in Italia (1862–1942)," now in Padoa Schioppa, *Saggi*, 213–226. See also Giuseppe Ferri, "La disciplina delle società nel codice di commercio del 1882," in *1882–1982: Cento anni dal codice di commercio* (Milan: Giuffrè, 1984), 93–106.

and legislative commissions worked to try to reform the corporation statute. On one hand, scholars called for stronger measures to protect shareholders and creditors, and on the other, business organizations called for more liberal corporate laws and for greater freedom for corporate management.[14]

To summarize, the complex of corporate law regulation stated in the Mancini Code of 1882 was in force until 1942, apart from a series of reforms made during the period when the country was under Fascist rule. Legal historians have already studied the different Italian company law reform drafts, particularly the two commercial code drafts of 1922 and 1925.[15]

Around these drafts there flourished a very brilliant doctrinal debate; also, the businessmen's associations showed a strong commitment to the reform process. The Chambers of Commerce continued to play a role, but the organizations which gained greater influence were two new associations founded around 1910, *Assonime*, the association of the Italian incorporated companies,[16] and *Confindustria*, the association of Italian entrepreneurs.[17]

In synthesis, a number of topics concerning what we nowadays call "corporate governance" were debated (and not only in Italy). Among the main topics under consideration were the powers of the shareholders' meetings (ordinary and extraordinary meetings); the different kinds of shares (in bearer and in registered form) and the right to vote which they carried: the issue of debentures (bonds); the role and the liability of the board of directors; the rules to follow in drafting the financial statements; and last but not least, taxation issues.

2.1 *The Winding-Up and Liquidation of Companies*

One of the most interesting topics which were under discussion in those times was on the winding up and liquidation of companies limited by shares. This

14 Padoa-Schioppa, "Disciplina legislativa e progetti di riforma," 228–239.

15 Gastone Cottino and Gustavo Minervini, "Le società per azioni a cento anni dal codice di commercio," in *1882–1982: Cento anni*, 109–125; A. Padoa-Schioppa, "La normativa sulle società per azioni: proposte e riforme, un concerto a più voci (1882–1942)," in Antonio Padoa-Schioppa and Piergaetano Marchetti (eds.), *Tra imprese e istituzioni: 100 anni di Assonime. IV: La società per azioni* (Bari: GLF editori Laterza, 2010), 7–81. See also Francesco Galgano, *Lex mercatoria. Storia del diritto commerciale* (Bologna: Il Mulino, 2010), 160–179; Paolo Ungari, *Profilo storico del diritto delle anonime in Italia* (Rome: GLF editori Laterza, 1974), 61–112.

16 See *Cinquant'anni di vita della Associazione fra le Società italiane per Azioni* (Rome: Castaldi, 1961) as well as the six volumes edited in 2010, *Tra imprese e istituzioni 100 anni di Assonime*.

17 Valerio Castronovo, *Cento anni di imprese. Storia di Confindustria 1910–2010* (Bari: Laterza, 2010); Giorgio Fiocca, *Storia della Confindustria 1900–1914* (Venice: Marsilio, 1994).

topic was chosen as an example of the nineteenth-twentieth century Italian debate on company law among a few relevant others, because through this topic many others were reflected. Liquidation worked like a mirror, so to say, of many problematic issues concerning what we call "corporate governance" today.

Here, I will refer specifically to an essay written in 1891 by a very brilliant Italian jurist, Angelo Sraffa (1865–1937),[18] who dedicated his first relevant work in the field to the subject,[19] and in the following years wrote on the failure of companies[20] and extensively on corporate law issues. His essays were mainly published in the *Rivista di diritto commerciale*, which he co-founded in 1903 and directed until 1937 with Cesare Vivante,[21] one of the most prominent Italian jurists of that time who had dedicated the first volume of his treaty on commercial law to the German scholar Levin Goldschmidt.[22]

In Sraffa's essay of 1891, the analysis of corporate law had a broad critical and comparative perspective, capable of holding together practices, lessons from other countries (especially in continental Europe), previous historical experiences, always favouring the problems of current events. His interpretative approach to commercial law and specifically to company law was praised by the well-known French jurist Raymond Saleilles,[23] who reviewed Sraffa's work on the liquidation of companies in the French journal *Annales de droit commercial*. Saleilles gave an eloquent title to his review ("Comparative commercial law. Contribution to studies of juridical methodology").[24]

---

18 See Annamaria Monti, *Angelo Sraffa. Un 'antiteorico' del diritto* (Milan: EGEA, 2011).

19 Angelo Sraffa, *La liquidazione delle società commerciali* (Florence: Cammelli, 1891).

20 Angelo Sraffa, *Il fallimento delle società commerciali* (Florence: Cammelli, 1897).

21 Paolo Grossi, *Scienza giuridica italiana. Un profilo storico* (Milan: Giuffrè, 2002); Alberto Sciumè, "Cesare Vivante," in *Il contributo italiano alla storia del pensiero. Diritto. Enciclopedia italiana. Ottava appendice* (Rome: Istituto dell'Enciclopedia italiana, 2012), 446–450, with more bibliographical references.

22 Cesare Vivante, *Trattato di diritto commerciale*, vol. 1 (Turin: Bocca, 1893).

23 Alfons Aragoneses, *Recht im Fin de siècle. Briefe von Raymond Saleilles an Eugen Huber (1895–1911)* (Frankfurt am Main: Klostermann, 2007); Frédéric Audren, Christian Chêne, Nicolas Mathey and Arnaud Vergne (eds.), *Raymond Saleilles et au-delà* (Paris: Dalloz, 2013); Paolo Grossi, "Assolutismo giuridico e diritto privato. Lungo l'itinerario scientifico di Raymond Saleilles," now in Paolo Grossi, *Assolutismo giuridico e diritto privato* (Milan: Giuffrè, 1998), 193–261, and also in Paolo Grossi, *Nobiltà del diritto. Profili di giuristi* (Milan: Giuffrè, 2008), 269–337; Marco Sabbioneti, *Democrazia sociale e diritto privato. La Terza Repubblica di Raymond Saleilles (1855–1912)* (Milan: Giuffrè, 2010).

24 Raymond Saleilles, "Contribution à l'étude des méthodes juridiques. À propos d'un Livre

However, returning to the topic of the winding-up and liquidation of companies, the major problem in practice was to determine the "legal nature" of a company in liquidation: what did it become? The Italian commercial code of 1882 stated that a company could be wound-up due to an expiry of term set forth (in the by-laws), or due to the attainment of the business purpose: the company was wound-up and could not be continued.[25] How should this norm be interpreted in relation to a company in liquidation? Some jurists thought that the tribunal's decree which put the company in liquidation was equivalent to the expiration of the term set forth, and no prorogation was possible.

Consequently, they thought that a company in liquidation became a mere co-ownership,[26] or something in the middle between a company and a co-ownership.[27] Others suggested that it could be considered a new company devoted to liquidation.[28] Some other authors also claimed that a company in liquidation was still alive in a fictitious way.[29]

The high courts of the Kingdom of Italy (*Corti di Cassazione*) decided that a company in liquidation continued to enjoy its legal personhood and its contractual obligations were still in force, even if the scope of the company was now different. Most of the legal doctrine agreed upon this position,[30] even Angelo Sraffa agreed on it.[31] In addition, Sraffa explained the fact that one possible destiny of a company was liquidation, and this idea could not be avoided. Therefore it was nonsense to think that the legal nature of the company faded as soon as the company reached one of its possible destinies.

---

de M.A. Sraffa. (La Liquidazione delle società commerciali)," *Annales de droit commercial français, étranger et international* (1891), 217–227.

25 *Codice di Commercio del Regno d'Italia* (1882), s. 197–207.

26 In particular, to this purpose Sraffa quoted the French colleague Claude-Alphonse Delangle, *Delle società di commercio* (Venice: Santini, 1851), 417–418.

27 Gustavo Bonelli, "La personalità giuridica dei beni in liquidazione giudiziale," *Rivista italiana per le scienze giuridiche* 7 (1889), 167–230.

28 Especially German authors followed this idea: Jacob Friedrich Behrend, *Lehrbuch des Handelsrechts* (Berlin: Guttentag, 1886), vol. 1/1, 566–568; Oscar Francken, *Die Liquidation der offenen Handelsgesellschaft in geschichtlicher Entwickelung* (Stuttgart: Enke, 1890).

29 In Italy this doctrine was followed by David Supino, *Diritto commerciale* (Florence: Barbèra, 1892), 149 *seq*. In France by Charles Lyon-Caen and Louis Renault, *Traité de droit commercial*, vol. 2 (Paris: Pichon, 1900), 265 *seq*.; in Germany by Achilles Renaud, *Das Recht der Actiengesellschaften* (Leipzig: Tauchnitz, 1875), 841–842.

30 Ercole Vidari, *Corso di diritto commerciale*, vol. 2 (Milan: Giuffrè, 1881), 636–637, and 657 *seq*.; Cesare Vivante, *Trattato di diritto commerciale*, vol. 2 (Turin: Bocca, 1903), 476 *seq*.

31 Angelo Sraffa, "Carattere giuridico delle società commerciali in liquidazione," *Foro italiano* (1891), 158–168.

In fact, it was possibly even more important that a company existed at this moment of its liquidation, when special procedures started to report to third parties what it had done. In particular, according to Sraffa, the company in liquidation continued during the liquidation itself as an entity separated from its members, able to assume obligations. However its scope had changed and the company continued only to fulfil the new scope connected to liquidation: to provide for the equitable and fair distribution of the assets.[32]

One more controversial point was the possibility for the shareholders of a company in liquidation to bring the company back into existence, once the company had been wound-up and put in liquidation. Sraffa argued against this possibility,[33] which however prevailed later on both in case law and in doctrinal opinions. Another major concern related to the liquidation of companies was the topic of the powers, duties and liability of liquidators: the legislation in force was not exhaustive, which meant that case law and doctrine had to work on it.

To sum up, the liquidation of companies brought every topic to the surface—the powers of the partners and those of the directors and then of the liquidators; legal personhood and the obligations toward third parties—and forced jurists and courts to face a number of controversial issues. They could not avoid dealing with them under the microscope of liquidation.

2.2 *The "Diffidence" towards Companies Limited by Shares* (società per azioni)

The heated doctrinal debate about company law to which we have referred, taking as its basis the specific example of the liquidation of commercial companies, was grafted onto a complex and constantly evolving economic reality, characterized, in the late nineteenth and the first fifteen years of the twentieth century, by an intense industrial development. What emerges, in the background, is indeed a kind of generalized distrust towards the use of the legal form of corporation.

In this regard, it could be interesting to refer to some recent empirical research in the economic field, based on data collected nowadays in different countries, which shows how business regulatory reforms are good for economic growth. The idea is that economic activity requires good rules, rules that establish and clarify property rights and reduce the cost of resolving disputes; rules

---

32 Sraffa, *La liquidazione*, 54.

33 Sraffa, *La liquidazione*, 59 *seq*. In 1899 published a second edition of this work and his conclusions were the same: Angelo Sraffa, *La liquidazione delle società commerciali* (Florence: Cammelli, 1899).

that increase the predictability of economic interactions and provide contractual partners with certainty and protection against abuse.[34]

I am not going to expand here on the hypothetical link between business regulatory reforms and economic growth, however, looking back at what happened in late nineteenth century Italy, the country and its firms were certainly still looking for the best rules. And one of the main problems was finding a “common ground” for the values to protect and promote through company law.

More specifically, what might be considered to be a clear symptom of that difficulty was the gradual spread of companies limited by shares in Italy and, this notwithstanding, the new Italian commercial code of 1882 provided for substantial freedom in the creation of such incorporated companies limited by shares which were generally considered to be the most important juridical “tool” in capitalist economies.

In particular, some statistical data collected in 1933 showed that in 1880, in the Kingdom of Italy, there were about 350 companies limited by shares, i.e. *società anonime*, joint-stock companies. Their number increased gradually and in 1896 there were *c.* 580: indeed, these were still “small” numbers. The later industrial development of the country certainly largely contributed to this situation, but once industrialization arrived, there were other reasons.

To explain the lack of success encountered by companies limited by shares, I would like to point out that what was still not appreciated from a technical and juridical point of view was the fact that the shareholders had limited powers compared to those enjoyed by the directors. One problematic aspect, particularly in the 1880s and in the 1890s, was that shareholders could not really cooperate in the administration of the corporation, which to us could be viewed as a ridiculous situation. In fact, this issue was to be one of the most discussed in particular in the legal doctrine, which played a non-secondary role in shaping company law rules during that time, and was especially concerned by the limited powers of the shareholders' meeting. The shareholders were the “owners” of the shares, but they could not really manage their “ownership”. Not only were the shareholders unable to manage their possessions, they actually needed to be guaranteed against the actions of the directors. Even after World War I, Italian legal doctrine was still tied to this older concept of companies limited by shares, which was characterized by the idea of the “dominance of the assembly”.

34 Jamal Ibrahim Haidar, “The Impact of Business Regulatory Reforms on Economic Growth,” *Journal of the Japanese and International Economies* 26/3 (2012), 285–307.

Legal scholars remained concerned by this topic at least until the end of the 1920s. Particular mention needs to be made to the ideas of Cesare Vivante, the "leading representative" of commercial law in Italy at the time, who always fought for the rights of the minority in the general meeting of the shareholders and, most importantly, played an active role in the legislative committees charged to draft new company law rules in the early post-war period.[35] On the other hand, however, businessmen were soon well aware of the indubitable advantages of companies limited by shares, especially when they wanted to collect capital to run their firms, and so they insisted for reforms which could allow them to better "exploit" this juridical form of company.

A second point which needs to be made in order to explain why there were so few companies limited by shares in Italy at the turning of the twentieth century is the fiscal question, and this directly concerned businessmen. Indeed, taxation issues were a profile of the Italian regulation on companies limited by shares, which apparently contributed (in a negative sense) to the scarce spread of this form of corporation in practice, especially among firms running smaller businesses. In fact, companies limited by shares were charged by the so called *imposta di ricchezza mobile*, a sort of income tax introduced in the Italian Kingdom after the unification: it was levied on company profits, even those allocated to reserves or capital increases. In practice, any company profit was hit, even if it was not distributed among the shareholders. I would also like to highlight that this fiscal problem was a very sensitive and delicate one, and it became the main point discussed by the Association of Italian Corporations (*Assonime*), mentioned above, since its foundation in 1910.[36] This Association immediately started a campaign to promote a reform of the fiscal treatment of the *anonime*. One could say that the campaign against this levy was the initial "core mission" of the Association of the *anonime*.

The delicacy of the problem of the excessive fiscal pressure that corporations were subjected to, indeed, also emerges from the lecture notes that were collected at college courses taught in the early twentieth century by one of the most famous professors of business law from the time, the aforementioned Angelo Sraffa—whom I had the opportunity to study in depth in recent years. He united an intense activity as a lawyer in the city of Milan with his academic activities.[37] Sraffa, rightly considered at the time to be one of the leading

35 On Cesare Vivante's doctrines see above, note 21.

36 Antonio Pedone, "Il contributo di Assonime alla formulazione della politica tributaria," in Antonio Pedone and Franco Gallo (eds.), *Tra imprese e istituzioni: 100 anni di Assonime. III: Imposte e sviluppo economico* (Rome: GLF editori Laterza, 2011), 5–23.

37 Monti, *Angelo Sraffa*, 176–189. On Sraffa's activity as a lawyer see also Tilmann J. Röder,

experts in corporate law, often took advantage of the lessons to illustrate current issues to his students at the Bocconi University[38] and to discuss with them concrete problems related to practice.

So, for example, in the academic year 1905–1906, when explaining to his students the classification of commercial companies according to the Mancini Code—on the basis of the type of responsibility of the partners in relation to creditors, according to the Napoleonic system—he complained about the improper use, in practical life, of one type of company instead of another due to artificial causes, which deformed, or rather, deeply altered the natural constitution of the company. "Miserably", in fact—this is the adverb ("*sfortunatamente*" in Italian) employed by him to express his full disapproval—one frequently chose to establish a limited partnership instead of a corporation only for tax reasons.[39]

Not even the cold transcript of his courses can hide his passion and interest in technical subjects, such as the taxation of commercial companies, behind which, however, were hidden far-reaching consequences. And still today we perceive from those lithographed pages how his lecture would quickly turn into a tirade against the exorbitant demands of the tax authorities and "predatory" rates on company profits from which the taxpayers were trying to defend themselves as they could by, among other things, avoiding establishing limited companies. Whether it was, therefore, the difficulty, from the doctrine and the legislature, in conceiving a company limited by shares in which the role of the directors were not subordinate to that of the shareholders' meeting, or a tax

---

Rechtsbildung im wirtschaftlichen "Weltverkehr". Das Erdbeben von San Francisco und die internationale Standardisierung von Vertragsbedingungen (1871–1914) (Frankfurt am Main: Klostermann, 2006), 274 *seq*., and 300 *seq*. In English, Tilmann J. Röder, *From Industrial to Legal Standardization, 1871–1914. Transnational Insurance Law and the Great San Francisco Earthquake*, Frederik Heinemann (trans.) (Leiden: Brill, 2012), 268–287. On nineteenth-twentieth century Italian lawyers see Alessandra Cantagalli, *Avvocati, banche e imprese* (Bologna: Il Mulino, 2010); Francesca Tacchi, *Gli avvocati italiani dall'Unità alla Repubblica* (Bologna: Il Mulino, 2002).

38 Marco Cattini, Enrico Decleva, Aldo De Maddalena and Marzio Achille Romani, *Storia di una libera università. I: L'Università commerciale Luigi Bocconi dalle origini al 1914* (Milan: EGEA, 1992) and *II: L'Università Commerciale Luigi Bocconi dal 1915 al 1945* (Milan: EGEA, 1997).

39 See for example Angelo Sraffa, *Lezioni pratiche di diritto commerciale, dispense compilate da S. Fedrigo*, anno accademico 1905–1906 (s.l.: s.n., 1906); *Diritto commerciale: anno accademico 1912–1913. Lezioni tenute dal chiarissimo prof. A. Sraffa* (Pavia: s.n., [1913]); *Società commerciali: anno accademico 1913–1914. Lezioni tenute dal chiarissimo prof. Angelo Sraffa* (Pavia: s.n., [1914]).

perceived as excessive by the business class, the fact is that the corporation was late to establish itself in Italy.

3 Final Thoughts on Cooperative Companies

This kind of "diffidence" towards companies limited by shares could explain—at least in part—not only the large use of partnerships limited by shares (*accomandita per azioni*), as I briefly mentioned, but also the spread of cooperative companies. In fact, the cooperative company, which could also be limited by shares, enjoyed great success during that time. Above all, the legislation in force considered, in a very positive way, the solidarity aims of cooperative companies, which could benefit from a number of fiscal discharges.[40]

Compared to corporations, which mainly had mere speculative finalities, cooperative companies bound to social but also (and often prevailing) lucrative aims definitely benefitted from a more favourable fiscal treatment. The great diffusion of cooperative companies in the northern and central parts of Italy is a social, economic and even political phenomenon already researched in the historiography and I am not going to expand on it at this point,[41] but it certainly deserves greater attention from a legal-historical point of view.[42]

---

40 Cesare Vivante, *Le società cooperative e la riforma del codice di commercio* (Venice: Ferrari, 1896).

41 Refer to Massimo Fornasari and Vera Zamagni, *Il movimento cooperativo in Italia. Un profilo storico-economico (1854–1992)* (Florence: Vallecchi, 1997); Maurizio Degl'Innocenti, Angelo Varni, Renato Zangheri, Zeffiro Ciuffoletti, Gianni Silei and Silvia Bianciardi, *Solidarietà e mercato nella cooperazione italiana tra otto e Novecento* (Manduria: Lacaita, 2003). See also Lia Gheza Fabbri, *Solidarismo in Italia fra XIX e XX secolo. Le società di mutuo soccorso e le classi rurali* (Turin: Giappichelli, 2000).

42 In those times, on cooperative companies besides doctrinal works authored by scholars—such as Cesare Vivante, *Trattato di diritto commerciale*, vol. 2/1 (Turin: Bocca, 1894), 1–37—there flourished more practical works written by lawyers and practitioners. For example, see the contributions by a Milanese lawyer who was involved in Milan social and political life as well as in cooperative movement: Pietro Manfredi, *Della necessità di disciplinare l'ordinamento delle società cooperative e con quali regole. Relazione al V. Congresso nazionale giuridico-forense* (Palermo: Barravecchio, 1903); Pietro Manfredi, "La cooperazione nelle leggi patrie," in *Rendiconti del Regio Istituto Lombardo*, serie 2, 25, fasc. 2, vol. 8–9 (Milan: Hoepli, 1892); Pietro Manfredi, *La società anonima cooperativa. Studi* (Milan: Hoepli, 1885). See also Giuseppe Gonetta, *Le società di mutuo soccorso e cooperative in Europa e specialmente in Italia, loro origine, scopo ed utilità. Studio storico-sociale, aggiuntivi alcuni discorsi sull'istruzione ed educazione popolare* (Florence: Vannini, 1884); Orazio Lenzi, *Delle società cooperative in genere e della cooperativa di produzione in ispecie*

One example will suffice: Angelo Sraffa, in 1894, on the occasion of his inaugural address of the academic year at the University of Macerata, significantly entitled "The commercial fight", launched into a plea in favour of cooperative societies and in particular of those associations that were set up by bodies of consumers. Looking at the results of unbridled competition among the large and small merchants, he identified the emergence of "a real and powerful merchant feudality" between the owners of big department stores, in particular in England and especially in France, and he was concerned about the fate—legal and economic, as well as social and political—of those who succumbed in the struggle, i.e., the consumers. In particular, Sraffa called for the need to temper the "excessive waves of individualism that have impregnated the mercantile life (...) with the spirit of mutuality and solidarity".[43]

The sources of inspiration for this contribution from his youth,[44] close to the positivist and sociological settings which were in vogue at the time, were, among others, *Les bases économiques de la constitution sociale* by a heterodox Italian economist, Achille Loria,[45] as well as the studies of an economist and evolutionary follower of "lorianesimo",[46] Ugo Rabbeno,[47] who dealt extensively with cooperation.[48]

(Siena: Torrini, 1893); Francesco Viganò, *La fratellanza umana ossia le società di mutuo ajuto cooperazione e partecipazione ed i municipi cooperativi* (Milan: Agnelli, 1873); Francesco Viganò, *Movimento cooperativo o le banche popolari tedesche e italiane e loro confederazione* (Milan: Civelli, 1873). From an economical point of view, Ghino Valenti, *Cooperazione rurale. La cooperazione in genere. Le forme e lo sviluppo della cooperazione rurale. La pratica della cooperazione rurale* (Florence: Barbèra, 1902).

43 "La lotta commerciale," in *Prolusione letta il dì 11 gennaio 1894 dall'avvocato Angelo Sraffa, professore di diritto commerciale nella R. Università di Macerata* (Pisa: Spoerri, 1894).

44 The same contribution was published as Angelo Sraffa, "La lotta commerciale," *La scienza del diritto privato*, vol. 2 (1894), 220–240. See Paolo Grossi, *"La scienza del diritto privato". Una rivista-progetto nella Firenze di fine secolo, 1893–1896* (Milan: Giuffrè, 1988), 79–80, and 187–197.

45 Achille Loria, *Les bases économiques de la constitution sociale* (Paris: Alcan, 1893). See Paolo Ungari, "In memoria del socialismo giuridico. I: Le "scuole del diritto privato sociale"," *Politica del diritto* 1 (1970), 245–246, and 267–268.

46 Among other studies on Loria's doctrine, Luigi Einaudi, "Achille Loria (1857–1943)," *The Economic Journal* 56 (1946), 147–150; Antonio Fossati, "Achille Loria nella storia del pensiero economico italiano," *Giornale degli economisti* (1953), 493–509. See also Riccardo Faucci, *L'economia politica in Italia. Dal cinquecento ai giorni nostri* (Turin: UTET, 2000), 210–215. In English, Riccardo Faucci, *A History of Italian Economic Thought* (London: Routledge, 2014), 119–124.

47 Sraffa in his contribution of 1894 quoted Ugo Rabbeno, *Il protezionismo americano* (Milan: Dumolard, 1893).

48 Ugo Rabbeno, *Le società cooperative di produzione. Contributo allo studio della questione*

More generally, in fact, it is known because the phenomenon of the Co-operative Movement, which rose in the mid-nineteenth century in England,[49] had a European dimension and in Italy it took form in those brief years at the end of the century, starting around the 1870s, just before the international economic situation favoured the industrial take-off in the centre-north of the country, as is mentioned above. The social structure was changing rapidly and the liberal ruling class favoured social solidarity. In fact, this solidarity was able to promote new economic and entrepreneurial initiatives and together they were a proponent of the controlled integration of the emerging classes.[50]

Consequently, the dominant political class agreed to the inclusion of cooperative companies in the Commercial Code of 1882 also by virtue of their educational and moral role, not only strictly economic.[51] In synthesis, cooperative companies were granted greater freedom of action in the form and manner of operation, even though they were subjected to special conditions, such as the creation by public act. Moreover, cooperative companies' shares could only be nominative and not to bearer. In addition, both cooperative companies' shares and dues could not exceed a maximum value.[52]

The discipline of the Mancini code was, in fact, the result of extensive preparatory work, in which jurists, economists and politicians participated: in the end, the cooperatives—which could be production, consumer, credit, banking, or construction companies—found their place in a special section of the title devoted to "companies and trade associations" in the first book of the commercial code. Some specific rules were reserved for them, which focused on the variability of capital and on the centrality of the person of the partner, all of which are principal characteristics of the cooperative form (head first,

---

operaia (Milan: Dumolard, 1889). See also the practical contribution Ugo Rabbeno, *Modello di statuto per le società cooperative di consumo* (Milan: Tipografia degli operai, 1888). On this author, Aurelio Macchioro, "Evoluzione sociale e cooperativismo in Ugo Rabbeno," now in Aurelio Macchioro, *Studi di storia del pensiero economico italiano* (Milan: FrancAngeli, 2006), 179–196.

49 Refer to Beatrice Potter, *The Co-operative Movement in Great Britain* (London: Sonnenschein, 1893).

50 Starting in 1886, the Italian cooperative companies' federation held a general meeting each year: *Il primo congresso dei cooperatori italiani, ottobre 1886. Relazione ufficiale* (Milan: Tipografia degli operai, 1887). See Maurizio degl'Innocenti, *Storia della cooperazione in Italia. La Lega nazionale delle cooperative, 1886–1925* (Rome: Editori riuniti, 1977); Gianni Silei, "La Lega nazionale delle cooperative e la Federazione nazionale delle società di mutuo soccorso dalle origini alla Grande Guerra," in *Solidarietà e mercato*, 87–134.

51 Maurizio degl'Innocenti, "Tra solidarismo e mercato," in *Solidarietà e mercato*, 7–46.

52 Pietro Sibert, *Le cooperative di consumo* (Turin: Unione tipografico-editrice torinese, 1920).

"the company", section VII, "provisions for cooperative societies").[53] However, the legislature of 1882 deliberately abandoned giving these companies a legal definition. From this descended articulated discussions in doctrine to determine how one should understand the cooperative, especially when it came to the consumer cooperatives,[54] widespread in practice particularly in the form of a limited company.[55]

In fact, these cooperative companies very frequently adopted the scheme of a company limited by shares, where shareholders enjoyed greater powers of governance and had one vote each in the general meeting which made its decisions following the majority principle. In addition and last but not least, as mentioned above, these companies benefitted from advantageous fiscal treatment.[56]

Of course, before reaching reliable conclusions on the role of cooperatives—especially in the form of a limited company—in the nineteenth and twentieth century Italian legal practice, further field studies are required, taking into account not only the contributions of legal theory, but also the case law.[57] Certainly, however, it is a search that will enrich the overall picture so far outlined by historiography, extending our gaze to the interweaving of social

53 *Codice di Commercio del Regno d'Italia* (1882), s. 219–228.

54 For example, Leopoldo Sabbatini, "Caratteristica delle società cooperative," *Il diritto commerciale* (1885).

55 *Statistica delle società cooperative. Società cooperative di consumo al 31 dicembre 1895* (Rome: Bontempelli, 1897); *Statistica delle società cooperative italiane esistenti nel 1902* (Milan: Tipografia degli operai, 1903); *Elenco delle società cooperative e mutue agrarie esistenti in Italia al 31 dicembre 1913* (Porto Santo Stefano: Tipografia Argentaria, 1914).

56 On the legislation in force and on prospected reforms, Ugo Rabbeno, "Il nuovo progetto di legge sulle società cooperative," *Riforma Sociale* 5 (1896), 1–13; Cesare Vivante, *Relazione sulla riforma delle società cooperative* (Turin: s.n., 1897).

57 Furthermore, one should consider that the diffusion of cooperative companies encouraged specific 'popular' literature: manuals and practical legislative guides to establish a cooperative company (or to join) were largely published. For example, Giuseppe Brambilla, *Le società cooperative, con cenni pratici di legislazione* (Turin: Roux & Viarengo, 1902); Luigi Buffoli (ed.), *L'organizzazione delle società cooperative di consumo* (Milan: Sonzogno, 1895); Luigi Buffoli, *Le società cooperative di consumo* (Milan: Sonzogno, 1885); Don Luigi Cerutti, *Manuale pratico per le società cattoliche cooperative di consumo* (Lendinara: Bufetti, 1895); Antonio Maffi, *Manuale per le società cooperative di produzione e lavoro* (Milan: Vallardi, 1902). See also Luigi Rodino (ed.), *Codice delle società cooperative. Annuario critico di Giurisprudenza pratica* (Florence: Paravia, 1893): the preface was written by a prominent Italian jurist, Pietro Cogliolo; Luigi Rodino (ed.), *Completo formulario degli atti concernenti le società cooperative. Annuario critico di giurisprudenza pratica* (Florence: Paravia, 1893).

and economic issues underlying the purely legal ones and resuming today the very topical debate of solidarity and market.[58]

---

58 Among other contributions, see Bruno Jossa, *L'impresa democratica. Un sistema di cooperative come nuovo modo di produzione* (Rome: Carocci, 2008).

Index

www.ingramcontent.com/pod-product-compliance
Lightning Source LLC
Chambersburg PA
CBHW071249180926
51613CB00002B/183
9789004348493